Ennd Ray Pf

VIETNAM

Inside Story of the Guerilla War

By WILFRED G. BURCHETT

With a New Introduction by the Author

D1213500

INTERNATIONAL PUBLISH

NEW YORK

Copyright © by INTERNATIONAL PUBLISHERS CO., INC., 1965

Two printings before publication, March 1965

Second Edition, December 1965

PUBLISHER'S NOTE

The author spent eight months in the areas of South Vietnam held by the National Liberation Front, mostly with the National Liberation Army (usually and erroneously called "Viet Cong" in the press). The body of the book is about his first journey of six months, during the last quarter of 1963 and the first three months of 1964. The Epilogue, written from South Vietnam and dated January 15, 1965, summarizes his impressions during a second visit of two months.

For this new edition, the author has supplied an Introduction in which he comments on the effects of escalation of the war by the United States since February 1965 and the prospects ahead as they appeared in the Fall of that year.

Library of Congress Catalog Card Number: 65–19627

Manufactured in the United States of America

209

AUTHOR'S INTRODUCTION TO SECOND EDITION

"Escalation" is the term used in Washington to cover the fact that "special war" has been defeated in South Vietnam and the involvement is now that of "limited war," including direct aggression against the sovereign state of the Democratic Republic of Vietnam in the North, without bothering about a declaration of war. The hopes of winning the war in the South with cheap, Asiatic cannon-fodder, the central point in General Maxwell Taylor's "special war," have faded and the general's return to Washington marked a spectacular punctuation point to that failure. Henceforth American blood and tears are to be added to American arms, treasure and prestige, uselessly expended to try and maintain in power whoever happens to be the latest in the series of shaky Saigon dictators. "Limited war" with American troops is the first stage of the "escalation," while a coy silence is maintained as to whether "limited war" is to be escalated into "global, nuclear" war, the third and last of the Pentagon concepts.

Involvement has been escalated to such a level that the Washington experts in the propaganda field are already peddling the idea that U.S. prestige is now so highly engaged that even if a Saigon government came to power cancelling the long-standing "invitation" for continued U.S. intervention, the intervention would have to go on "invitation or no invitation." This seems to fit a new situation in which many observers see an American war of aggression against the entire Vietnamese people, north and south of the 17th parallel.

In early 1965, Washington had a chance of getting out of the war with as much honor as was possible to salvage at that point, more than it will ever be possible to salvage henceforth. The military pundits, including General Westmoreland in Saigon, had drawn some correct conclusions from the Binh Gia battle that took place at the turn of the year (briefly touched on in the Epilogue). It was now clear that the Liberation Army had grown up and was able to engage in daytime classic battles with

i

elements of war of movement and positional warfare, cutting to pieces the best of the elite troops the U.S.-Saigon command could put into the field. It also enjoyed the all-out support of the population in an area which the U.S.-Saigon command had regarded as the "safest" in all of South Vietnam. In that battle, two and a half battalions of the total 11 battalions of the strategic reserves were wiped out to a man and all their weapons seized. Massive use of U.S. air power could not influence the situation. The "writing was on the wall" for the rest of the Saigon army. At the same time, political chaos in Saigon was reaching a climax, as the most die-hard of the puppet politicians and army leaders came to realize the game was up. The idea of negotiations was in the air everywhere. The proposal for a new Geneva Conference, or at least one to guarantee the neutrality of Cambodia, had wide support, including Peking, Hanoi and the National Liberation Front of South Vietnam. This was the moment for the United States to have bowed out gracefully.

Instead the decision was taken to bomb North Vietnam and commit U.S. ground troops to battle; any prospect of negotiations was deliberately bombed out of existence. Such as Maxwell Taylor or Westmoreland could not admit that they were being whipped by South Vietnamese peasants with captured American weapons. At least it had to be North Vietnamese with Chinese or Soviet weapons! And how quickly the pretext for the air attacks changed, justifying the reasonable suspicion that U.S. air power was poised on land and on sea to make the attacks and it was left to those on the spot to provide the pretexts. At first it was a reprisal for one of many Liberation Front attacks against U.S. bases, in this case at Pleiku; within days the pretext had been "escalated" to the necessity to halt the "flow of arms and men" from North to South. Later it was changed to "bombing the North Vietnamese leaders to the conference table" and punishing them until they ordered their compatriots in the South to lay down their arms.

In fact, to repeat a constant theme of this writer since he first visited the liberated zones of South Vietnam, nothing the United States could do to North Vietnam could affect the military situation in the South except to drive the patriots there into still greater efforts to crush intervention and the interventionists. The process started at Binh Gia could not be halted or modified even if North Vietnam disappeared from the map. There are hard facts to illustrate this.

During 1964 the three-year old Liberation Army often succeeded in wiping out entire units of Saigon troops at company (100-120 men) level but was rarely able to wipe out an entire battalion (500-700 troops) because of the superior fire-power and mobility of the Saigon forces. Nevertheless, even in 1964, they did manage to wipe out eight entire battalions. During the first six months of 1965 they wiped out 20 crack battalions of Saigon's regular army, as units, starting with the 4th Marine battalion at Binh Gia on New Year's Day. (A Ranger battalion was destroyed in the same battle two days earlier.) Of these 20, nine belonged to the 11 battalions of the strategic reserve, as it existed at the end of 1964. The strategic reserve is comprised of Ranger, Marine and Parachutist battalions, the only ones maintained at full strength, heavily armed and specially trained by the U.S. "advisers."

By mid-1965 the strategic reserve—the only troops not tied down in fixed garrison duty, guarding towns, bases and other strategic targets—had virtually ceased to exist. During the same period the Liberation Army carried out a series of shattering attacks on the Special Forces training centers where U.S. "counter-insurgency" experts trained the "elite" units.

By this time the Americans were refusing to commit whatever mobile forces were left, preferring to let even key posts be overrun rather than attempt to save them by sending reinforcements. They learned a bitter lesson on May 31, 1965, at Ba Gia (Quang Ngai province) where two of the strategic reserve battalions, the 39th Rangers and 3rd Marines, were completely wiped out when sent in vain to reinforce the 1st and 2nd battalions of Saigon's 51st regiment. All four battalions were destroyed, all military installations dismantled and all weapons seized. At the Dong Xoai battle, north of the Bien Hoa jet bomber base, on June 9-12, 1965, after three battalions, including the 7th Parachutists, had been cut to pieces, U.S. "advisers" turned a deaf ear to requests for more reinforcements. In fact there was nothing to send, not even from the four strategic reserve battalions normally kept in Saigon to deal with possible uprisings.

With four-fifths of the territory and ten out of South Vietnam's fourteen million population in the liberated zones, where was the U.S.-Saigon command to get its replacements, let alone meet the absurd targets for expansion of the army? Most of the four million still under Saigon control were in the big cities, two million in the twin cities Saigon-Cholon alone. The Liberation Front had ten million peasans—the basic raw material of an army in any such war—among whom to recruit, Saigon had four million urban dwellers. The harsh reality of the situation was that the hard core of the Saigon army had been cut to pieces and there was no prospect of replacements; the rest had no stomach for the fight. And stomach for the fight faded proportionately to the rate of U.S. direct intervention. The unfortunate youths rounded up by Saigon's press gangs outside cinemas, restaurants, stadiums, etc., could be forced into uniforms and "statistically" added to the size of the Saigon army but nothing could make them fight—except against those who had press-ganged them or stood behind the press-gangers. Western news agencies began carrying reports of youths in Saigon and other urban centers dressing up in girl's clothes—an effective form of disguise in Asia—of mutilating themselves, taking disease-producing drugs, or simply moving out to join the "Viet Cong" rather than fall into the hands of the press gangs. "Total mobilization" orders issued by the latest dictator, General Nguyen Cao Ky, were a joke, as his regime controlled only a tiny fraction of the territory covered by his "orders."

These were Washington's real problems when they decided to intensify intervention—not the myth of intervention from the North. By the autumn of 1965, in fact—after six months of bombing North Vietnam—Washington was in the embarrassing situation of having to admit that either mighty U.S. air power was shockingly ineffective, incapable of halting supplies moving over a couple of hundred miles of road and railway networks, or admit the complete falsity of its thesis that the war in the South depended on the North. For the scale of Liberation Front attacks mounted month by month after the bombings, inflicting the greatest defeats on the U.S.-Saigon forces since the war started. This process will continue despite the replacement of Saigon's destroyed strategic reserves by U.S. combat forces. And Washington's problems are in South Vietnam, not in the North, unless they commit another monumental folly and attack the North with ground troops.

When I last saw him in January 1965, the president of the National Liberation Front, Nguyen Huu Tho, in discussing the prospects of escalation to "limited war" made a prophetic remark: "If the Americans continue to intervene in a small way, they face a small defeat; if they decide to intervene in a big way then they face a big defeat."

The pretext for continued U.S. intervention is getting a little obscure; the rapid fall of the Saigon dictators and the complete absence of a legal base for any of them, is making the "we are there by invitation" argument wear rather thin. "We are there because our prestige demands it," is also an argument that does not go down well either at home or abroad. One begins to notice a new line emerging, the father and mother of all the whopping great lies that have ever been invented. I noticed it first in printed form in a book called *Mission in Torment* by John Mecklin (Doubleday, 1965) late (and once again) correspondent of *Time* magazine. But in between, 1961-1964, Mecklin headed the Saigon Bureau of U.S. Information Service. He stepped off the "special war" bandwagon when he saw it was headed for catastrophe to become the most fervent advocate of "limited war." As for U.S. aims in South Vietnam, Mecklin writes blandly (page 297) that Washington had always sought no more than to defend "the status quo ante, i.e. an independent South Vietnam as provided by the Geneva Agreement of 1954." This thesis is subtly becoming the official U.S. pretext, namely, we are there in defense of the 1954 Geneva Agreements. Now if there is one thing that the Geneva Agreements do not provide for, nor make any mention of, it is an "independent South Vietnam." On the contrary, it is specifically spelt out that the temporary demarcation line along the 17th parallel, drawn to permit the separation and regrouping of the combatants, should in no way constitute a permanent boundary.

Mecklin admits that the war in the South was being lost, not by intervention from the North but because the "Viet Cong" was winning on the countryside "in man-to-man confrontations and this was a weakness that could not be corrected with planes or bombs or by making faces at Ho Chi Minh. Talk of bombing Hanoi or V. C. supply lines sounded, in fact, like a palliative for failure" (p. 304). One could think Mecklin might be heading up to the conclusion: better extricate ourselves from this and let the Vietnamese settle it among themselves. His answer is the opposite, for he sees as "the only choice remaining" direct involvement of U.S. combat forces against the "Viet Cong" inside South Vietnam: "The moment had come to do this, to go to war as quickly as possible. With every day of procrastination the danger mounted of a sudden upheaval such as a neutralist coup d'état, which would make it more difficult." One must go to war quickly before a Saigon government cancellel the "invitation" and insisted on negotiating a settlement with the Liberation Front, something definitely possible at that time. Mecklin goes on (page 307) to repeat the Great Lie as the supreme justification for not doing that: "Our mission would be rigidly limited to surgical intervention to enforce the Geneva Agreement of 1954 in support of the legitimate government of South Vietnam, hopefully at the invitation of this government." Not necessarily at the invitation!

Thus the gospel from a "Quiet American" who was the No. 1 official in Saigon for three years in charge of propaganda, explaining to the American public among others what the war was all about. Either he has never troubled to read the Geneva Agreements or he has been given the job to turn them upside down and stand truth on its head. One can find there no reference to a "legitimate" or "independent" government of South Vietnam. If it were not for the fact that Mecklin's theses have since become Washington policy—or are fast becoming so—the book would be hardly worthy of attention.

From the end of July 1965 onwards, and almost every day at the time of writing, eight-engined B-52 bombers fly 2,500 miles or so from bases in Guam initially to discharge their huge loads of bombs on forests, rubber plantations and rice fields 10 to 30 miles from Saigon. More recently, after Saigon patrols reported they were unable to find any "Viet Cong" corpses, the bombers from Guam as well as locally based jet bombers were switched to the Mekong Delta which has one of the highest concentrations of populations per square mile anywhere in the world. And since August, the air attacks against North Vietnam have been concentrated against dams, irrigation networks and flood control systems.

The only criteria seems to be to wipe out anything that lives or moves; to destroy anything that shows signs of life or habitation and to provoke mass slaughter by famine or flooding. If bombers do succeed in breaching the Red River dikes in the North, they will inevitably cause floods that will drown two to three million peasants. Is there any moral difference in gassing them in Nazi-type gas chambers? It is a question being asked not only in Vietnam but in every other country in Asia. Hanoi has taken the decision to put on trial pilots who take part in such raids. The Nuremburg verdicts preclude any defense that the pilots were obeying "orders of their superiors" and also established various other precedents under which U.S. pilots could be convicted, even if there was a state of war between the United States and North Vietnam. These are aspects of "escalation" that the Pentagon computers may or may not have taken into consideration. The war is being escalated to a bestiality that blurs the exclusive image of what one used to think was the unmatchable and never-to-be-repeated bestiality of the Nazis.

In the light of "escalation" what are the perspectives? In the North, everything will be done to avoid giving the United States any chance for direct confrontation with the Soviet Union or China. Short of a massive U.S. ground attack on North Vietnam the North Vietnamese will continue to fight back in their own way, in their own time and with their own men, the latter handling even the most sophisticated types of weapons. Hanoi insists in having complete control of its war. In the South every effort will be made to limit the ground fighting to South Vietnam itself. North and South are agreed that everything should be done to contain the war within its present boundaries; that no action on their part should give the Pentagon "lunatic fringe" the pretext for the next stage in escalation.

"We are going over to wartime socialism," a leader of the Democratic Republic of Vietnam told me, "but we do not want to interfere with the socialist countries' building of peacetime socialism. We do not want one drop of blood from the fraternal countries to be spilt because of our problems."

"Wartime socialism" has a specific content; it means key factories buried deep in the mountains; rearranged hours of work to avoid peak bombing periods; autonomous food zones to reduce the effects of destruction of irrigation systems and the stress on communication networks; strictly just distribution of food and consumer goods "according to needs"; long-range economic planning based on a long war, taking into account that it would not be beyond the United States to destroy Hanoi, Haiphong and other cities. The only thing long-range planning does not take into account is surrender. "We fought the French without having Hanoi, Haiphong or any other city in our hands and with the French in physical possession of all the towns and strategic highways," explained this veteran leader of the Vietnamese revolution. "How can the United States expect to impose policies without being in physical control of the country? That they will never be in a thousand years."

In mid-September 1965, I met Tran Bui Khiem, in effect the Foreign Minister of the National Liberation Front. Answering my question as to the perspectives in view of the new, massive U.S. intervention, he replied: "We still prepare for a long, protracted war, because we had taken such U.S. intervention into account a long time ago. Secondly, as there is much talk about negotiations, we say if there are any negotiations they must absolutely be based on a complete American withdrawal from South Vietnam. We can not agree to any negotiations which puts the attacker and the defender on the same basis, the interventionists and those who defend themselves, the aggressors and those who are the victims of aggression. We realize that it might take them a long time to accept this, but there is no other way, and our people are prepared for the sacrifices that such a long war entails. But to leave the Americans here means that any talk of independence and sovereignty would be a mockery." Tran Bui Khiem insisted, as did leaders of the Liberation Front earlier this year when I met them in the liberated zones, that the question of "neutrality" for South Vietnam remains and will remain a key point in the Liberation Front program and is regarded as the most realistic basis on which a settlement could be arranged among Vietnamese without harming the legitimate interests of any other country, including the United States.

WILFRED G. BURCHETT

Along the Frontier of South Vietnam,
October 1, 1965

AUTHOR'S FOREWORD

Apart from my general interest in the peoples of the former states of Indo-China and my special sympathy for the South Vietnamese people in their heroic struggle, I had an important, added reason to visit the Liberated Areas and battlefronts of South Vietnam during late 1963 and the first three months of 1964. The United States is experimenting with a new type of warfare in South Vietnam, so-called "special warfare," the theoretical father of which is General Maxwell Taylor. When he was projecting this theory, in 1960-61, he was special military adviser to the late President Kennedy. Later as Chairman of the Joint Chiefs of Staff, he was called upon to develop the strategic concepts of "special warfare" for South Vietnam; still later he was sent on the spot to Saigon as super-ambassador, with full military and political powers, to apply personally the strategies and tactics of his new concept.

Maxwell Taylor's thesis was that in this nuclear era, the United States must prepare to fight three types of war—global, nuclear war; limited or local wars, and "special" wars. The "special" thing about the latter is that U.S. combat troops are not involved. The expensive lesson of the Korean war made it imperative that the "cannon-fodder" be provided in such future wars by "local" populations, fed and supplied at a fraction of the cost of U.S. troops, and the shedding of whose blood would bring no tears to American homes. Maxwell Taylor's thesis in fact was merely a military extension of the late John Foster Dulles' creed: "Let Asians fight Asians."

South Vietnam was selected as the first testing ground for "special war," and I went there to find out on the spot what was really special in this new military concept and what were the special means the South Vietnamese people had in countering its strategies, tactics and techniques. It seemed to me that this was important in view of the declared U.S. intention to wage this type of war wherever revolutionary movements threatened what were imagined to be American interests. It seemed, in

other words, that in the age of nuclear stalemate and upsurge
of national liberation struggles, humanity was to get used to the
idea of "special wars" all over the globe, particularly if the
experiment in South Vietnam succeeded.

Shortly after I arrived in South Vietnam, a guerilla group of
the National Front of Liberation (on the night of November
23-24, 1963) overran an American-run "Special Forces" training
camp at Hiep Hoa, about 20 miles northwest of Saigon. Apart
from completely destroying the military installations, seizing
enough arms to equip a couple of NFL battalions and capturing
four American sergeants—whom I later interviewed—the partisans
found a pile of interesting documents. Some related to the training and operational plans of Cambodian traitors—the Khmer
Serei, organized on South Vietnamese soil with U.S. dollars, arms
and instructors to overthrow the neutralist regime of Prince
Sihanouk. These were immediately forwarded to the Cambodian
government. One document particularly interested me, a Manual
for Special Warfare personnel. An introductory article by General
Paul Decker, then U.S. Army chief of staff, laid down the
"ideological" concepts of special war.

According to Decker, the collapse of old-style colonialism had
given birth to dozens of newly, independent states, economically
weak and politically immature, "easy prey for Communist sub-
version," as he put it. The U.S. armed forces must be organized
and streamlined to intervene anywhere in the world to prevent
"Communist takeovers." To this end the Pentagon, asserted
General Decker, had divided the globe into four strategic areas
in which the United States might have to wage special warfare.
For each of the four areas, a special general staff had been created
and "special forces," the shock troops of special warfare, were
being trained and organized on a stand-by status for action at
any moment.

Decker did not specifically name the four areas, except Southeast Asia where the first experiment was being waged (the
Manual was published in 1962). But he did refer to training
schools at Fort Bragg, North Carolina, at Okinawa and the
Panama Canal zone, where French and Spanish-speaking officers
were being trained along with their English-speaking counter-

parts. Decker made several references to the growth of "subversive" movements in Latin America and left no doubt that this was a second special warfare area. Current U.S.-backed operations in the former Belgian Congo with U.S. airpower involved together with white mercenaries and "native" troops and the training of French-speaking officers, obviously means that Africa, with its numerous former French colonies, is a third area. The fourth may well be Europe.

"Special warfare" in fact is nothing less than the military expression of American neo-colonialism, just as the Expeditionary Force was the military expression of classical colonialism. Neo-colonialism tries to present a different face to old-style colonialism, ruling up to a certain point by remote control, through a Synghman Rhee, a Ngo Dinh Diem or a Tshombe. But when that fails, the military machine moves in, "invited" of course by a complaisant puppet. The old Expeditionary Force was based partly on the colonial power's own soldiery, plus those conscripted from its colonies and such shock troops as the French Foreign Legion. But in "special warfare," the Americans supply the arms and dollars, the planes and the pilots, the strategic and tactical command from a General Staff down to officer "advisers" from divisional to company level, everything in fact short of the "cannon fodder." In the book that follows I have tried to illustrate how this works in practice and what forms of defense were developed by the South Vietnamese patriots.

Another major question was how, when and where the war in South Vietnam started, because this is a war which seemed to have no precise starting point in terms of time and place, a war which only gradually impinged itself on the public consciousness. All of a sudden it was there with half a million South Vietnamese and 20,000 Americans engaged in a major war against what appeared to be jungle shadows. But it was the jungle shadows who were winning, inflicting an endless series of defeats against a superbly equipped modern army. I spent a good deal of time trying to track down precise details as to how it all started, where and when the decisive first shots were fired.

At the moment these lines are being written, Washington is threatening to avenge its defeats in South Vietnam by "escalating" the war; that is, by attacking North Vietnam, by spilling the war over the frontiers of South Vietnam into Cambodia, by linking up their undeclared war in Laos with their overt war in South Vietnam, by creating in fact a generalized war in all the former states of Indo-China. The reply of the peoples of Indo-China is to close ranks and form a united front of all patriotic forces and peoples of Indo-China in defense of peace and a final end to U.S. intervention in this part of the world.

The lunatic fringe in Washington is certainly capable of the ultimate madness of bombing Hanoi, Haiphong and other towns of North Vietnam. But they can never alter the outcome of the war in the South by this. They can never bring the people of the North or the South to their knees by bombing towns or anything else in the North. Washington would do well to ponder the fact that the Viet Minh fought and beat the French without having Hanoi, Haiphong or any other major city in their hands, and this despite the physical presence of a French army and administration inside Vietnam. An attack against North Vietnam automatically brings People's China into the war and Soviet military aid as well. The United States, even if it wished to repeat the folly of Korea can never physically occupy either North or South Vietnam. By attacking North Vietnam, the United States would have taken the initiative of creating a single military front in Vietnam which would very quickly result in the military reunification of the country. To enlarge the war in the former states of Indo-China—and the continued use of U.S. bases in Thailand—would be to start a process that would erase every trace of U.S. presence in Southeast Asia, clear down to Singapore.

There is only one way out: complete withdrawal from Vietnam.

— WILFRED G. BURCHETT

Phnom Penh, Cambodia
November 30, 1964

CONTENTS

Illustrations

PART I

THE WAY THINGS ARE

Chapter 1

DOWN FROM THE HIGHLANDS

ENCOUNTER IN THE JUNGLE

During four days the track had led over a series of steep ridges, our little group clambering up, stone by stone, for hours on end what must have been roaring cascades in the rainy season. Occasionally we were rewarded by a magnificent panorama, serried folds of mist-covered forest stretching away into purple infinity. But they were only tantalizing glimpses through the thick foliage. The almost vertical watercourses were dry, except for occasional deep pools, but the stones were greasy with humidity. Clambering up was the more tiring, like climbing an endless and terribly steep staircase from which every now and again two or three steps were missing altogether and you exerted arms as well as legs to haul yourself up to the next level. Fortunately, a tough training program had prepared my muscles for this. Going down was more difficult because every now and again you slipped on a greasy boulder, or the stone in which you had placed your trust went slithering away and unless you did some fast footwork, you could go rolling and bumping away after the stone. This never in fact happened to me, but there were some horrified gasps from my companions at what seemed the inevitable at times.

I preferred the watercourses to the zig-zagging trails; for hours on end the latter were mere tunnels in the undergrowth. I also preferred doing my own climbing to hanging on to the mane of the fierce little ponies available in some areas and which climbed like cats and skidded like a car out of control, but never fell. Although it was almost the dry season, there was still occasional misty rain, the undergrowth was often dripping wet. But it was not the ice-cold drops of water on my neck in the early morning that worried me; it was the little green leeches that dropped down from the branches as you brushed past; softly and coldly,

like drops of water. You only knew the difference when the blood
started trickling down under the singlet, from the tiny triangu-
lar bite in which the leeches so ingeniously inject their anti-
coagulant saliva. There were the ordinary black kind, too, which
attacked the feet on the humid earth tracks, but with the open,
rubber-tire sandals and trouser legs rolled up, they were easily
seen. With a touch of a cigarette end they curled up and dropped
off. By following the watercourses one could avoid the cold caress
of both undergrowth and green leeches. Ground leeches were also
less of a bother in the stony trails carved out by the madly racing
streams in the rainy season.

This was my leanest period as far as eating was concerned.
We were too close to the adversary's posts to shoot game. Try
as we would it was impossible to produce fish from the pools,
although they were there and the guerillas looked speculatively
at their grenades sometimes—their most effective fishing gear.
As the smoke from fires would have attracted planes, cooking was
done in the pre-dawn hours. From that sunrise breakfast of
steamed glutinous rice—which I could never eat because of a
life-time habit of drinking tea only for the morning repast—till
fires could be lit around dusk to roast some manioc roots, we
nibbled at the solid balls of cold, glutinous rice prepared over
the pre-dawn fires. Wrapped in parachute nylon, they looked like
fair sized bombs attached to the guerillas' belts.

My worst trials always came when we had to cross the innumerable rustic "bridges." The deluxe ones were swaying con-
traptions suspended from cables of jungle creepers, with woven
matting laid across lengths of bamboo as a footway and creeper
handrails on each side. Although the swaying created a sense of
great insecurity and one speculated on how effective were the
knots which sometimes joined two or more creepers in the sus-
pension cable, at least there was something flat and reasonably
wide for the feet. The next best were those with a few sections
of bamboo bound together for the footway and fixed bamboo
or sapling handrails. The worst were those from a single perfectly round tree trunk or giant bamboo, tapering from one
foot down to about six inches and with a single, usually terribly
loose, creeper at about waist level. This was useless for sup-

port but did help in correcting one's balance in the way that a long baton helps a tightrope artist.

Although the rubber-tire sandals were wonderful for everything else, they were no good for crossing single-log bridges, especially if the latter were humid or greasy from the recent passage of muddy feet. One always tackled these barefoot, walking in a slightly splay-foot fashion, to give each foot its maximum grip over the width and curve of the trunk. I only discovered this trick by carefully watching the tribespeople. At first glance they seemed to skip effortlessly across but in fact they placed their feet very carefully. One got used to feeling with the feet and keeping the eyes on the far bank, because looking down to watch where each foot was going was unnerving when there was a fifty-foot drop to a rushing stream or some sharp rocks. As for the lissom "handrail," you let it lightly slide through the hand, using it for orientation rather than support.

On the fourth day of that particular journey we had everything, all variants of bridges, green and black leeches, our usual watercourse tracks. Towards late afternoon our troubles seemed over. We came out into level country with sparser timber and every now and again some open clearings with tufts of giant, feathery grass and reeds. Suddenly I was thrust into a thicket and there was an air of great urgency. Carbines were cocked and after a whispered conversation, two of my companions—M'Nong tribesmen—slipped away through the forest in the general direction of the path we were following. One had a rifle, the other a light machine gun. With extreme caution, I was led back into a denser clump of the forest we had been crossing. My interpreter pointed to a similar patch the other side of the clearing, but try as I may I could see nothing. I could hear voices, however, and the interpreter whispered one word "enemy." By his gestures, I undertsood that our two groups were following almost parallel but converging trails which came together a couple of hundred yards further on. We stayed where we were, our few guerillas having spread out and taken up positions behind logs and inside big tufts of grass into which they had wriggled on their bellies like snakes.

The voices receded and all of a sudden the complete calm

was shattered by a volley of automatic fire, from the general direction of the converging paths. Thanh, my bespectacled interpreter from Saigon who had left his studies as a medical student to join the resistance, pressed me into the ground behind a stout tree and I noticed he had that pained look, compressed lips and furrowed brow that always appeared when something happened that was not on our program. Within seconds there was lots of firing; fire and counter-fire in a sort of bow-and-arrow pattern, I decided. Light automatic and carbine fire seemed to come from an arc-shaped area directly ahead of us; the counter-fire seemed to be coming from a straight line, much closer to us. There was a pause, then I could hear voices again, excited ones this time and I noted our guerillas were hugging the ground and sighting over their barrels; now I could see hurrying dim forms through the heavy, green filter of the undergrowth.

Shots crashed out again and little spurts of flame from the guerillas' carbines and the last I saw as my head was pushed into the ground again were forms scurrying faster than ever back in the direction from which they had come. The guerillas fired, then rushed to positions parallel to the line of flight and fired again, moving with incredible speed through the undergrowth and firing all the time. There was no return fire and soon all was calm again.

After a few minutes the two M'Nong returned, grinning all over, and our group reassembled again for more hurried discussion. "The enemy has fled," Thanh said, "but we must move off quickly. There is a big open space to cross and these troops will alert a post in no time, even if they have not already heard the firing." I asked about casualties.

"Our people fired to scare them off, not to kill or wound," Thanh replied, after consulting the guerillas. "The comrade with the machine gun and the other one who went first, fired from many different positions in front of where the enemy troops were marching to give the idea that if they advanced further they would run into a big force. But we did not want to hit them hard because there might be air reprisals and our task is to deliver you safely to tonight's rendezvous. It was an enemy platoon on patrol, very rare in this area. We think they are pulling back to their post, but one of our comrades is following them to make sure."

We shouldered our haversacks and moved off again through lightly timbered country and, after about 30 minutes walk, came to a clearing about a half mile wide, with a patch of what seemed to be dense jungle on the other side. Despite my protests, my haversack was taken by one of the M'Nongs and Thanh said: "We must move at maximum speed." That had been part of my training—to march at very high speed, starting with 15 minutes without a break and working up to two hours at maximum speed without a break. Just for situations like this, I thought.

We set out very briskly and as we approached the center of the clearing, I noticed the M'Nong—mighty hunters of elephants and noted for their big ears—gazing skywards behind us. Sure enough within seconds, there was the heavy roar of helicopters. Then we really did put on speed. I estimated that even if we jog-trotted we still had five minutes ahead of us and although the 'copters were not yet in sight, what they could do in five minutes from the time they made such a noise was obvious. The noise grew to shattering dimensions and four ungainly, dark shapes, flying quite low appeared over the patch of jungle we had just left, bearing down towards us like vultures on their prey as if they knew precisely where we were. We were jog-trotting by now, and while some of the guerillas selected firing positions and made their weapons ready, I was given the signal to run as fast as I could. Four of us raced across the last couple of hundred yards at full speed. The firing had already started when we literally jumped into the forest and I was guided to a grotto in a tree-covered, rocky outcrop.

There were bursts of machine gun fire from the helicopters and a stream of automatic and carbine fire from the handful of guerillas. From the faces of my companions, as well as by the facts of the situation, it was clear we were in the toughest spot I had been in since the start of my journey. Four 'copters could lift a company of troops—80 to 100—and we were ten, including myself. The roar of the helicopters, hovering now and seeking their targets, was shattering; it seemed there was no space in the ears for anything more, but still above the motors was the devas-

tating clatter of their machine guns and the pitifully unequal
reply of the guerillas' two light machine guns. The 'copters
circled and hovered, as if trying to make up their minds where
to land.

Suddenly the motors roared louder than ever, the squarish,
whale-like noses pointed skywards and they soared up and away,
flying right into the rays of the setting sun. We rushed to the
edge of the forest and I was near tears of joy as one by one the
guerillas got to their feet and headed towards us. "Anyone hurt?"
was the first question, and as none had been I asked why they
had not landed.

"Look around you and you'll see why they didn't land," said
Dinh, the stocky little chief of the unit. Then I noticed what
had escaped me as we raced for cover, that there were evenly
spaced, sharply pointed poles, covering the latter half of the
clearing, each 10 or 15 feet high. "They couldn't land here without getting spiked or fouling up their propellers," Dinh said,
"these poles are planted in a very scientific pattern. That's why
they hovered so long, looking for a gap."

"Why didn't they land on the other side where there were no
poles?" I asked.

"Because it would have been useless. These helicopters can be
effective only if they dive straight down on their prey in what
the puppets call 'eagle-catches-chicken' tactics. If their troops have
to advance even a few hundred yards against our fire, they will
take casualties and once they have casualties they will break off
any action. In any case, they knew we were near the edge of the
jungle and by the time they had crossed half a mile of clearing,
if we wanted to avoid action we could have faded away into the
jungle where they dare not follow. Also it was near sunset and
they don't stay out after dark. And we had certainly drilled some
daylight into their machines. We were hitting them. I could see
the tracers going in, but you have to hit a vital part to knock
them down. Our experience is that once you start hitting them,
they always pull out. So although the situation must have looked
a bit black to you," he said with a grin, "there was really nothing to worry about."

"Their machine gun fire sounded very impressive," I said.

"Huh! It's always like that," Dinh replied contemptuously. "They make a lot of noise; fire their guns like mad but have no idea what they're blazing away at. At first it used to impress us, too. This time I watched some of their bullets going in; I could see one of them firing his gun from the 'copter doorway but by the firing angle it was clear the bullets were going nowhere near our men; I think they fire to keep up their own spirits. By the way," he concluded, "in another 15 minutes we will be in a safe area where the enemy never dares penetrate."

Sure enough, shortly after the sun had gone down, we were met by a small, smiling group of M'Nong guerillas, who guided us for another half hour to a small group of huts, where the cooking fires were already blazing under pots of rice—and what turned out later to be an excellent monkey stew.

IN THE NAM BO

I awoke to a light touch on my shoulder, and there was my slim, copper-faced guide smiling down at me, his fingers across his lips for silence. As I slowly swung out of my hammock where I had been resting all day and far into the night, my hands were clasped in turn by those of half a dozen smiling guerillas, all new faces to me. The lithe M'Nong tribesman who had been my guide swiftly folded up my hammock as he had done a score or more times before, tucked it into a haversack, then turned to me and held out his arms. We hugged each other and there were tears in his eyes. After weeks of travel together mainly on foot and horseback, difficulties and dangers shared together, his final role had been to steer me through to this rendezvous point, then hand me over to others. The newcomers, rifles at the ready, motioned me to my place in the little column and with a last wave to my M'Nong friend, standing by the tree from which he had unhitched my hammock a few minutes previously, we set out and he and the tree were immediately swallowed up by the jet black tropical night.

Not a word had been spoken and this was not so much because of lack of means of communication as of the fact that we were filtering through enemy country, the nearest post less than a thousand yards from where I had been resting—and we had to pass still closer before we reached friendly territory. The M'Nong guide had scratched a little map on the ground to emphasize the need for caution.

At first I held on to the barrel of the shouldered rifle of the guerilla ahead of me, but soon my eyes could distinguish the white triangle of his haversack and I was able to follow him closely enough to avoid taking a wrong turn on the narrow, winding track. We walked as fast and as noiselessly as the crackling, dried leaves under our rubber sandals would permit. After about an hour we sat down on a log, while signs were made indicating extra caution. We were at our closest point to the post. A few minutes later a seventh guerilla turned up to indicate that all was well; we could continue, which we did for another two hours. The most difficult moments for me, as always, were when it came to shuffle across the single tree-trunk bridges.

Finally we halted, haversacks were dumped on the ground. Now there were broad smiles, more handshakes and the word "Nam Bo." Cigarettes were lit and everyone relaxed. We were again in friendly territory. For me it was an emotional moment because it meant that I was now in the real South, in Nam Bo (Cochin-China),* and on my way to what I felt sure would be the highlight of my visit—the outskirts of Saigon where I hoped to touch the very essence of this war at the gates of the capital itself. Conversation now was limited only by language difficulties, my too few words of Vietnamese and their too few words of French.

While we were resting, I noticed two guerillas take out their knives and hack down a small sapling which they proceeded to trim and then attach the cords of my hammock to each end. A new way of slinging my hammock, I thought. Perhaps it is tiger

* For Vietnamese their country is composed of three parts, the Bac Bo or what the French called Tonking in the North; Trung Bo or Annam in the Center—now sliced through by the demarcation line along the 17th parallel—and Nam Bo, or Cochin-China in the South. The Tay Nguyen (Western Highlands), where I had been for many weeks previously, is in the Trung Bo.

country and they are putting me high up between the forks of two trees. When the cigarettes were finished the unit chief made signs that I should enter what was now transformed into a palanquin, suspended between the shoulders of two guerillas, each about half my size. With some indignation I invited them to test the steely quality of my leg muscles. There were some smiles and appreciative murmurs as a result of which the hammock was untied and the pole thrown away.

I learned next day, when an interpreter turned up, that the guerillas had been informed that I was "old and not used to walking." This was a slander on my 52 years and previous months' activities—and the only occasion on which I found the guerillas to be misinformed.

They now lit their bottle lamps and our march continued, this time with an occasional exchange of conversation between the guerillas to emphasize that we were in safe territory. Every now and again one of them would snatch a broad leaf which they held behind the lamps and used as reflectors to throw the light forward on the path. Would not electric torches be more convenient, I had once asked? The reply was that apart from anything else, storage of batteries in that climate was very difficult whereas kerosene could be stored indefinitely in secret caches along the communication routes. The lamps were made from French perfume bottles and an ingenious wick enclosed in a copper tube, which fitted into a 303 cartridge case with a tiny spring that made the wick pop out the moment the cap was unscrewed; they were invaluable in lighting the guerillas' path to their famous night attacks.

We were still in very dense jungle, on a path that was little more than a tunnel through thick undergrowth and groves of bamboo. But it was well into the dry season in the Nam Bo and there were no leeches to worry about. Only the cries of night birds and the crackling of leaves under our own feet broke the heavy silence of the night at first, though later there were a few muffled explosions of artillery shells in the distance.

After four hours of march and a final crossing of one of the hateful log bridges, we arrived at a tiny cluster of huts where we were to spend the night. My escort chief insisted I sleep on

a bed inside a hut though I always preferred my hammock between the trees. He indicated it was tiger country, so I com-
plied and thus spent my first night in the Nam Bo on a brutally
hard bed of split bamboo, with a straw mat contributing little to
cushion the hardness, and surrounded by what seemed to be
hundreds of pigs of all ages. One or more came from time to
time to scrape their backs against the legs of my bed, with appreciative grunts. Every now and again there would be tremendous collective squealing and the whole herd went scampering
off into the forest only to race back a few minutes later with the
same speed and squeals. I assumed there must be some wild
animals in the vicinity and some porcine system of signals and
shelters.

Later next day I discovered the huts belonged to a tiny Liberation Army unit which, like most units, went in for agricultural production. Pig and poultry raising was part of their job
and later I visited a splendid vegetable garden, lined with papaya, coconut and banana palms, the whole thing cunningly
blended with jungle growth to provide maximum camouflage
against marauding planes. One of the soldiers working on the
plot shinned up a coconut palm and threw down half a dozen
nuts. It is traditional, as a first gesture to a visitor to the Nam Bo,
to offer a drink of that delicious ice-cool liquid stored in the
well insulated coconut. While we were still smacking our lips,
a small group, rifles over their shoulders, emerged from the
jungle, heading our way. It was a new escort, complete with
French-speaking interpreter. After greetings and introductions,
the latter began to make cautious inquiries as to whether I could
ride a bicycle for a relatively long period. As, except for one
or two very short rides in the Tay Nguyen, I had never done
any real cycling for over 30 years, I said I supposed I could, but
I really enjoyed walking.

We set out in the late afternoon for a four-hour walk which
brought us to another, more impressive cluster of huts equipped
with Dien Bien Phu kitchens. As the name suggests, the latter
were developed during the famous battle at which the French
suffered final defeat, the ovens arranged below ground level in a
big trench, usually hacked out of the floor of a bamboo and

thatch shelter. Instead of chimneys, there are long tunnels leading from each oven in parallel or diverging directions into the
jungle. Most of the smoke is absorbed by the earth walls of the
tunnel, the rest dispersed in the undergrowth. This is important
when the slightest wisp of smoke is a primary target for the U.S.
pilots who run the South Vietnamese air force.

There's no smoke without life, seems to be their motto; and
life itself, outside the cities and concentration camp villages, is
the enemy as far as those who direct the air war are concerned.
Any life at all or any sign of life, human, animal or vegetable—
in the case of food crops or orchards—is a target for their bombs,
napalm or air-sprayed chemical poisons. In the Tay Nguyen, I
had heard of any number of cases where parachutists had been
dropped or troops helicoptered in, just to root out a crop of
maize or rice as soon as it started to show green. Napalm is used
against ripening crops as a matter of course. A peasant hoeing
in the field; a buffalo wallowing in a pool or its calf frisking in
the rice stubble, a flash of green from a cultivation patch—all
these are primary targets for the American airmen who alone
keep the air war going. According to figures given by General
Nguyen Khanh after he took over in Saigon at the end of January 1964, half the casualties claimed by Saigon to have been inflicted on the "Viet Cong" in 1963, were from air action. How
the pilots were able to distinguish between "Viet Cong" and the
peasants was not explained.

So the Dien Bien Phu kitchen introduced in the South was a
major development, especially in military units and other organizations with permanent bases and plenty of manpower to dig the
underground chimneys. The latter usually extend for several
scores of yards and lend a blast-furnace draught to the fires.

Next morning I was introduced to a bicycle; despite a dubious
start, in the weeks that followed I was to cover about 500 miles
on bike, plus quite a few more on foot and in sampan. My comprehensive training for the trip, incidentally, had not included
bicycle riding and nothing could have simulated the reality in
any case. A narrow, winding trail, never more than three or four
yards straight, with roots and snags everywhere; tiny stumps
where the undergrowth had been slashed close to—but not level

with—the earth, jabbing at your pedals and angles; overhead
creepers waiting to strangle you while you are looking down
to avoid a stump; trellises of bamboo banging at your head no
matter how low you bent over the handle bars; a multitude of
spikes reaching out to rip your shirt and flesh to shreds; a combination of traps, snags, loops and spikes trying to trip you up
and unseat you at every turn. And in the beginning, the bike
invariably insisting on taking the very direction one wanted to
avoid. Worst of all, added to the previous terrors of the log
bridges, was that the bike as well now had to be maneuvered
across, usually on one's shoulders. But when we emerged after a
few hours of snag-ridden, serpentine trail on to what still bore
resemblance to a hard-topped highway, I began to appreciate
being on wheels again. The old sense of balance soon returned
and the miles began to whizz by. It was better than being in a
jeep because with the silence of bike travel we always had plenty
of warning of approaching planes and could pull into the undergrowth.

GIFTS OF THE U.S.A.

My first Nam Bo bike was a Mavic, and although it was
French-made, the frame and both wheels were stamped with
clasped U.S.-Vietnamese hands under the Stars and Stripes and
the legend that it was a "gift of the people of the USA." Just like
the bombs and napalm! The same with the haversacks of the
guerillas and troops we passed on the road. Haversacks were almost invariably white flour sacks, stamped in big letters: THIS IS
A GIFT OF THE PEOPLE OF THE USA. NOT TO BE SOLD OR EXCHANGED.

It was ironic, to say the least, to see long lines of troops moving along the road to attack a post or take part in a counter-
mopping up action, each prominently displaying on his back:
"GIFT OF THE PEOPLE OF THE USA." In the Nam Bo, it seemed,
the clasped hands of friendship were more in evidence in Liberation Front areas than their own yellow-starred red and blue
flag. Apart from the captured U.S. weapons themselves, almost
every other bit of equipment I came across, from generators to
spot-welding machines and X-ray equipment, bore the clasped
hands and the standard legend.

When one looked at a regular soldier of the Front, the extent of U.S. "gifts" became even more impressive. Attached to his U.S. webbing belt are: the tiny bottle lamp already mentioned and in which U.S. cartridge cases play a vital role; his U.S. nylon hammock which is standard sleeping equipment, with parachute cords for hitching it to trees; a water bottle with a big U.S. stamped on the cloth container; a cluster of hand grenades made in the Front's own workshops, and finally the round bomb of rice—a 24-hour ration—wrapped in U.S. parachute nylon. His shirt is often enough of the same material as that around the rice, camouflage nylon. His standard arm is the U.S. carbine, but a percentage of his comrades-in-arms will be carrying Garands, tommy guns, 37mm machine guns, a variety of bazookas and mortars, and in battalion-sized units, a few of the highly appreciated 57mm recoilless cannon.

The Front soldiers, like those of the Vietminh before, march on the famous "Ho Chi Minh" sandals; the only difference being that U.S. Goodyear has replaced the French Michelin as the main supplier. The soles are from tires—ten pair can be cut from an average truck tire, or a hundred pair from an American ten-wheel General Motors truck—almost standard in South Vietnam. The four thongs that keep them in place are strips from inner tire tubes. They are the finest solution for footwear in heat and jungle conditions ever devised. I wore nothing else for nearly five months. With such equipment a Front battalion can march 15 miles after sundown to destroy an enemy post and back to their own base before dawn with the booty.

After a 25-mile ride on that first morning of cycling, we came to a quiet, brown stream where we laid up for the rest of the day. Toward evening a couple of sampans arrived, one with an outboard motor towing the other. We abandoned our bikes to board the boats. The outboard motor bore the clasped hands of friendship and the mark: "Kohler. 7 h.p. Made in USA." Throughout the night we puttered down this calm stream between luxuriant vegetation bordering the banks with an occasional glimpse of a village among the trees. Nothing but the brilliant white sparkle of the stars overhead and the occasional roar of a plan, transports off on commando-dropping missions.

So we traveled uneventfully for several days—nights, in fact.

since we usually rested up in daytime and traveled by night when
we used sampans, the streams not having that same wonderful
overhead protection from planes that the jungle tracks offered.
At various rendezvous points our group was gradually added
to until, in addition to an interpreter, there was a doctor, cook,
Liberation Front press officer, cadre in charge of security, body-
guards and guides who changed from region to region. At a
certain rendezvous point another set of bicycles awaited us, well
decorated with the hands of friendship.

As our group was established we settled down to a fairly
regular routine, once we were on bicycles again. We set out
as soon after dawn as possible and tried to reach our destination
before the great heat set in around midday. In the Nam Bo,
the heat did not vary much from around 38C from 11AM till
sunset. In the late afternoon we visited villages, army units,
Front organizations, workshops, had interviews and meetings,
avoiding travel or too much work in the great heat of the day.
The temperature was always bearable at night and except when
artillery shells were coming close, one slept wonderfully well
in the hammock under a mosquito net topped by a nylon fly
to keep off leaves and insects.

"You are in Saigon Now"

Messengers turned up every few hours during our travels with
tiny envelopes such as those used for visiting cards. They brought
the latest news of the adversary's movement and this became
especially important as we started to funnel into the complex
of military positions at the approach to Saigon. Our itinerary
was often changed from hour to hour, according to the contents
of those envelopes, the little notes inside covered with miniscule
writing which was studied with the greatest attention by our
security chief and his colleagues. Sometimes they would squat
down and scratch a whole series of maps on the ground, effacing
one and replacing it with another, before a satisfactory route
was agreed upon. They were exciting days as we headed straight
for Saigon. My notes, jotted down each evening, for a typical day
read as follows:

NGUYEN HUU THO
*President, South Vietnam
National Front of Liberation*

HUYNH TAN PHAT
*Secretary-General and Vice
President, NFL; Secretary-
General, Democratic Party;
and Pres., Saigon-Gia Dinh
Executive Committe, NFL.*

Bridges like these can be made in minutes.
Negotiating bikes over them is a problem.

Tiny lamps made from perfume bottles
light the path for night attacks.

Standard haversacks are
wheat sacks, "Gift of USA."

*Planes overhead all day today. B-26's, AD-6's, HU-IA heli-
copters and what my companions, even those who speak no
French, call* mesdemoiselles, *in reality French-built Morane reconnaissance planes. The jungle is thinning out with many
open stretches of grassland and rice field stubble and we have
to pay real attention not to be caught by planes while crossing
one of the clearings. Also we are passing closer to military posts
and sometimes through Saigon-controlled territory or zones which
the Front controls effectively only at night. Our guide has to
be perfect. A few green twigs placed in a certain pattern indicate which track we should follow at intersections; it is the
guide's responsibility to place them correctly. A minute or two
along the wrong path would mean disaster. Hard for me to tell
the difference between Saigon-controlled and Front-controlled
zones, except for the lack of people in the former. They are all
locked up, the soldiers in their posts, the people in their concentration camp villages. The guide said we must pass through one
very open area at night, because the track leads between two
posts at six and four miles distant with very open country in
between. In fact, because of the little notes that kept arriving
we did it in daylight, I being informed only when we arrived.
We passed the night in a thick clump of trees about two miles
from another post. The escort had their weapons very much
at the ready all day.*

The following day the track led through lots of open country
and in and out of rubber plantations. Lots of plane activity.
One *mademoiselle* started very early in the morning, at first
in big circles, then tighter and tighter ones with our little group
always in the center, in a patch of small trees and bushes in
which we had taken cover when she seemed too inquisitive.
The main concern of my companions was that someone may
have reported back about a "European with the Viet Cong"
and the Americans may conclude I am one of their POW's being
transferred. They offer rewards of 10-30,000 piastres* for that
kind of information and are liable to launch anything from
helicopter-borne troops for a quick snatch, to operations in-

---

* At the official rate, 35 piastres to the U.S. dollar.

volving several battalions to make a recovery. We decided to push on fast to a safer area the moment that *mademoiselle* went home. Before she left, however, another took her place flying much lower and again with our little group in the center. By now it was clear that we were the object of special attention. We were in a sort of large "no-man's land in which everything moving—from Saigon's viewpoint—was "hostile."

We had to play "hide and seek," pushing on when the plane's tail was turned to us, hoping she was blind in that position, hiding in whatever skimpy cover was available when we were clearly under observation. But she called up a sister plane to have us constantly in view. The two of them buzzed around like blowflies, flying in ever tighter circles and then cutting diagonals through the circles, zooming down lower and lower while we sped along, taking chances, by now trying to reach the comparative shelter of a rubber plantation. Our security chief feared helicopter troops might be moved into the various clearings and the escort troops were very much at the ready again. By the time the planes had zoomed down to near tree-top level we had reached Olympic standards in a final burst of speed that took us into the shade of a rubber plantation—not the same perfect camouflage roof as the jungle gives, but enough to cover our nakedness, of which I had been acutely conscious for the previous hour or so. The "hide and seek" had gone on for three hours by now; the sun was well up and the sweat pouring down. Our guide kept up a high speed, however, until we reached what was pronounced to be a "safe area." Within three minutes the planes dived down and to my surprise—I did not suspect that reconnaissance planes carried weapons—they dropped napalm bombs on a tiny cluster of huts they had sighted in the plantation, a few hundred yards from where we had slung our hammocks. One of the huts was hit and a nine-year-old girl was killed—which depressed me greatly because the planes were undoubtedly led to those huts by following our trail.

In the afternoon we moved on again, passing within 1,500 yards of a post, some green twigs fortunately indicating which tracks we should *not* follow. Lots of plane activity, but nothing

so specifically in our direction. There were plenty of explosions
from high-level and dive bombers, but as the sun dropped low
on the horizon this slackened off. I was cautioned to follow the
bicycle ahead very precisely because the road was "mined" by
the guerillas with spiked traps and some explosive ones. Part of
the road here had been destroyed with big ditches cut straight
across it in places and cut out in a cog-wheel fashion in others
so that a bicycle could wind its way in between the cog "teeth."

We entered a village where everything was gay and lively,
decorated with banners of the Front and slogans on red cloth
hailing the Lunar New Year; there were cozy scenes in the huts
as we passed, families taking their evening meal out-of-doors,
children playing under the trees, dogs barking at our arrival—
the atmosphere of normal, peaceful village life. There was
even a rare, friendly mechanical noise—electric-powered irrigation pumps for the local-market gardens.

I was astonished on being escorted into a hut to see a bottle
of John Haig whisky on the table. My host, a wispy-bearded old
man whose face was a myriad of wrinkles and who was introduced as a "veteran revolutionary from the November 1940
uprising," asked whether I drank it neat or with soda. Within
seconds he produced a bottle of soda and a basin of ice. The
reply to my wonderment as to where the ice came from was:
"But you are in Saigon now!" In fact, we were about six miles
from the outskirts.

After a full day's rest and talks with the villagers and local
guerillas, we set out on a zig-zag course which was to bring us
still closer to the capital. And about the time the year of the
Cat was transforming itself into the year of the Dragon—that is
about midnight on February 12, 1964—I was gliding down a
small canal toward the golden halo of Saigon. The outboard
motor puttered away gently; some escort troops, carbines across
their knees and fingers on the triggers, peered earnestly into
the darkness; the guide scanned every tree and cross canal.

The motor was cut. We were either very close to the rendezvous point or we had missed it. A minute or two in the
wrong direction now would be fatal. The striking of even a
match could bring a shattering artillery barrage in reply. As

we rounded one bend however, a tiny point of light did flash twice from within the depths of a bamboo grove, and as we veered towards the feathery profile from which the flashes had come, there were some whispered exchanges between shore and boat, as a result of which we entered a tunnel in the bamboo and within seconds, hands clasped my arms to guide me out of the boat and on to a path.

Without a word spoken apart from those hurried whispers, the escort troops fanned out each side and ahead of me and we were hastening along a path through a pineapple garden towards the next rendezvous point, a grove of trees for our hammocks. We were then about five miles from the southwest tip of Saigon. It was comforting to be assured that the sharp explosions in the immediate vicinity, some of them like rippling bursts of machine gun fire, came from the petards of New Year revellers, ignoring the strict ban that General Nguyen Khanh had ordered on any use of fireworks in welcoming the New Year of the Dragon. Khanh was frightened the explosions might prevent him from recognizing in time the sounds of a new coup; he had only been in power a little over two weeks and was still acutely coup-conscious.

Chapter 2

STRUGGLE AROUND SAIGON

In Whose Territory?

A trim, smiling man with twinkling eyes and a thin line of
moustache, dressed as if he had stepped straight out of his
Saigon office, came into the peasant's hut where my hammock
had been slung for the night. I had slept late, and had been
musing over the constant roar of planes and helicopters which
neither seemed to grow nearer nor to recede into the distance.
It had just been explained that they were warming up their
motors at Saigon's main airport.

"Welcome to Saigon," said the smiling man in French of a
Parisian quality, both hands stretched out in greeting. "Meet
the members of our Committee." They were 12 altogether out
of 16 members of the Executive Committee of the Liberation
Front's Saigon-Gia Dinh branch (Gia Dinh is Saigon's province).
Four of them had secretly slipped out of Saigon the previous
night to attend our meeting. The smiling man was Huynh Tan
Phat, a well-known Saigon architect. Apart from heading the
Saigon-Gia Dinh committee, he is one of the outstanding national
leaders of the Liberation Front, as the Secretary General of
its Central Committee and head of the Democratic Party, one
of the three political parties affiliated to the NFL. Like so many
of the Front's leaders, he had temporarily abandoned his profession and city comforts for the hard, dangerous life of the
liberation struggle. I already knew that his wife was serving
a life sentence under the terms of Law 10/59.*

Among the Committee members, as Huynh Tan Phat presented them, were two journalists, a writer, a musician, two
peasants, a factory worker, a representative of Saigon youth

* Enacted in 1959, this law set life imprisonment or the death penalty
for anyone "committing a crime against the security of the state or har-
boring an intent to commit such a crime."

33

whose profession I did not note, a housewife, one student, one schoolteacher and of course the architect himself.

One of my first questions was whether we were meeting in "liberated" or "enemy-occupied" territory. On numerous occasions while cycling, I had been warned to keep my head down and lower my hat—that splendid Vietnamese conical straw hat which keeps the face in shadow all the time and completely conceals it in an emergency—or to lay down flat in the bottom of a sampan because we were passing through enemy territory.

"We have to live very closely integrated with the enemy," explained Huynh Tan Phat with a marvellously humorous twinkle that rarely leaves his eyes. "They think, for instance, that this hamlet is theirs. In fact it is ours. People often come out from Saigon and have no idea they are in one of our liberated areas. We don't bother them, never ask them for papers unless we smell an agent. In that case we would have been warned in advance. Our territory and the enemy's is closely interlocked, especially here so near to Saigon. But you only come up against the enemy if you run right into an enemy post or get within the sights of his artillery or machine guns. We have a policy called 'corking up' enemy posts, meaning they are surrounded by our guerillas day and night and the garrison can only move out with our permission."

He produced a map to illustrate the situation. He showed me the hamlet in Binh Chanh district, where I had spent the first few hours of the Year of the Dragon, and I was astonished to note that we appeared to have spent the night and most of next day a few hundred yards from a post. "Actually that post no longer exists," he said and put a cross through it. "It was taken out a couple of months ago. For months previous to that, it was encircled day and night; the garrison had to ask our guerillas for permission to visit the market, or draw cooking water from the Kinh Xang canal right alongside. They feared an attack at any moment so they have now abandoned it." The post had been held by a company of Saigon troops and it was about four miles from Saigon. More alarming, however, seemed the situation in the immediate vicinity of the hamlet where we were meeting in a peasant's hut.

Posts—with no crosses through them—were all around, two of them at a distance of 1,000 and 1,500 yards, respectively. And suddenly, there started a tremendous noise of exploding artillery and mortar shells, heavy machine gun fire, the roar of diving planes and the dull crack of exploding napalm bombs. It was very difficult to hear Huynh Tan Phat's voice and even more to accept the calm assurances that the enemy could never move out. "Yes," he said, "it does look rather frightening on a map. We seem to be completely encircled by enemy posts but, in fact, it is they who are encircled by us. The garrisons can't move out except in big, combined operations with Saigon's mobile reserves."

When a pause was proposed, I asked about the noise of what seemed a very fierce battle in our immediate vicinity, but of which no notice was taken. "Didn't anyone tell you about that?" asked Huynh Tan Phat, with an apologetic smile. "That's the U.S. Parachutist Training Center at Trung Hoa, a couple of miles from here. They can't train their conscripts in parachute jumping any more because too many used to fall into our areas, some of them purposely. Now they give them infantry training under simulated battle conditions. It goes on nearly every morning; someone should have warned you."

On the map of Gia Dinh province, the "interlocking" of Front and Saigon-controlled areas was expressed in red and green splotches of color with large yellow patches in between to denote areas nominally controlled by Saigon by day and effectively controlled by the Front at night. Red areas are what Liberation Front cadres refer to as "guerilla bases" and yellow denotes "guerilla zones." Apart from the great blob of green which represented Saigon-Cholon, other smaller green islands showed Saigon-controlled district centers and groups of "strategic hamlets," each with one or more military posts in the immediate vicinity. The yellow areas were bigger than the red and green taken together and extended up to the very outskirts of Saigon. "We wiped out an enemy post less than half a mile from the outskirts a few weeks ago," Huynh Tan Phat said, as I expressed surprise that guerillas should reach the threshold of the city.

"Saigon," he continued, "is not only the administrative capital,

it is also the enemy's military and political nerve center. Here
are also concentrated the main military installations, munitions
depots, air fields, training centers, the U.S. command—everything
for running the war. Of late there have been two tendencies:
one, the city spreads out into the countryside as new military
installations encroach on the peasants' land and hamlets are
bulldozed out of existence to make way for new supply dumps
and training areas, airfield extensions and so on; the other
tendency is the more the U.S. puppets are defeated in the
countryside, the more they withdraw into Saigon. Gia Dinh
itself, they consider, a sort of armored belt to protect the capital.

"As you can see," he said, as he turned to the map again, "this
whole area is intersected by a big network of roads, strategic
highways and 'strategic hamlets.' Movement is difficult for our
forces because of this and the barbed wire, ditches, enemy posts
and other obstacles. But as you yourself have experienced, we
do manage to move." He dispatched someone to keep an eye
on the planes that were buzzing around. Air-raid shelters were
nearby and there would be time enough to jump into them
between the "bombs away" signal and the explosions.

IN A STRATEGIC HAMLET

"As part of their defenses, the enemy set up 282 'strategic
hamlets' in Gia Dinh province," Huynh Tan Phat continued,
"to form a belt of human armor around the city and to eliminate any they considered as 'Viet Cong.' They formulated a
policy of 'letting the water out of the pond to catch the fish'
but the fish, as you see, were a little too agile to be caught that
way. As this area is so close to the capital and the seat of
their military-police power, they could concentrate very big
forces and did succeed in setting up the hamlets. Some of them
were so-called model hamlets—show pieces for U.S. military brass
and visiting foreigners. But after last November's coup against
Diem*, the people rose and destroyed many of them. By the end

---

* Ngo Dinh Diem ruled South Vietnam from 1954 to November 1963,
when he was assassinated, together with his brother Nhu, during the
generals' coup.

of 1963, over 50 were completely dismantled, including some
of the 'model' ones; the peasants went back to their old villages
and put their own land back into cultivation, right under the
noses of the enemy. In almost all the rest, the grip of the enemy
was broken and our organizations were set up."

"Could I visit a 'strategic hamlet' still under enemy control?"

"If you don't mind taking a bit of a risk, of course you can."

"One fairly close to Saigon?" I asked. He produced the map
again, and after consulting with his fellow committee members
he underlined one village.

"That could be interesting to you," he said, "because there
is a liberated village right alongside. You'll see what 'living
integrated' means."

Next day, I travelled by bicycle, sampan and on foot and
about an hour before sunset, I was clambering down a moat
and then over some earthern ramparts of the "strategic hamlet"
of Tan Thanh Tay, in Hoc Mon district some six to seven miles
from the Saigon outskirts. A small escort of troops had come
with me and people rushed out to embrace them, thinking
that liberation was at hand. It was not really a typical "strategic
hamlet" because the people had successfully fought against
being encircled by a palisade and barbed wire. But it looked
like no other Vietnamese village I had seen till that time. Houses
were hovels, huddled together with no trees or greenery—so
typical of Vietnamese villages south or north of the 17th parallel
—no gardens or fish ponds. A skinny old man, with a frame like
an Auschwitz victim, acted as spokesman for a group that gathered around as soon as my guides assured them I was a "foreign
friend."

"This is no life at all," he said. "Just when we should be
going to the fields in the cool of the evening, we have to come
back. We have to be inside the gates half an hour before sunset
or we'll be beaten up. No trees for shade, they cut everything
down; just cleared the bamboo away with bulldozers. No chance
of raising pigs or chickens, with houses on top of each other
like this; not even a fish pond. They suck our blood dry with
taxes and they invent new ones all the time. Taxes for everything. On top of that, the troops from the post come and say:

'Give me that chicken. Give me this, give me that.' If you refuse
they say you are 'Viet Cong' and beat you up, then drag you off
to the district jail. Your family will be lucky to hear from you
again once that happens."

Others spoke up to tell of the living death that life in this
glorified concentration camp represented. No place for children
to play; they stood around listlessly, hanging on to their mothers
with pallid, unhealthy faces. There is no room "even to breathe,"
as one woman with a babe at her breast expressed it, "and we
always live in terror of what will happen next. Day or night,
there's no security; the troops come and steal and terrify the
older girls."

We could not stay long because word soon came that four
enemy soldiers happened to be inside the hamlet near our entry
point and had raced back to their post at the opposite end
of the hamlet, about 1,000 yards away. There was no likelihood
of the garrison launching an attack, but it was explained to me
that the post had two 81mm mortars and they might start
shelling. So we walked away rather briskly until the security
expert said we were out of mortar range. The sun was just
setting by then. We rested on a rice field terrace, drank some
bottles of Saigon beer and watched bombers roaring down the
runway of Saigon's main airport.

As the tropical dark swiftly descended, the twinkling lights
of the Saigon outskirts came into focus and the glowing red tips
of the antennas at the American Quan Tung training centers,
just outside Saigon. We moved off to visit the neighboring
village of An Nhan Tay less than a mile away. The road leading
into the village had been destroyed by cutting yard-deep trenches
right across it and packing the dirt and rocks removed into
ramparts between the trenches.

"Isn't there any attempt made to put it into service again?"
I asked.

"At first they used to try and repair," my guide explained,
"but what they repaired by day, the peasants destroyed by
night—if not in exactly the same place then somewhere else.
In the end they gave up."

The population in An Nhan Tay had also been concentrated.

On the way to the "strategic hamlet" I had visited the original hamlet around which An Nhan Tay and some other hamlets had been concentrated and saw stacks of trees and bamboo that had been cut down to remove any hiding places for guerillas. Now people had rebuilt their homes in their original hamlet; houses were well spaced, surrounded by fruit trees and clumps of bamboo, with pigs and chickens snuffling and scratching around; children were running about with the shrieks and whoops one can hear in most parts of the world at the last hour or two of evening play; peasants were out watering their vegetable gardens; everything bespoke peace and a normal life. I saw the heap of rubble to which the post which used to control the "strategic hamlet" had been reduced and talked with a cadre who had lived underground for almost six years, physically underground, because he lived in a secret trench not a hundred yards from the post, at the end of a tunnel the villagers had helped him dig from the hamlet, and along which they brought him food. He came out at night to continue organizational work and keep hopes alive during the worst years of the Diemist* repression. In the end, it was from his secret hide-out that the attack against the post was launched, with a few more tunnels leading to the very foundations of the post's fortifications. A sturdy little man, relaxed and gay like so many of those I met in the Saigon-Gia Dinh area.

"The enemy acted in a very barbarous way in this region," he said. "People were killed indiscriminately at the whim of the local tyrant. Although we are so close to Saigon, this was a strong resistance area even under the French so the Diemists were specially severe; terror and violence were used to cow people into submission. People fought against setting up the 'strategic hamlet' but after a two months' struggle, the enemy brought in bulldozers and with the whole area encircled by several battalions, they started to bulldoze trees and everything green out of existence to make a devastated zone around the

---

* The term "Diemist" is used throughout to designate the policies, actions and forces of the regime of Ngo Dinh Diem, who has since been replaced by others, without changes in the nature of the Saigon government.

'strategic hamlets.' But the people fought back every inch of the way. When the bamboo hedges were bulldozed away, they fought to protect their fruit trees. When these were hacked down they fought against having palisades and barbed wire, and on this they won. When the post was built, the troops could observe but not control the concentration of houses.

"Meanwhile the villagers, especially the young men and girls, started digging underground tunnels at night, creeping closer and closer to the post. Most of these young people are now in the Liberation Army," he said. "During that period, the people several times broke out and went back to their old village in the devastated 'no-man's land.' The enemy sent troops after them and brought them back. It was only after we wiped out the post after the November coup against Diem that we could stay back in our own village and build up a normal life again."

I walked into one An Nahn Tay home at random; the table was piled high with fruit and New Year sweetmeats and red paper streamers hung from the ceiling with Chinese characters for "Happy New Year Of The Dragon." A dignified, tiny old lady appeared, a member of the "Soldiers' Mothers" organization. The cadre said she was one among many who performed miracles of courage in feeding and hiding "activists" on the run from the Diemist police. The old lady listened calmly to the eulogy and said: "Any sacrifice old people like me can make is little compared with what these lads risk every day to serve the people." She spoke of the hopeless life in the "strategic hamlet" and the new, free life now they had struggled to liberate themselves. Within seconds her house was filled to over-flowing and the courtyard as well at this absolutely unprecedented visit of a "foreign friend." The only foreigners they had ever known in their village before were the opposite of "friendly," a point made by the old lady. After a symbolic drinking of the strong, bitter tea that the South Vietnamese adore—they despise the big pots in which tea is served in the North and treasure tiny affairs in which they claim the real essence of the tea is preserved—and many expressions of good wishes for my health, we took our leave.

An Open-Air Show

That night I was to have visited an open-air show put on by the district theatrical ensemble. As it had been a tiring day, I said I would decide only after the evening meal. About the time we should have been setting out for the open-air theatre, artillery opened up, shooting 155mm shells in our direction, the first salvo landing close enough for headlong dives into the shelters, with clumps of dirt showering on our necks from the explosions. After the first few salvos, four shells coming at a time, a battery of heavy mortars from a nearby post joined in, their screaming whine clearly distinguishable from the heavier drone of the artillery shells. The firing kept up for about 90 minutes. Then there was silence, broken by the comforting normal sound of a Lambretta transport taxi starting up—probably delivering ice from Saigon.

The enemy had got wind of the show, probably because people had converged on the area for hours beforehand from all the surrounding hamlets, including some enemy-controlled ones, and their target was the open-air theater. Almost all the shells fell in the area we would have been crossing had we decided to go. Nobody had been hurt. Lights had been immediately doused at the theater; the audience lay flat on the ground until it was all over, the show starting up again immediately afterwards.

Next night we attended a show in the same place, the master of ceremonies first announcing the security precautions; in the case of planes appearing or artillery opening up lights would be doused and the audience should move into trenches, dug since the previous night's experience. No applause by request because it might drown out the noise of approaching planes. A lone bomber did appear shortly after the show started; the powerful kerosene pressure lamps were extinguished but as the plane did not circle, everyone stayed in their places. It roared away into the night, a red light blinking in its tail, like some malignant spirit come to spoil the charm of the evening. The show opened with songs and choruses, with delicate, charming music played on traditional wind and stringed instruments and composed by a member of Saigon's executive committee.

There was a drum dance with very effective use of the tom-tom by fluctuating rhythms and volume to denote the ups and down of life and struggle in South Vietnam; the first resistance struggle, the joyous reaction to the coming of peace, the black period of repression with grief and mourning over the whole land; the call to arms for a second resistance war; victories and life in the liberated areas. There was a fantastic "Sorcerer's Dance" based on highland tribal dances and rhythms.

The ban on applause was repeatedly violated during a one-act play about soldiers in an enemy post demanding permission of their officer to accept the Front's offer to visit their families during the Lunar New Year ceasefire period which the Front had proclaimed. The officer refuses and after lots of semi-comic argument, the troops hand in their guns and leave anyway, and in the end the officer decides to do the same thing. (This was not far-fetched, as tens of thousands of troops did just that. Even 250 trainees at the Trung Hoa parachutist training camp ignored their officers' protests and took off for their homes in Front-controlled territory. Troops and officers from a post near one of the hamlets where I spent a night during the New Year period, came over to see an open-air show by the same district theater group.)

After the "live" show, there was a film which I did not wait to see, but the audience—well over 2,000—remained rooted to the spot. The director of the group told me the shows were always well attended and that they gave performances within a mile of Saigon's outskirts. "Those shows always draw huge crowds," he said. "At one of the early ones, some Saigon theater people turned up. They had come to scoff, but went away delighted and told us we were doing a good job in preserving our national culture while they had to dabble in western themes of sex and sensationalism." I asked if the Saigon regime tolerated such activities as theirs.

"Of course not," came the reply. "You witnessed what happened last night. They would like to wipe us off the face of the earth and all those that come to our shows. But the people support us everywhere. Local guerillas protect us and we have our own means of self-defense. Within a few hundred yards of

Saigon itself, it is difficult for the enemy to bomb or shell even if he knows a show is going on. And our own self-defense people would take care of any night operations against us."

A FORTIFIED HAMLET

Among those I met the following day were two dimpled and demure girl guerillas, whose names in Vietnamese meant "Blossom" and "Lissom," respectively. They were both from the same village and the district guerilla leader had mentioned them as having helped, with five lads from their village, to repulse a company of enemy troops. They were in spotlessly clean black cotton shirts and trousers; hand grenades dangled from their U.S. webbing belts and each had a U.S. carbine. They looked 15 years, but "Blossom" said she was 19 and "Lissom" assured me she was 22.

"Blossom" was the real heroine of the action and she made it sound quite simple. "When the enemy came very close, I rushed from one firing position to another firing my carbine and one of the puppets fell each time I fired. We all shifted our positions so they would think there were a lot of us. Actually most of our self-defense unit was away that day and we were only seven," she explained in a light, babyish voice. "The enemy started to set up a machine gun to fire at one of our positions, so I ran there and threw a hand grenade. It killed the gunner and put the machine gun out of action. By then the enemy had nine killed and wounded and they withdrew. Later they fired some shells but they did no damage." That was all. It seemed incredible to me that a company, 80 to 100 men, would break off an engagement with nine casualties or that they would not have tried to take the positions by assault.

Then I was taken to have a look at the "fortified village" which the two girls had helped defend. The defenses consist of a maze of tunnels, about 20 miles in this one hamlet, I was told, leading into spacious fire positions which cover every approach. They are big enough for some one of Vietnamese size to run doubled up from one fire position to another, as "Blossom" had described.

I was taken to inspect a single clump of bamboo and told to look very carefully for anything suspicious among the roots. I found nothing. Then I was taken into the tunnel and to a firing position which could accommodate three or four people. Someone took a stick and poked it through what seemed to be blind slits with earthern gun rests behind them. The slits opened up to cover the road along which we had cycled a few minutes earlier into the hamlet. Again I was taken to the bamboo clump and there my attention was drawn to the tiny slits which had been opened up among the bamboo roots, impossible for anyone to detect at even a few yards.

Other firing positions which I inspected were also perfectly camouflaged and as the guerillas changed places constantly, even if the gun flash or smoke gave a position away, it would be little use firing at it. All roads, paths and canals approaching the village were adequately covered. To jump for cover at the time when the firing started was inevitably to fall into a terrible series of traps, most of them deep pits with bamboo and steel spikes; others with grenades and anti-personnel mines made in a local arsenal. I understood why an action was broken off after nine casualties. To take even the outer perimeter of such a fortified hamlet would be a very costly affair. If attacking troops were to penetrate the tunnels, all sorts of hand-operated traps would go into action. The attackers would probably be diverted to a section which would be blown up with everyone in it. If an assault force attacked in the center it would be fired on from the flanks, if it attacked the flanks it would be fired on from the center; if it overran the outer perimeter and penetrated further, the second and third and fourth lines of defense would go into action. If the odds were too overwhelming, the guerillas could pull out altogether through the system of escape tunnels which might lead into the forest, to a river bank or to a neighboring hamlet.

The "fortified hamlet" of "Blossom" and "Lissom," was the first of such perfection I had visited. I was later to visit other tunnel systems which linked a whole group of hamlets and had over 500 firing positions and successive traps to block off sections in case flame-throwers or some sort of poison gas was used.

A hundred thousand work hours had been put into building the tunnel defenses of some of the hamlets. They were built almost entirely by the young people of the villages, the older ones keeping up supplies of rice, tea and fruit while they worked often from dusk to dawn.

'The enemy builds big posts with huge watch towers to try and control the countryside," said the military chief of Saigon-Gia Dinh. "We build our fire positions as close to the ground as possible and the rest underground, because our people are defending their own homes. They need to see the enemy—over their sights—only when he comes with evil intent to the gates of their hamlets. The enemy cannot move along the roads and paths near our villages without being continually in the sights of our guns. This is what we mean by people's war."

There were about 4,300 such fortified villages in South Vietnam at that time, mostly in the Mekong Delta region, but they were being added to every day in Central Vietnam. It seemed to me that those who devised them had pooled the experiences of General Vo Nguyen Giap and his creeping system of trenches used so effectively at Dien Bien Phu, the tunnel system used by the Chinese guerillas in Hopei province during the anti-Japanese war in which whole counties were linked by underground defense and communications networks, and the system of defensive tunnels built by the Korean-Chinese forces across the waist of Korea near the 38th parallel. If one such hamlet could keep a company at bay—and I heard of plenty of cases where even battalions were repulsed—one only has to multiply by 4,500 the magnitude of the task of any regime or any military machine in trying to reconquer them.

From midnight onwards on the night after the meeting with "Blossom" and "Lissom," there was intermittent artillery fire, but none coming close enough to make us leave our hammocks —they were slung in a rubber plantation. At dawn the firing was more intensive and coming our way. *Mesdemoiselles* were also very active, showing a special interest in our little corner. About the time the Saigon morning papers were delivered to my interpreter, one of those tiny envelopes arrived. It was for the Saigon-Gia Dinh military chief who happened to be with us—a brisk, cheerful man with that alert, decided way about him that marks a good staff officer in any army. After studying the note, he scribbled a reply; showing both to my companions and buckling on his Colt, with a few terse words and a sunny smile he strode away.

"A company of parachutists moved in to the other end of the plantation about midnight," said Huynh, my journalist-interpreter. "We have had them under observation and they are moving this way at the moment. We had better put you in the secret trenches." By that time, there was considerable activity all around. The doctor was checking his medical pack, our baggage—always packed for instant moves—was being carried with some speed deeper into the plantation. "They're still about a half mile from here," said Huynh laconically. "We also have some troops around. We'd better not dawdle because bullets will soon be flying."

I did not favor spending an unlimited period in the secret underground tunnels which were not tailored for my girth. A compromise solution was found by letting me move into a well-camouflaged semi-circular trench, with communication trenches leading well to the rear. The parachutists in mottled green camouflage uniforms were advancing, cautiously, weapons at the ready in two groups, one about 50, the other carrying some mortars, about thirty. There were three U.S. advisers with the larger group.

At about a hundred yards distant, they sighted two trenches with some Front troops in them. The parachutists flopped down and opened up with heavy machine guns, from both columns. The Front forces replied with a short burst from each of two heavy machine guns, wounding three paratroopers. From where I was I saw the Americans drop into a trench at the first shots and could see their hands gesticulating, urging the unit to advance. But the troops wavered a moment, then swept up their machine guns and the mortars they had been just setting up and started retreating into the trees, the Americans scrambling to their feet and leading the way once the retreat started. They fled so precipitately that they left their lunch rations in the trench. Guerillas followed them up and little envelopes started arriving with news that the parachutists had withdrawn one, two, three miles—back to their training base at Trung Hoa. There had been no casualties in the Front trenches, and the position in which I was installed had not fired at all.

A local guerilla leader came over as soon as the "all quiet" was received and a few excited words were exchanged between him and the unit commander of the regular forces which had done the firing. "The guerilla is angry because they fired so soon," the interpreter explained. "He wants to know why they fired at 100 yards, instead of 10 or 15 yards like the guerillas. The whole unit could have been wiped out and their arms captured." The unit commander explained that his aim was to scare them, not to wipe them out. His job was to protect a "foreign friend." If they had been wiped out and the Americans killed, there would have been a big action to recover the bodies, the village would have been bombed as a reprisal and such results would violate instuctions to give "maximum security" to their foreign charge.

The locals explained that the parachutists were trainees who were just about to "graduate." The exercises under simulated battle conditions which I had heard a few days earlier was the last but one phase before graduation. The last was an actual combat engagement, usually against lightly-armed local guerillas. To their surprise, this batch had run into regular troops who also had heavy machine guns. Doubtless those particular graduates were put through another conditioning process of simulated battle conditions before being sent out to face enemy fire again. "In any case the trainees run after we fire a few shots," the guerilla leader said, "but we usually get some of their weapons."

About an hour later, as we cycled through the hamlet near which the action had taken place, a girl from the local information office was striding through the street with a megaphone, announcing that an attack by enemy forces had been repulsed and that news "of casualties and booty will be announced later."

The incident in the rubber plantation was the start of an exciting few days in the Saigon area and I was able to sense something of what "living integrated with the enemy" meant.

Chapter 3

HIDE AND SEEK

One thing that constantly astonished me was the absolute precision with which the Liberation Front forces operated. The contact to steer us past enemy posts was always waiting behind the right tree at the right time; a tiny signal light would wink at us out of the jet black night at the very moment the second hand of the watch moved up towards rendezvous time, a winking point of light that could be taken for a firefly unless one knew it should be there at that precise time and place. The sampan was always where it should be to cross a stream in enemy-controlled territory; the barbed wire was always cut within yards of the rendezvous point to cross a strategic highway; the guide to the secret tunnels never failed to be when and where he should be.

This was all the more surprising, as I rarely found anyone who could tell me the date or what day of the week it was, except when we were close enough to Saigon to get the morning papers. Even high-ranking cadres told me they had to make elaborate calculations at times to arrive at the correct date. But when it came to hours and minutes, they were as precise as sputniks. They had to be, especially in those frontline areas around the perimeter of Saigon. But I never failed to be surprised when, for instance, cycling along a tiny track through dense jungle, the cook would suddenly lean over and, without slackening speed, extract a chicken for my lunch, its legs tied together with a bit of jungle creeper. I never understood how such rendezvous with chickens were arranged and even less the mystery of how the cook knew behind which bush it had been deposited.

A more important example was the precise information the Front military cadres had, not only about their adversary's movements, but his intentions. At some point along the jungle track, or canal, or mountain trail, whoever happened to be chief of the group would suggest a rest. Within minutes, a partisan invariably appeared with one of those tiny envelopes already mentioned. I quickly developed a great affection for them because they brought us continuous news of what the adversary was up to. Often enough, they came from a guerilla unit stationed day and night around some enemy post; or brought information from a contact inside the post. Sometimes, especially in the Saigon area, these little notes caused us to change our travel plans abruptly. After studying such a note, the chief of the group would pull out what looked like a small pack of playing cards and in consultation with whoever happened to be the guide through that particular area—a guerilla who combined the duties of mail courier with that of guiding cadres past enemy posts—the group chief would thumb through the cards, checking them carefully with the news in the letter and selecting one with which the guide agreed.

The cards were covered with letters and numbers and one would think at first, by the intense, serious expressions, that some game for very high stakes was being played. In fact, the numbers and letters were coded symbols for every road and track, every stream and canal in the region through which we were passing. Each card represented a different combination, all the possible variants of moving from point A to point B. According to news of the adversary's movements, the card was chosen and liaison established with the guerillas whose territory we would be traversing.

When we travelled on bicycle our small convoy inevitably got spread out along the tiny tracks that wind through the forest like a fast-wriggling snake, at times leading to a hub of tracks the spokes of which radiated out in all directions. The duty of the guide was to indicate by signs known only to the guerillas which track was to be followed so that those lagging behind would not go astray. This had to be exact, too. As we often passed, in daylight, within one or two miles of a post, only a few minutes of cycling might bring one up against a post. Although the garrison was "corked up," as Huynh Tan

Phat had expressed it, their shells and machine gun bullets were certainly not.

On one memorable occasion a tiny envelope arrived and faces were more serious than usual as the contents were perused. It was the evening before we were to leave the Saigon-Gia Dinh area and head off to the northeast. "In two days time," explained the area military commander, "the enemy will start a big mopping-up operation, employing five battalions, about 4,000 men. This operation will take place in the very area you have to traverse; they will occupy the roads you have to travel or cross; their patrol boats will be active on the rivers you have to travel on. It will last four days. We propose that you stay here where we can protect you."

Sure enough, two mornings later, there was great activity by planes and helicopters, *mesdemoiselles* buzzing around from the first streak of dawn, seeking out targets for the bombers. Whatever information they signaled back, I could never even guess. But by 8 AM two B-26 bombers came over and started a raid that lasted four hours. They stuck to a single flight circle, dropping a few bombs each time they came round. My interpreter, an expert on the direction of shells, now proved his merits by estimating the flight of bombs. As the planes came round, he watched them with an eagle eye, reporting when the bombs were leaving the bomb bays and whether they were coming close enough to jump into the shelter or not. The bombs were always whooshing down as we jumped and the fearsome crash of the explosions about coincided with the thud of our feet into the shelter. We avoided going in as much as we could, because the earth ceiling was covered with long-legged spiders, the shock of the explosions invariably detaching some of them on to our necks.

THE TUNNEL SYSTEM

In mid-afternoon, envelopes having poured in all day, one arrived with the information that Saigon troops had pushed down and occupied a road only a half mile distant, so I and a few members of our group were to be hidden in a secret tunnel.

The others had to get ready for "military affairs." Five battalions were being employed, as the warning had predicted, and were accompanied by 23 M-113 tanks. Artillery and mortar shells were coming quite close and there was an alarmingly sharp rattle of machine gun fire, as we were guided through a patch of rubber trees to a square manhole through which we dropped —in my case squeezed—down into a tunnel. When we were all in, the manhole was covered over with earth and leaves, all traces of our tracks erased and various sentries took up vantage points in well camouflaged positions to keep an eye on events. I was assured that the tunnel was a very long one and part of a maze of tunnels connecting various hamlets. Before we entered, a set of cards had been consulted and precise instructions given to an expert tunnel guide as to which direction we should take in case of a "real emergency."

Such tunnels are not built for my size; where others double up and walk I could only crawl and for a few moments I had a feeling of claustrophobia. I have always had a secret dread of being underground in a confined space and have marveled that anyone could choose mining as a life job. Breathing was difficult at first because our group was huddled together, all breathing heavily after the exertions of getting ourselves and our baggage into the tunnel.

Later, when the rest of the party moved off in the direction given by the guide, the air got better and I found, stretched out on the ground that breathing became normal again. There were moments, however, when I felt I must burst out of that manhole again at all costs. But they passed. There were miniscule worms in the ground, no bigger than a speck of dust, which manage in a surprisingly short time to burrow into the skin, causing a prickly feeling when one touches the spot. This was explained to me when I started to scratch. Apart from the irritation, it seems, they do no harm. Someone brought me a nylon sheet to lie on and all but the early worms were frustrated, but those that did burrow in stayed with me for several weeks.

The noise of battle was somewhat muffled here but distinct enough for me to know that it was quite close and moving in our direction. The baggage was pushed up the tunnel ahead of

us; in guerilla conditions any separation from one's baggage
is likely to be final so we had brought it all along. Mine was
full of precious notes and exposed films and I was anxious that
they, at any rate, should be destroyed in case of any risk of them
falling into unfriendly hands. My thoughts were very much
on this because while I was still squeezing myself down through
the manhole, there had been another sharp burst of machine
gun fire very close, I judged not more than 100 yards, immediately followed by several carbine shots within 20 or 30 yards.
I thought the shots were aimed in our direction, that the Saigon
troops had infiltrated and thus must have sighted the hideout.

In fact, as I discovered later, a patrol had come within a few
hundred yards; the Front forces had given them a few bursts
of a heavy machine gun, the carbine shots were fired as warnings to us by sentries who had also sighted the patrol. But I
only knew this some hours later. Huynh, my interpreter, who
also could not know exactly what was going on—firing seemed
to be coming from all directions by now—told me "not to worry"
and that "we will certainly get you out of this." I explained that
one of my worries was the matter of my notes and films and
the other was that I had not been able to send word for
weeks past to my wife in Moscow. He crawled away and returned
within a few minutes to say:

"If you want to send a very short message, only three or four
words, we can send it off from here. But you must do it immediately. So I wrote down my telegraphic address and the banal
words: "Perfect Health Greetings," and tore the page out of
my notebook. Huynh crawled away with it and returned to say
that a "courier" had immediately left for a dispatch point. Three
days later my wife received the telegram in Moscow, breaking
a long period of suspense. Had she known the conditions under
which it was sent, the suspense would have been understandably
still greater. Huynh also announced that the bag with my notes
(over 300 typed pages, by then) and films had been sealed up
in one of a number of holes in the tunnel walls, designed for
such emergencies. I was then guided a few score more yards along
the tunnel to a place where there was a tiny, horizontal air
hole, leading from the tunnel into an abandoned spiked trap.

I lay with my face close to a marvellous flow of air and dozed off to sleep; the rippling crashes of artillery seemed to have receded a bit.

I was awakened by the interpreter shaking my shoulder and bringing news that after suffering some casualties, the Saigon troops had pulled back a few miles. We could emerge into the fresh air for a while. Envelopes converged on us from all directions, confirming that about an hour before sunset the adversary was licking his wounds and had dug in about three miles distant. After much consultation, it was decided to shift our position to a point a bit further from the enemy and where there were "more comfortable tunnels and first-class air-raid shelters." So we set out for a brisk hour's march. When we arrived at the spot, on the banks of a fairly big river, urgent discussions again took place. There was the disturbing noise of a motor of some sort of heavy river craft, not too far downstream from where we were. Within minutes an envelope had arrived with the news that an American landing craft was moored at a wharf about a mile downstream, with the motor running and only the crew aboard.

"There are two possibilities," said the military chief after consultations were completed. "Either that landing craft is to ferry the troops back to their base, or it is waiting to take troops aboard for a raid into this area. I think the second is more likely as the operation should continue three more days according to original plans. So we must move you again."

It was a splendid moonlight night and we were soon on our way, marching over rice fields, the short, dried stubble pricking at our feet through the open sandals. After we had marched quickly for half an hour, we could hear the landing craft's motor revving up and it was clear it was under way, heading in the direction we had just left. Almost immediately salvos of shells started coming in our direction and we had to throw ourselves on the ground for the bursts, keeping on the move in between. After a good three hours' march, with the shelling providing the only rests, we slung our hammocks in a thick belt of forest, my "own" trees being on the edge of a crater from a 1,000-pound bomb. Half an hour after we arrived, there was one sharp burst of automatic fire in the distance. Later, an envelope arrived with the news that a cadre, following the path we had taken, was surprised by a patrol from the landing craft and was killed with a burst from a tommy gun.

Military Manhunt

Early next morning the operation was in full swing, the main body of Saigon troops having moved into the area. *Mesdemoiselles* were soaring overhead like wasps, trying to spot defense positions and direct artillery fire. It was easy to distinguish the attackers artillery, mortar and long bursts of machine gun and automatic fire from the lighter, shorter bursts from the defenders' automatic weapons and single shots of rifle fire. The guerillas never like to fire a single unnecessary shot—cartridges are too precious.

It sounded like a terribly unequal combat with bombs and shells thundering down in between the exchanges of the lighter weapons. But the guerillas do not accept battle on the adversary's terms. They slow them up, make them pay a little and then fade out. When they give battle, it is on their terms and not too close to populated areas. And this was what was happening now. When I asked what was the main aim of the operation, the Front area commander said:

"It's just a large-scale manhunt and to destroy crops and livestock. The main aim is to round up as many men of military age as possible for conscripts. Apart from that, to destroy rice stocks and pigs and chickens. But our people are very experienced in hiding their stuff. Everybody has his or her task at a time like this. We are always warned of such raids in time. The young people look to the defenses or just disappear if it is not in our interest to fight back; children move the livestock to hiding places; older people set the temporary traps and make sure the permanent ones are in good shape. The older people stay on even if the enemy comes into the hamlet; they warn the troops to stop away from houses and gardens because the 'Viet Cong' have laid traps all over the place: 'What a pity it would be if fine, healthy young chaps like you were to get your legs and stomachs all pierced through with those terrible spikes the Viet Cong put everywhere,' some motherly old woman will say—probably after she has sat up all night sharpening bamboo spikes and laying some traps herself. The old people will also argue with the officers if there is any destruction of property and tell them they will protest to the district and provincial authorities and demand compensation for any property damage."

I asked what was the role of the Front's armed forces and local guerillas in the operation that was going on at present. "If the enemy moves against the fortified villages we will hit them," he said. "Preparations have been made; otherwise our job is to frustrate the main enemy aim of grabbing manpower and to avoid any contact on terms unfavorable to us. But while the enemy has concentrated five battalions down here, our regular forces have gone into action in the area from which the battalions were withdrawn. Several important posts have been destroyed in Tay Ninh province and more will be destroyed in the next couple of days."

"What about the artillery and mortar fire?" I asked. "What are they actually shooting at?"

"Sometimes they spot some of our defense positions," the area commander replied, "but more often they just bomb and shell blindly at any patch of forest or bamboo, at anything they suspect might be sheltering people. And half the time I think they shell to try and inject some morale into their troops. They must have long given up any idea that the noise terrifies our people; they've had too many experiences that prove the contrary."

As the artillery started up again after an hour's relative peace, I listened to the 11 AM news from Radio Australia and heard a Reuter dispatch: "Senior U.S. officers and high-ranking Saigon government officials are demanding that the war should be extended to Communist North Vietnam to offset Viet Cong pressure in South Vietnam." The rest of the broadcast was blocked out by two dive-bombers roaring down in an attack about a half mile away. They each made three dives, releasing two half-ton bombs each time. In a fourth dive, they released rockets and fired their machine guns.

Later in the day, when things got a bit quieter, some of us went to see the results. A delegation of U.S. taxpayers would have

been impressed! There were 12 craters spread over a strip of
jungle about 300 yards long by 100 yards wide and some holes
not more than three inches deep with remains of rockets around
them. The target was a tiny patch of jungle track that showed
through the trees, on which one bomb had squarely landed. Perhaps there had been a column of troops passing? I thought, but
a check was made. Nobody had been in the area and troops in
any case would have been well under the trees with planes
about. It would take the guerillas five minutes with their knives
to hack out a new bit of track around the crater.

"It's typical," said the area commander when we reported
back. "They'll bomb and strafe for hours at any tiny bit of
track they see. Every day there is this fantastic waste of shells and
bombs."

The action never came any closer to our hide-out and on the
morning of the third day the firing had receded well into the
distance; on the evening of the fourth day, the operation ended.
About noon of the following day, after sufficient tiny envelopes
had arrived to confirm the enemy was back in his barracks, we
set out for Binh Duong province to the northeast.

In the meantime I had a slight touch of influenza—apart
from a scorpion bite, the only ailment I had during my whole
tour. It so happened that we had to cross many open spaces,
sometimes with thick sand, and put on extra bursts of speed
because of the danger of enemy planes or helicopters. Contrary
to our normal habits we were travelling in the great heat of the
day, about 40 C. At one moment, when we had to dismount because of the deep sand in the middle of the biggest clearing we
had to cross, there was the noise of dive-bombers coming our
way. We had to put on a very special burst of speed, carrying
the loaded bikes on our shoulders. The planes sounded horribly
close and we still had several hundred yards to go. Some guerillas
in the area took up firing positions at the edge of the clearing
and we ran, the sweat streaming down my body as though someone had thrown a bucket of water over me. We barely got into
a thicket as the planes came, circling for a target. The troops
had orders not to shoot unless the planes actually attacked; after
a few circles they roared away again.

I was exhausted, for the first and only time during the trip. The 'flu had weakened me just enough to make the extra effort knock me out. But it was necessary to move. The planes may have been only the preliminary to a helicopter operation, for which the clearing was perfect—no spiked poles this time. When I tried to stand up I felt my legs giving way and trees and sky were suddenly mixed up with the sandy track. Two husky soldiers who had noted my plight came over and there were discussions, as a result of which a young sapling was hacked down and my hammock attached. I could not refuse a palanquin this time because to stay where we were could endanger our whole group. But then the miraculous cook started walking toward me with a large bottle of Saigon La Rue beer, the white foam oozing out of its neck. I drank it slowly and immediately felt my strength returning. The doctor explained that my exhaustion was due to loss of liquid from my body and the beer was helping restore the balance. Within half an hour I was on the bike again, having escaped a second time the indignity of the palanquin, and we were on our way to a "safe" area for the night. Whatever the scientific explanation, I have never enjoyed a bottle of beer as much as that one. But how it happened to be there—and cold— was one of those mysteries of Liberation Front organization which was never fully explained.

Later, when the most dangerous part of my visit was over and we were installed in a secure base area, the group chief directly responsible for my security asked me for advice and criticism before we parted. I replied that the fact that he had steered me past and around so many enemy posts to the very gates of Saigon and back and that I was safe and sound proved there was no reason for criticism. It was "an amazing piece of organization," I assured him, and that was an understatement. "Ah," he said, "indeed, you should criticize me severely. There was one terrible moment which I can tell you about now. You remember the day, when . . .?"

I did remember an occasion when, at the end of the day, the group chief had been in a rarely agitated mood and it seemed to me that our guide for the day had been in some sort of disgrace. It was an evening when our group was handed over, as far as security was concerned, to that remarkably efficient military commander of the Saigon-Gia Dinh area.

"We did not tell you about it at the time," he continued, "but our guide took a wrong track in one of the most dangerous areas we had to traverse—it was less than 10 miles from Saigon. The wrong track took us within a few hundred yards of an enemy post in one of the few areas that swarms with enemy agents. You remember asking who were the three soldiers in camouflage uniform, buying coca-cola at a roadside kiosk?" I did remember and was puzzled by the reply that uniforms of Front and Saigon soldiers were difficult to distinguish, because I had never seen such camouflage green worn by Front troops. "Well, they were three enemy paratroopers. We had delivered you right into the arms of the enemy, it seemed. By a miracle they did not spot us and no one denounced us. We managed to slip back to the right track again, but that was a very terrible moment for us all. Our group had a meeting that night at which we criticized ourselves very severely and instituted measures to see that it could not happen again. We agreed not to tell you about it until we had delivered you back to safety."

If this incident seems to contradict my eulogy of Front organization at the beginning of this chapter, then it must be accepted as the one exception that proved the rule.

Chapter 4

INTEGRATED WITH THE ENEMY

In the Mekong Delta

It became a standard joke during the latter phase of my travels to ask from time to time whether I was in "liberated" or "controlled" territory and, if troops were around, to ask if they were "theirs" or "yours." On numerous occasions I stayed in hamlets which were "liberated" while on the other side of a river or strategic highway was another hamlet belonging to the same village which was "enemy-controlled." In one such case, I asked the head of the local village committee if the enemy ever came over to have a look.

"Yes," he replied with a broad peasant's grin, "in this region we let them send in a patrol from time to time and even the district chief may come because officially they pretend this is 'their' hamlet and we do, too; in fact they know it's 'ours.' They round up a few local people and threaten them: 'We know you're all "Viet Cong" here. You just watch your step. We'll fix you some day.' But the people say: 'What can we do if you abandon us? How can we help it if the "Viet Cong" come? Why don't you come back and have a garrison again?' The district chief can only fume and rage. He knows very well that if a garrison is reinstalled, it will be the very people he's speaking to who will either win the troops over by propaganda or will wipe out the post one night. But he dare not play too tough. He remembers what happened to his predecessor who was a thorough despot and murdered many patriots until he was dealt with himself. He also knows that if his troops start any rough stuff, most of them would never leave the hamlet alive. He can do nothing about that either."

So, "living integrated with the enemy" was not only a phrase I was often to hear, but it was a habit to which I was becoming accustomed. The situation around the Saigon area seemed complicated enough, but this was nothing compared to that in the Mekong Delta, as explained to me over a map by Nguyen Huu Tho, the Saigon lawyer who as President of the National Front of Liberation qualifies as "Viet Cong No. 1," in Western press terminology. He is a mild, professorial person of great charm, with much of the city-bred, liberal intellectual about him. When we met for the first time, deep in a patch of jungle which had taken me many months of tough travel on horseback, on foot and by sampan to reach, it was he who wore the silk shirt and slacks of a Europeanized Saigon host, and I who wore the black cottons and rubber-tire sandals of the "Viet Cong."

My mind went back to almost exactly ten years previously when another Vietnamese leader had emerged from the jungle shadows with similar outstretched hands. A cape thrown over his thin shoulders and brown cottons of the North Vietnamese peasants, his famous wispy beard straggling down from a gaunt face, it was Ho Chi Minh; the place, the Tay Nguyen jungle of North Vietnam; the time, the beginning of the battle of Dien Bien Phu. Six months after that meeting, I entered Hanoi with the first units of the victorious Vietnamese People's Army. I mentally noted that I must *not* ask President Nguyen Huu Tho if six months later I would be entering Saigon with the first units of a victorious Liberation army.

As to my question about the Mekong Delta, Nguyen Huu Tho showed me how, for military and administrative purposes, the Front divides the Mekong Delta into two parts, Zones 1 and 2, which roughly correspond to Saigon's "Fourth Tactical Zone." With the main channel of the Mekong as the dividing line, Zone I lies to the West, Zone 2 to the East. In Zone 1, President Tho explained, there were 368 villages of which only 36 were completely liberated at the end of March 1964. But these villages comprise 3,200 hamlets of which 2,500 were in Front hands. In the liberated hamlets lived 2,000,000 of a total of 3,100,000 inhabitants of Zone 1. "We can collect taxes and recruit for our armed forces in the liberated villages," explained Nguyen Huu Tho. "The enemy cannot touch our population and is having increasing difficulties in trying to collect taxes and conscripts in the 700 hamlets under his nominal control."

Most peasants carry rifles while working in the fields

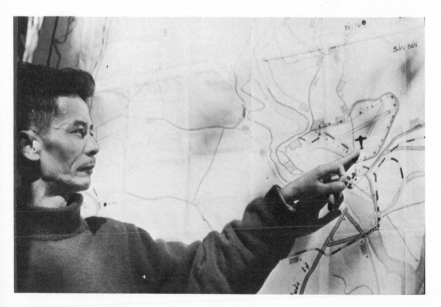

HUYNH MINH *commanded the attack on Bien Hoa airfield. Such attacks are carefully planned in advance.*

(Above) Announcers at
Liberation Radio; the young man
is the son of Nguyen Huu Tho.

(Left) YBIH ALEO, Rhade chief; Vice President of NFL and Chairman of
Autonomy Movement for Western Highlands Minority Peoples.

Liberation Front troops on the march

The situation was similar in Zone 2, where of 494 villages, a little over 100 were completely liberated, 91 under Saigon control and the rest "from half to two-thirds liberated." Of the total population of 2,700,000, about 1,800,000 lived in liberated hamlets; another 400,000 in urban centers, provincial and district capitals, and the remaining 500,000 in "guerilla zones" controlled by the Front "at least at night."

This sort of situation is possible only under conditions of "special war" which has to look different from the old type colonial war, since it has to operate under a "national" government and army. The fact that during the decisive Ap Bac* battle, the villagers of Ap Bac could march off to the local provincial governor to protest that their village was being attacked by "their" government is another example of the "other side of the medal" of the American "special war" invention. In the first resistance war,† it would be impossible to march off to protest to a provincial governor—he was French—and each side mutually accepted the other as the enemy. That was clear. But the Ap Bac villagers could protest to the governor: "You represent the government. Your job is to protect us. Why have you sent planes and artillery to destroy our village? We demand compensation for every house and tree destroyed." I do not know the results of the Ap Bac protests, but in very many cases, the population from liberated villages did extract compensation for property damage during "mopping up" operations and enemy raids. In such demonstrations people from "liberated" and "controlled" hamlets often took part together and the local authorities had no way of distinguishing them. "The pretense that the Saigon regime is a national government," said Nguyen Huu Tho, "opens up unlimited possibilities for coordinating military with political struggle."

It is obvious from looking at the military maps that many Saigon-held roads could be cut; many provincial and district centers, especially in the rich Mekong Delta, could be captured by the Front and I wondered at first why this was not done. But

---

* See pp. 85-88.
† The war against the French, which ended in their defeat at the battle of Dien Bien Phu in 1954.

then it became clear that these roads are also the Front's own supply lines; and especially for the population in the Front-controlled villages, urban centers are distribution centers for the surrounding countryside in Front hands. To cut the roads and capture the towns would paralyze the supply system. Saigon knows this, but what can be done? Abandon the roads and towns? This would mean abandoning vast areas, with a tremendous loss of prestige. It would mean also, in the case of the Mekong Delta, abandoning the rice supplies that feed Saigon and much of the rest of the country. To cut consumer goods supplies would produce roars of protests from peasant customers who will all claim they are loyal citizens of the government, even if the latter has "abandoned" them, and from local merchants and manufacturers for their lost market. In the old straight-out colonial days, such protests could be ignored, but under "special warfare" conditions, they have to be taken very much into consideration.

For the Saigon regime to withdraw from predominantly "Viet Cong" areas in order to deny them supplies would mean a virtual withdrawal from the countryside altogether. It would have to concentrate in a few main cities, abandon any pretense that the government represented anything "national" and declare total war against the peasantry. The U.S. government would have more difficulties than ever trying to justify its continued participation. So despite withdrawal from a few hundred posts in the Ca Mau Peninsula, the U.S. command has also to tolerate the "living-integrated-with" situation for want of an alternative. The inevitable result these days of trying to take back any more of the hamlets on the "other side" of rivers and roads is to lose more of those on "their own" side. So for prestige reasons the Saigon authorities have to maintain the pretense that they control many more villages than they actually do, a pretense which suits both sides but especially the Front.

City Demonstrations

One of the forms of "coordinating political with military struggle," as Nguyen Huu Tho expressed it, was that of mass demonstrations to thwart enemy military activity, or to support that of the Front. From one early spontaneous example, a whole system was worked out. Villagers of Tranh Banh district of Tay Ninh province had been tipped off that troops were on their way to their village on a "mopping up" operation. The whole population left *en masse,* old people and children, everyone with all the belongings they could carry, driving their pigs and buffalo ahead of them and poured into the district center—with 800 buffalo. They occupied the whole town, paralyzed traffic and at the office of the district chief, they said: "We heard troops are coming to destroy our village. We don't dare remain there. You are the government, you must protect us. Find a place for us to sleep. We must have rice and food for the children." The district chief, who always combines the functions of district military commander, had to call off the operation and spent the next few days getting the town cleaned up from what the pigs and buffalo left behind them.

Word of this soon spread and similar actions started to take place on a more scientific basis. Le Thi Thien, a dimpled, peach-skinned young beauty from Ben Tre province—southwest of Saigon and justly famed for the beauty of its women—is known throughout the Delta as an efficient organizer of demonstrations.

"After the success at Tranh Banh," she said, "we in Ben Tre decided to calculate the exact space of the streets and squares of all district centers and even the provincial capital. It took some time, but we had to know how many people were needed to fill up the whole space. Then we could organize the necessary number from the countryside. This had to be done carefully, too, so the exact numbers would arrive from different directions to be in the town by 5 AM. The leaders of each group had to know which streets and squares they were to occupy. We arranged things so that every square yard of space was occupied by our 'human sea' so the target town would be paralyzed by dawn. In this way it was impossible to repress us, because troops and police couldn't move; nothing could move, in fact, except us. We organized demonstrations of up to 20,000 people, almost all women, in my province and neighboring My Tho. If the authorities were able to call out troops and they threatened to open fire, we had special spokeswomen, with high political consciousness, usually from the Soldiers' Mothers organization of the first resistance. A conversation would go like this:

" 'Sons, you could all be my children. My two lads are in your army.' She would pull out a couple of photos of soldiers in Diemist uniforms. 'They look just like you,' she would continue. 'If you shoot at us, it would be like shooting at your own mother. You shoot at the young women behind me, it would be like shooting at your own wives. Their husbands are also in your army. Why have we come here? To stop people getting killed. Maybe your mother is in a village being bombarded at this very moment. Or your wife is being raped by Diemist troops. If you don't believe that such things happen, I'll introduce you to two soldiers' wives from our hamlet who were raped a few weeks ago.' "

One particular demonstration Le Thi Thien described was at the Ben Tre provincial capital and was to protest the use of air-sprayed chemicals to destroy crops and livestock. "Villagers carried branches from fruit trees, leaves from banana palms withered by the chemicals; dead pigs, ducks and chickens—a real exhibition of destruction. They hurled them into piles in front of the troops and shouted:

" 'Look at that. That's why we're here, to protest about that. We don't carry arms, we've not come to harm you or cause trouble. Keep your bullets for the enemies of the people, for those who are killing your own mothers and wives. But if you feel some glory in shooting at us, do so. But in shooting at us, you'll dishonor your own wives and mothers.' Those who do the talking," continued Le Thi Thien, and I suspect she did a good deal herself, "are real 'peace technicians' who snatch peace out of seemingly impossible situations because the authorities have standard instructions to use maximum force in putting down demonstrations. The only way massacres are avoided is by talking the troops out of using their weapons. The spokeswomen have cool courage and natural tact, mostly peasants' wives and mothers who speak the language of the troops. There is no trickery in this. Their words come from their hearts and from the soil. 'If you don't believe me, come and look,' one will say. 'You can shoot me afterwards. That's not important. But see first with your own eyes what the U.S.-Diemists have done. Maybe your unit doesn't do things like this. But first look at what the others have done, then shoot me if you like.' "

All this has a devastating effect on the morale of the soldiers who are all peasants and some of whose wives and mothers may very well be in the crowd. It is another aspect of "special war" which General Maxwell Taylor probably did not take into account when he laid down the principle of using exclusively local troops under a U.S. command. Once the war started to go badly these "local troops" were wide open to disaffection and the Front's "chignon battalions"—as they were called because of the chignon style of hairdo favored by the women of the South —exploited this to the full. Saigon officers were said to be more terrified of the "chignon battalions" and their activities than the "Viet Cong" proper. Certainly, desertions made up a high proportion of Saigon's monthly casualties and these were largely the work of the skilled women propagandists.

Demonstrations did not always pass off as peacefully as the one described, especially the early ones, before the Front had started large-scale operations, and the Diemists could concentrate unlimited military forces. One incident which is known all over Vietnam—North and South—took place in My Tho province in mid-1960. Thousands of women marched on the provincial capital to protest against a specially savage "mopping up" operation in which half a dozen villages had been burned. When they arrived at what is known as the "Bird's Cross Roads"—because of a five-way road junction in the form of a bird's foot—the demonstrators were met by a solid bloc of Diemist troops, rifles at the ready. A young, expectant mother who was carrying the first banner was shot and fell dead with the cry, "Compatriots, advance." A second girl grabbed the banner and was also shot dead; then a third—all of them under 20 years. The marching women halted only long enough to pick up the bodies which they carried at the head of the procession. A fourth girl had seized the banner, and the troops, stupified by such courage and determination and already swamped by the marching, furious crowd, gave way. The procession continued on to the provincial governor's office where they displayed the bodies of the three dead girls, demanded compensation for the burned villages and for the families of the three heroines. A huge crowd of city residents gathered around and supported them; the governor ceded to their demands.

The "Bird's Cross Roads" incident has entered into the history of the South Vietnam liberation struggle and certainly inspired innumerable other examples of heroism by women patriots.

One of the most extraordinary of the demonstrations was in Saigon itself, in the early days of May 1960. When Diem peered out of his presidential palace windows at 7 A.M., the square below was completely packed with peasants, squatting on the paving stones, dressed in the worst rags they could lay hands on and eating the most miserable scraps of food. They had been brought to the spot from all sides of the city in buses and boats and, because of impeccable organization, appeared almost simultaneously in the palace square, 70,000 strong. Banners were soon in evidence demanding an end to the burning of villages, the massacre of peasants, the slaughter of livestock.

People going to their offices, students and pupils to their schools, stopped to talk to them and were horrified at the endless tale of atrocities. Shopkeepers brought them tea and food; a huge crowd of Saigon residents started building up around them —all contrary to police regulations. The peasants demanded that Diem himself should receive a delegation. This was refused. A high police officer arrived and said he would listen to their petitions. They refused and demanded at least a high government official. Troops were rushed to the spot to dislodge them, but were "neutralized" by the "explanations" from the peasants and the Saigon residents who kept arriving in bigger and bigger numbers.

Eventually a high official appeared and accepted written petitions and verbal protests on condition they went home. But the crowd refused to move until the troops were withdrawn. When this was done, they agreed to leave. The police wanted to end this terrible fraternization between peasants and townspeople as quickly as possible and offered to take the demonstrators back to their villages in trucks. The demonstrators refused the police offer—they preferred to go on foot. And they dawdled along the

streets and country roads, accepting cups of tea whenever they
were offered and answering the myriad questions about conditions in their hamlets. When they got back, reception committees
were awaiting them, with more tea and sweetmeats and the entire population assembled to hear how the townsfolk had received them.

There were demonstrations in Saigon and other urban centers where the participants got nowhere the first day, except
to be dispersed by the police. There was no possibility of fading
away into the jungle as the partisans did, but there were markets
and quiet side streets where they spent the night and at dawn
next morning were all in place again in the main town square.
Such demonstrations never broke up until at least a moral victory had been won.

It was difficult for the police and local authorities to be too
brutal with demonstrators who all claimed they were loyal supporters of the government and only came so that the government
should know what was being done in its name in the countryside.
And as high authorities of the government could not admit that
atrocities were authorized in its name, the demonstrators had a
useful weapon to take back with them in their arguments with
local authorities. But in subsequent demonstrations, participants
were sprayed with colored water, or women's hair was clipped
short with shears, so that village police could make arrests embarrassing for the central police to make in front of Saigon and
other urban residents.

'CANNON-SPIKERS'

Apart from those who organize or participate in the actions
at district and provincial centers, there are in every village
groups of women known as "cannon-spikers."

When troops start setting up artillery or mortars to bombard
a village which they suspect is "Viet Cong," a goup of women
turns up. The most experienced, a babe in her arms, approaches
the officer in charge: "You must be very tired. Better come in
and have some tea. Or a nice, cool coconut." The others move
among the troops, asking what is going to happen. "If you think

you're going to dissuade me from bombarding the village with your tricks, you're mistaken," might well be the officers' reply.

"But what are you going to do that for?"

"To wipe out the 'Viet Cong' that you've got hiding there."

"But there aren't any 'Viet Cong' in our village now. There were some but they heard you were coming and have gone away. If you shell the village, you'll only kill women and children like us. I assure you there are no 'Viet Cong' left. I'll take you into every house and show you if you like."

Meanwhile the other "cannon-spikers" are working on the troops, showing them photos of husbands and relatives in their own army: "We are just like your families. Are you going to fire on your own kith and kin?" If the officer insists on going ahead, the "cannon-spikers" line up in front of the weapons and say :"Well, better kill us first. We'll be dead anyway if we go back into the village and you shell us."

Usually, I am assured, this works. It is one thing for troops to fire from a few thousand yards at some anonymous targets from which they only expect to see smoke and flame, and quite another to fire point-blank into the warm flesh of those who could be their own mothers, wives and babes. Had they been Foreign Legion troops or those of the French Expeditionary Corps, such activities would have been impossible. Apart from barriers such as language and race, no Vietnamese would have demeaned themselves by begging mercy of foreign invaders.

In one "cannon-spiking" operation I heard of, the village women and children raced towards the artillery team as they were making their preparations, driving pigs and buffalo ahead of them, carrying chickens under their arms; within minutes, chickens were all over cannon and shells, pigs and buffalo were milling around. Women and children jammed in around the guns and squatting on the piles of shells were wailing and shouting: "If you're going to shell our village, this is the only safe place for us to be." The cannons were "spiked" on that occasion, too. Such incidents multiplied by the thousand build up to a terribly effective politico-military weapon, wielded with consummate courage and skill.

An example of "living-integrated-with," in a different sense than that described earlier, is that of the Saigon garrisons, bottled up in isolated posts, encircled by a Front-controlled population, subject day and night to perhaps the most effective propaganda weapon ever used in any war. When the Front takes over an area, one of the first steps is a land reform which though not affecting existing property rights—except in the case of those judged as traitors—does provide land to the poor and landless peasants and eases the lot of those who rent land. In distributing land, a portion in also set aside for those serving in the armed forces, whether those of the Front or of the Saigon regime. This is done in recognition of the fact that the overwhelming majority of the troops are press-ganged peasant conscripts.

Every night in some part of South Vietnam or another, whereever there are Saigon posts there are hundreds or thousands of girls, megaphones in hand, creeping around in the grass or trees around the posts. Whenever possible the girl at any particular post will have a relative inside. She starts the evening "program" by chanting a poem, evoking memories of home and village life. There may be a couple of shots fired in her general direction, as the first response. She will call her relative by name:

"Chanh, Chanh, it's your cousin Thi Lan. Why do you shoot? I'm only a village girl. I don't have any arms. I thought you and your friends must be lonely and bored there, so I came to chant some poems." The program continues with softly chanted poems and songs, carefully chosen village tear-jerkers. Then: "Chanh, Chanh. Are you listening. There's good news from your village. Little Chi has done very well at school. By the way, your village has been liberated and a nice bit of paddy-field along the river has been set aside for you. Some of your friends in the army, too." More songs and poems. "Chanh, why don't you give up this dishonorable life, leave the bad road you are on and come back to your village. Be on the side of the people, before it is too late. Why should you get yourself killed for the Yankees?" There may be more shots at this, but the real shots have gone home, not only in the mind of Chanh, but in those of the whole garrison. The next time he is called out on an operation Chanh will be thinking of that bit of rice-field down by the river, bent only on surviving to sink a plough into it. And very probably he—like 45,000 other Chanhs and Nguyens in 1963—will slip away one night to contact the Front forces, either to join them or to get a pass to return to the bit of rice land down by the river. The poems outside the posts never fail to produce deserters, I was assured by both poem-chanters and deserters themselves. An incredibly effective form of "special counter-warfare!"

The most spectacular result of this sort of activity that I heard of was in a village of Ben Tre province in September 1961, when a group of women talked an entire garrison into surrendering. It was beautiful and eloquent Le Thi Thien who told me of it and I suspected she directed the action, but with typical Vietnamese modesty she admitted only to having "taken part with the others."

"It was a very bad post," she said. "The officer in charge was a landlord's son from the North and the troops were Catholic émigrés whom he had handpicked. They were very cruel and the officer had encouraged them in killing by disembowelling. The families of the garrison lived in a village not far from the post. A group of us went to talk with them. We told them straight that their husbands had behaved badly; that the officer was a real brute who had killed and tortured many people and we, the NFL, had decided to wipe out the post. Three posts had recently been wiped out in the same district, so they believed us. Some of your husbands are real enemies of the people, we said. This is the worst post in the district. But still we are human and don't want to shed blood unnecessarily or to kill decent soldiers. But unless they surrender, we will wipe them all out together with the post. If you want your husbands to remain alive, then come with us and try and persuade them to surrender, otherwise they will be destroyed tonight. The families were eager to try and grateful that we had given them the chance. 'We will do our best to try and persuade them,' they said. 'If we fail you must decide what to do.'

"So we took off together. These families were not on the side of the people; they were only anxious to save their husbands and sons. About 30 or 40 came, some with children. They called their relatives by name and then started: 'The NFL people say you have committed many crimes but they are prepared to pardon you if you come out and lay down your arms. Think of us and save your lives.' Mixed with the voices of wives and mothers appealing to family emotions with plenty of tears, were ours sounding a more political note. 'We suggest you choose the road of life, not of death, the road of justice, not of crime.' Children were calling for their fathers, mothers for their sons, wives for their husbands. The soldiers wanted to come out, but the tyrant officer stopped them, so they shot him and came out to lay down their arms. Actually," concluded Le Thi Thien, "we didn't have any arms until they put them into our hands. But we pretended the post was surrounded with guerillas and kept calling out: 'Section One move round to the flank; Section Two, guard the road; and so on. They thought they were surrounded."

All of the activities described above from "living-integrated-with" to "cannon-spiking" and talking individuals and garrisons into deserting, were possible only because of the inherent weakness of "special war" waged without any popular backing; in fact, waged to impose policies that were detestable to the overwhelming majority of the population. Thi Lan could have chanted poems till she was blue in the face extolling the virtues of landlordism and exhorting her cousin and his comrades-in-arms to shed their blood to protect the landlords' interests, but it would have had no effect. And Le Thi Thien and her friends could have argued in vain all night with the families of the garrison, had it not been that they knew of the atrocities that had been committed and the total hatred that ordinary people felt towards the Saigon regime and those who served it.

On the face of it, the Saigon regime seemed invincible. It had a complete monopoly of tanks, planes, artillery, gunboats and motor transport—to say nothing of dollars at the rate of a million and a half per day. The countryside was dotted like a rash of measles with its posts and fortresses but it had no base in the hearts of the people. The Front had.

Tran Nam Trung, the representative of the armed forces on the Liberation Front's Presidium, summed up the situation just prior to the November 1963 coup which overthrew Diem:

"The enemy set up posts all over tne place but they could not control the population through the posts. In fact most of them were encircled by our forces. Posts with squad, platoon and even company strength were immobilized, encircled by the people's forces which had the political and military means of isolating them. They could only move out with the aid of mobile forces and take part with the latter in large-scale military operations. But the enemy could not accumulate the necessary mobile forces for the 'general counter-offensive' because such a high proportion were tied up in the posts. The civil administration, chief of canton and districts, police chiefs and others were also immobilized in the posts. They could not move out to collect taxes.

"The population controlled the posts and not vice versa. The garrisons had to get permission from the guerillas to draw water, to take a bath or go out to market. If the guerillas agreed, they could move out a few yards to draw water but were limited to a certain number of men and for a set time. If you looked at the military maps, you could see posts everywhere but in fact the surrounding territory was liberated, in the hands of the people. It was the posts that were encircled, not the people. Over vast areas, where the enemy insisted on staying in the countryside, he was forced to live integrated with us, on our terms."

And that was still the situation at the time of my visit, only more so. Had it not been thus, I could never have traveled through the heart of the massive defense complex which surrounds Saigon.

Chapter 5

OF ARSENALS AND HOSPITALS

A Jungle Arms Factory

"We started up in 1960 and our only raw materials were bits of scrap iron and some powder from unexploded bombs. At that time, we had only one department; now we have ten. Then we thought we were performing miracles to produce 15 grenades a month; now we produce 5,000." He was a tall, gaunt and balding Vietnamese; around me workers in aprons and with white masks over their faces were ramming powder into anti-personnel mines; working spiral presses that jammed wooden handles neatly into hand grenades; grinding in queer, canoe-shaped receptacles caked gunpowder from bombs into a finer variety for grenades, mixing and sifting powder as if we were in a bakery instead of a jungle arsenal. A *mademoiselle* was buzzing around overhead. If she could only have seen what I was looking at! But the jungle is kind to its friends.

"At first we had no skilled workers," continued my informant, the director of the arsenal. "But we trained peasants, some of whom can now be regarded as skilled workers. Gradually we developed and expanded until now we can to a certain extent meet the Front's requirements in this region. In the process of production, we also trained cadres who now head the various departments. Imbued with the spirit of struggle against the enemy, the morale of workers and cadres is higher every day. Some specialized workers have come from Saigon to help us."

He handed me a couple of aluminum beer mugs, inscribed with my name and that of my host organization, the Quarter-master General's Department of the Liberation Army. "They are made from rocket cylinders," he said. "We have no primary raw materials, so we gather all the scrap available from the enemy: plane parts, bits of bombs and rockets—the beer mug handles are from napalm bomb canisters—wrecked trucks, bridge railings, bits of railway track, any metal we can get hold of. The population do their best for us—look at these brass incense burners an old woman brought us the other day."

I stopped to watch a welder in a masked, steel helmet, welding fins on to rifle grenades and followed the acetylene gas line to the parent machine. It was marked: "Portaweld—Onan, Minneapolis," and also bore the clasped hands of American Vietnamese "friendship." "Yes," the director said, "we cannot complain about the quality of U.S. machinery. If they had come to our country only with machines like these instead of their planes and tanks, it would have been better for us all." In one of the departments for mines, I was astonished at the variety of special service mines, small cylindrical and flat anti-personnel mines, long cylindrical ones for dealing with barbed wire entanglements, others like sauce pans of various sizes for M-113 tanks; big ones for special jobs; others for exploding under rail tracks or for use against naval craft. The director placed one of the latter in my hand (it was empty) and said: "We sunk two naval vessels in the Saigon river a couple of weeks ago with mines like these."

Most of the installations were laid out in well spaced thatch-roofed huts, covered with fresh green every morning where there were any gaps in the green of the jungle roof. Buildings were far away from each other so that no single bomb could destroy more than one. Lathes, generators, boring and polishing machines—all of them American—were in underground dugouts. There was enough staff available to transport by hand everything to another area in case of an emergency.

To get to the arsenal was a complicated affair because of the most fantastic maze of traps I had ever encountered, an integrated system of spikes and their own mines. I was shown new secret weapons, based on principles developed in their own workshops, and perfectly adapted to the type of war they were fighting in which light weapons, transportable on human backs, had to replace motor-hauled artillery. Every worker had his own weapon alongside him at his workbench. They were keen, smiling young chaps, obviously and justifiably proud of their productions. It was pleasant again to hear the humming of machinery; to hear mechanical noises which were not from the adversary's planes or gunboats. One of the impressive sights was a long line of Saigon watchmakers, lenses screwed into their eyes, heads bent low over delicate springs and coils of copper and fine magnetized wire for various delayed action fuses. Later I was to hear a "Voice of America" transcript of a McNamara press conference in which the U.S. Defense Secretary cited as "absolute proof" of intervention from North Vietnam, "the appearance in South Vietnam of more sophisticated types of mines, including some naval mines and others with delayed action fuses." I saw these "more sophisticated" types of weapons in serial production in the jungle arsenal.

Laboratories and the building housing the chemical processes for explosives manufacture were spotlessly clean, the bamboo huts lined with U.S. parachute nylon. In one such hut, girls with delicate balances were weighing the miniscule quantity of explosives necessary for various types of detonator caps and one fifteen-year-old lad was in charge of an improvised machine for fitting the detonator caps into the cartridges. The director assured me there had not been a single accident at the plant.

"The increase from 15 to 5,000 grenades a month since 1960 is typical of a very rapid increase in all departments, every year," the director said, as I took my leave. "And we will continue to expand our activities at this tempo."

FIELD HOSPITALS

The rapid expansion of arms production was typical of rapid expansion in every field of the Front's war effort. One of the most remarkable results has been in the medical field.

A typical front-line hospital which I visited did not look very different from an ordinary hamlet at first—the same bamboo huts each consisting of barely more than a steep, overhanging palm roof supported by poles and a waist-high, pleated bamboo outer wall, designed to give maximum shade and air. In fact, each hut was a "ward," and one slightly bigger and more enclosed than the others was the operating theater. Ceilings of the wards, and ceilings and walls of the operating rooms, dispensary and out-patients' clinic, were lined with white parachute nylon.

In the first ward I visited there were three patients. One was a rubber plantation worker who had been shot in the neck by Saigon troops while he was making his normal morning rounds collecting latex from the rubber trees. The bullet had been removed and he was "doing fine." Another was a middle-aged woman who had been wounded in the stomach with a grenade burst. Sections of intestine and part of her liver had to be removed and she was still very weak. The third, a young guerilla lad, had lost one hand and part of another in a tragic accident with a grenade only two days previously. In a nightmare he had imagined his hamlet was under attack and reaching for his grenade pulled out the pin and was just about to throw it when he woke up. Realizing he would probably kill his comrades if he threw it, he held on to it, plunging his hands under some bags of rice alongside his bed. By a miracle, only his hands suffered. One and part of the other had to be amputated. He was still suffering from shock.

This was a real front-line area; alongside each building were air-raid shelters, including those wide enough to take stretcher cases. It was an area subject to almost daily bombings, nightly shellings and frequent "mopping up" raids.

"During 1963," said Dr. Tran, the surgeon in charge, "we handled 247 surgical cases. They included stomach, head, chest and limb surgery; the results were 98 per cent positive." Apart from Dr. Tran there were four medical assistants, with two years' medical college training, and nine nursing sisters. The hospital had been set up in late 1960. "At that time," reminisced Dr. Tran, a short, energetic man with a thick stubble of hair and sensitive, square-tipped fingers, "there were only three nursing sisters in this whole district, no other medical worker. Now in the district we have 13 medical assistants, 105 nursing sisters, 120 nurses, 13 midwives and 52 assistant midwives. The Front tries to have at least one sister for each hamlet." I visited a medical school attached to his hospital where 36 nurses and 15 midwife trainees were being given six-month accelerated training courses.

Later I was to visit a much larger unit, referred to by Dr. Ky, who was in charge, as a "regimental hospital." The buildings were much larger, but still of pleated bamboo walls and palm leaf roofs. It had also been set up in 1960 but was enlarged and modernized in 1962, when Dr. Ky took over. I asked about equipment and medical supplies: "Of course, we are short of some things," he said. "But on the surgical side, things have improved a lot since our lads captured a portable X-Ray unit." (I inspected it later, it was made by Picker of Cleveland, Ohio.) It was not only the X-Ray unit that was "made in USA"; there were all sorts of other things including, of course, the generator that powered the unit. Tweezers and some other simple surgical implements were made from rocket and napalm bomb casings; nylon thread of various calibers was used for sutures, in some cases reinforced by a local product. As in the district hospital, all buildings were lined with snow-white parachute nylon.

"We use plenty of penicillin and streptomycin, despite the enemy's blockade of medical supplies," said Dr. Ky, "but we also use a lot of oriental medicine which we can produce from local products. Our snake-bite antidote, for instance, is more effective than any Western one." (There is a specially deadly snake in many parts of South Vietnam, similar to the Australian "death adder;" not more than a foot long, it jumps at its victims. Within three minutes one is paralyzed and in two hours dead. The Liberation Front chemists have developed an antidote in tablet form, and every guerilla carries two as part of standard equipment. I always slept with one of these in a handy position for immediate application and was warned never to stray far from my hammock at night and constantly to use a flashlight.) Among substitutes for western medicines, Dr. Ky cited hemoglobin serum in injectible form, obtained from buffalo and pigs; a substance from tiger bones which acted as a powerful stimulant in cases of prolonged weakness; an extract from the placenta of new-born buffalo calves, good for malaria and rheumatism.

I asked what was the average time in his area for medical treatment during a military operation. "Any casualty," replied Dr. Ky, "can count on first-aid treatment at a company medical

station within 30 minutes of being wounded; within one hour
he receives first surgical attention at battalion level, and within
two hours fundamental surgery at regimental level. Only exceptionally serious cases have to be sent back to the main
hospital; normally the front-line hospitals can handle everything
that comes their way. If the scene of action is not more than
one or two days away from the base hospital, then serious cases
will be sent back there, but in case the action is to be further
than two days—in terms of our communications possibilities—
then we establish a field hospital, never more than two days
distant. The latter can handle serious surgical cases and patients
can be hospitalized there for weeks on end if necessary." Dr.
Ky estimated that once wounded got into the hands of the
medical staff "over 90 per cent are saved." He was specially
proud of two brain surgery cases and insisted on my seeing them.
Both had had bullets removed from the brain; both had been
completely paralyzed in half their body. Now, the first one
operated on is walking around and talking normally, the other
one is able to move and Dr. Ky was certain that he would also
be walking soon.

Such results are obviously possible only with a very high
standard of surgery and post-operational care, difficult to
associate with the primitive appearance of the hospital buildings. The hospital had its own pharmaceutics section where
various medicines were being prepared in liquid, pill and injectible forms. Dr. Ky explained that part of the medicines came
from a central pharmaceutics department which was run by the
Committee for Public Health.

Later, I was able to meet Dr. Ho Thu, a French-trained pharmaceutical chemist, who is a member of the Liberation Front's
Central Committee, a modest, greying scientist who, other
Presidium members assured me, had "performed miracles" in
producing medical supplies. He astonished my by saying that
the Front now produces 70 per cent of its medical requirements.
"This had been possible," he said, "because we made a careful
study of traditional oriental medicine and based ourselves on
the great wealth of our forest products. In some fields we have
surprised ourselves. For instance, we have been able to solve

the question of flesh and bone gangrene." When I asked how, he smiled and said: "We are keeping this a secret, because we consider this a source of national wealth for the future. I can only say that it is based on a forest product. It was only when we made a proper inventory of local vegetable, animal and forest products and checked these off against ancient oriental medical manuals, that we realized how rich we were." While I was still expressing my surprise over the success with gangrene, Dr. Ho Thu said: "We have had an even greater success with the preparations of animal organisms transformed in injectible water. In France, any manufacturing chemist needs a special ministerial decree to produce this because it is an extremely complex process, needing most complicated equipment. But we were able to solve this with rudimentary means and the result is of highest quality, in no way inferior to the French product. We have also developed a serum protein which is a perfect replacement for plasma."

Dr. Thu said they maintained big stocks of serums and vaccines and had enough always on hand to halt any "normal" epidemics of typhus, smallpox, cholera, etc. Thanks to this, and speedy action, they had halted a recent cholera epidemic which had started in Saigon and which the authorities there had confidently hoped would spread into the liberated zones. "As for malaria," continued Dr. Thu, "this has always been a major problem in the South Vietnam countryside. But we have waged a big campaign against it and the percentage is down enormously. It is down to five per cent in even former seriously infested regions and we hope to reduce this still further—to eradicate it completely, in fact—by using our local resources and the full cooperation we get from the local population."

Medical attention is free in the liberated zones and it was interesting to learn, and to confirm on several occasions, that many people come from the Saigon-controlled areas, including from Saigon itself, to have treatment in the liberated areas. This was especially striking during the 1964 cholera epidemic in Saigon when tens of thousands of people came to get their anti-cholera injections in the liberated zones. "This is not just because our service is free," Dr. Thu explained. "People appreciate the professionally responsible attitude and the devotion of our medical cadres who are trained to serve the people. The main line in the liberated zones, as far as public health is concerned, is to concentrate on social hygiene and preventive medicine, in raising living standards and introducing modern notions of hygiene to the peasantry." Considering the small lapse of time and great difficulties, concluded Dr. Ho Thu, "very rapid progress has been made in the development of the pharmaceutical industry, in the training of medical cadres and the setting up of hospital and public health facilities."

Chapter 6

RATIOS AND BATTLE TACTICS

OF ARMS AND MEN

The Liberation Front's armed forces have obviously not been behind other branches in rapid expansion. How many effectives the Front has is a secret, but I am sure there are more than the highest U.S. estimates I have seen published. Dang Thanh Chon, who is vice president of the Liberation Youth Federation, told me that 500,000 young people between the ages of 16 and 25 were enrolled in the Federation. Of these, 100,000 had "left their villages to enlist in the armed forces and other Front organizations." This did not include those in local self-defense units and Chon said that at least half of Federation members who remain in the villages are expected to enlist in them. Chon, a quiet, earnest young man with thick-lensed spectacles, listed the main immediate tasks of his organization as:

Get the maximum number of youth in the liberated zones enlisted in the Front's regular armed forces and guerillas.

Use all forms of struggle to prevent youth in the Saigon-controlled areas from being conscripted.

Appeal to the youth in the Saigon-controlled zones to come to the liberated zones and enlist in their armed forces.

Push ahead with dismantling "strategic hamlets" in the Saigon-controlled areas.

Consolidate and develop the "resistance" or "combat" villages in the liberated zones.

Nguyen Huu Tho estimated that the Saigon forces had increased from 370,000 in 1961 to 577,000 by the end of 1963, including all services. "They increased quite rapidly," he said, "but our forces increased far more quickly; the ratio of the enemy's numerical superiority is fast being whittled away. The ratio changes in our favor every day and this is a process which cannot be reversed. The area in which they can recruit also shrinks every day. As for morale, there we have complete superiority."

As to how fast the Front forces are expanding, a regiment I visited provides a good example. It was formed in October 1961 with only 300 men and 120 rifles, the latter either home-made or old French models, contributed by former combatants of the armed religious sects. Their first engagement took place within a month of the "regiment" being formed, an ambush in which they captured three machine guns and 25 rifles, killed a district commander and captured his deputy. Every month for a year, they carried out at least one operation, including (in June 1962) an audacious attack against the Trung Hoa parachutist training center near Saigon which yielded a rich haul of arms. Then in November 1962 they took four months off for a political and technical training course, summing up all their experiences, negative as well as positive.

"We had one operation which we did not consider successful," the regimental commander, a 38-year-old, former village guerilla leader told me. "In February 1962 we attacked the Ba Tuc stronghold in Tay Ninh province near the Cambodian frontier. There was a complex of three posts; we destroyed two, captured 25 guns and 20 prisoners. But we do not consider this action successful because we did not destroy the whole post and we had some casualties. But morale was high and we used this lesson to avoid future failures. Our preparations had not been as thorough as they should have been." Among other actions, a team had penetrated into Tay Ninh city, in October 1962, to attack the U.S. advisers' office, killing five and wounding three Americans. "There were a number of casualties in the platoon assigned to protect the Americans," said the commander. "The remainder were arrested for having failed in their task, the platoon was disbanded."

It was typical of the nature of the Front forces and of the war that the regiment could decide to take four months off from the war for political and technical education. It meant that by the end of 1962 they were "calling the tune" in the area where they operated; it was they and not Saigon who decided when and where there would be engagements.

"After the course," continued the commander, a straight,

soldierly figure, "we had a clearer idea of our mission. We saw it better against the background of the whole struggle; our men had a firmer political stand and their morale was heightened further. Our first operation afterwards was March 24, 1963, when we attacked the key Sam Xoo stronghold. We wiped out the garrison and the enemy was forced to withdraw from three more posts."

The regiment carried out 14 operations during the next 12 months. On the last one I was taken along with a battalion on a two-day operation. It resulted in three posts being wiped out, and the "strategic hamlets" they controlled were dismantled. By the end of 1963, the regiment was up to full strength in men and arms. Nearly 600 pieces of its present armament are captured U.S. arms, including $37mm$ machine guns, highly appreciated against helicopters and planes, $57mm$ recoilless cannon which are so efficient against tanks and blockhouses. The rest of their arms were made in the local arsenals. Most of the American weapons were captured in the first 12 months. During 1963, the unit kept only one third of what it seized, the rest were distributed to the self-defense units set up when the "strategic hamlets" were dismantled. From the beginning of 1964, all arms captured were distributed, except heavy weapons and any specially required ammunition. Such regiments are small by western standards, probably not much over 1,000 men, divided into three battalions, but as every member is a front-line fighter, the combat effectiveness is very high.

Between the end of 1961 and 1963, this regiment had trebled its effectives and had captured five modern arms for every old one it started out with. I believe this is a fair average of what has been going on in all Front units. It illustrates the magnitude of the problem of the U.S. High Command in Saigon. The original idea of General Maxwell Taylor and the highest military pundits in the Pentagon was that in guerilla warfare a ten or eleven to one superiority is essential as a starting point in anti-guerilla operations.

At the end of 1961, when the USA moved into South Vietnam in a big way, setting up a U.S. command in Saigon under General Paul D. Harkins, they calculated that Diemist numerical superiority was around ten to one. It seems this was not far out. General Harkins' plan was to increase this to a 20 to one superiority by the end of 1962. According to British experience in Malaya, the pundits believed, the remaining resistance could then be cleaned up within six months. The more favorable ratio was to be achieved by a speedy expansion of the Saigon forces; the wiping out of a substantial part of the guerillas. In fact the expansion targets were never reached; the desertion rate on the contrary was stepped up; the guerilla forces expanded instead of diminishing. The result of that first year of U.S. command was to reduce a ten to one superiority to one of about six or seven to one.

What the ratio is in mid-1964 is another of those secrets as far as the Front is concerned. But if it is more than four or five to one, I would be surprised. And this applies only to the Front's regular and regional forces. If one considers all those garrisons pinned down in their forts by local self-defense guerillas, one can understand that Saigon's mobile reserves are more and more often forced to meet their opponents on grounds of something like numerical equality. Difference in fire-power is canceled out by difference in morale. Superiority in mobility is canceled out by superiority in intelligence work—a couple of days advance notice, or even a few hours, is enough to get the Front's forces into position if they intend to do battle.

It must not be thought that Front communications are restricted to the notes in tiny envelopes of which I have spoken so much. Regular units have U.S. communications equipment, field telephones and radios; such predicaments as arose during the early battles, when there were no communications between command post and attacking forces, no longer exist.

EVOLUTION OF TACTICS

In the question of tactics and techniques, too, there has been a steady evolution which makes a fascinating study on its own. At first it was defensive actions with spikes—to deny enemy entrance to homes and gardens but no attempt to keep him away from hamlets and villages; and no use of fire-arms. Then spiked traps on approaches to villages and ambushes to get arms, but only to keep the enemy away from the villages and deal with him more efficiently if he came. Then diversionary actions in one area to keep the enemy from concentrating on one particular village or district. And as the war developed and "strategic hamlets" were established and maintained only by the military posts set up in the vicinity, the night attacks on military posts—another big move forward. At first, only self-defense forces at hamlet and village level, but when it was necessary to start hitting the enemy before he came to hamlet and village, then regional forces were necessary to thwart the opponent's regional forces who came to the defense of the local posts. When Saigon's mobile reserves were sent on massive, large-scale operations, then regular armed forces were necessary to deal with them.

The tactics of the swift night attack were insufficient once helicopters were used on a massive scale to track down next morning the forces which had struck at night. This was a period of crisis, the solution of which was found at Ap Bac, a battle which deserves to be described in detail, since it marked a significant turning point in the war.

On New Year's Day, 1963, U.S. reconnaissance planes sighted a couple of hundred "Viet Cong" guerillas close to the village of Ap Bac, in My Tho province, almost due south of Saigon. January 3 would be Ngo Dinh Diem's birthday. It was decided to present him with a special birthday present which would start with the wiping out of the "Viet Cong" force that had been sighted and follow up by destroying all guerilla forces in the area. At 2 AM on January 2, armored river craft started disembarking troops of the crack 7th Division at hamlets just north of Ap Bac. Then a convoy of trucks unloaded another batch at a cross road to the south. By 5 AM armored cars and M-113 amphibian tanks were transporting troops to a series of posts that surrounded the hamlet; at 5:30 helicopters ferried in more troops to the north and at 6 AM another unit arrived by road at a point east of the village and started to link up with others to complete an encirclement.

By this time, according to the Liberation Front battalion com-

mander Duyen, who was in charge of the Front forces of two
companies and one platoon—about 230 men—the Diemists had
brought in three battalions from the 7th Division, two companies of Rangers, four companies of Civil Guards, four companies of Self-Defense Corps, one squadron of 13 M-113 tanks,
six 105mm cannon and a company of 106mm mortars. Promptly
at 6 AM, planes and artillery started a furious bombardment of
the Liberation Front positions—they were dug in on a strip of
land over a mile long by about an average of 350 yards wide,
in interconnected trenches which led to firing positions in groves
of coconut palms and bamboo. In charge of the Diemist troops
was Col. Bui Dinh Dam, commander of the 7th Division. At
6:30 AM, the air and artillery bombardment lifted and two companies of Civil Guards started the assault, wading up to their
knees across rice-field mud.

"Our men held their fire until the first line was only a few
yards away and the last line was within range," said Duyen,
a handsome man in his early thirties with a shock of black
hair that he constantly had to throw back from his forehead.
"Then they fired. Within seconds there were about 40 enemy
casualties, and they retreated. Between then and 7:30 there
were three more assaults, each preceded by heavy air and
artillery bombardment. In the fourth attack, the Diemists sent
two platoons in an outflanking attack while the main force
attacked in the center again. They were all beaten back, and
by that time they had taken about 100 casualties. That ended
the first phase of the battle.

"The second phase took place between 8:00 and 8:30 and
the enemy used two companies in three assaults," continued
Duyen in his dry, factual report. "We used two platoons in
counter-attacks and the result was that the Diemists withdrew
about a half mile behind the front line. During this action the
enemy used 15 helicopters and tried to land troops right in
the center of the battlefield. We had been expecting something
like this from the beginning. Our 37mm heavy machine guns
opened up and three helicopters were shot down immediately.
The rest tried to gain height and withdraw but two more were
downed as they flew over Van hamlet, just to the north. Within

half an hour, assaults had been launched from the south, center and north and the Diemists had suffered 60 to 80 casualties. It was difficult for us to verify exactly, because they fell in the rice fields and immediately after there was air and artillery bombardment which made our lads keep their heads down.

"There was more shelling and bombing as the troops from the second attack withdrew and then a third attack was launched with four fresh companies. We used one of our companies; after four of their assaults one of their companies was completely wiped out. In that action we had our first casualties, one killed and two wounded. But the heavy air and artillery bombardments prevented us leaving our trenches to collect enemy weapons.

"After the third attack failed, Brig. General Huynh Van Cao, commander of the Third Army Corps, came over from Can Tho and personally took command. There was a heavy artillery bombardment, over 200 shells fired in about 20 minutes, and then eight infantry companies were thrown into the central sector. The first wave advanced to within a hundred yards of our positions, fired and then withdrew. The second assault was spearheaded by the M-113 tanks, the troops following on behind. We held our fire till they were about 30 or 40 yards distant, then opened up. Our special 'steeled squad' moved out of the trenches with their anti-tank grenade launchers. Within seconds four of the M-113 tanks were ablaze and four others were damaged. All but two of our lads in the 'steeled squad' sacrificed their lives in this heroic episode. The enemy was forced to withdraw one mile, the fourth phase ending midday.

"Huynh Van Cao had done no better than Dam. Dam had lost five helicopters and another eight had been damaged of a total of 20, but Cao had succeeded in putting eight out of 13 amphibious tanks out of action. So the commander-in-chief of the Diemist army, Major General Lee Van Ty, came from Saigon to assume personal command. He brought with him the 1st Airborne Battalion and reorganized all the forces that were left. At 3 PM, he launched the first of two major attacks from the center and from the north, but both failed. At 5 PM, the battle was over.

"Between the fourth and fifth phase, there was a curious incident. The Americans sent in technicians to salvage the damaged M-113 tanks. We fired at them but at the same moment their own artillery started pouring in shells. A lot of Americans were wounded, either by our fire or their own. U.S. officer 'advisers' ordered Vietnamese troops to go in and rescue them, but they refused. The Americans had to mobilize their cooks, technical personnel and others to go to the rescue of their tank repair teams. Some Diemist officers were court-martialled for this afterwards."

Around midnight the same night, the Front forces withdrew and, after more bombing and shelling from dawn next morning, at 10 AM the Diemist forces penetrated the defense perimeter only to find the position abandoned. The Front forces were resting about two miles away. Their losses had been 13 killed, of whom eight were in the "steeled squad" action against the M-113's, and 15 wounded, while the Diemists had about 400 casualties, according to Duyen. The U.S. press made no attempt to conceal the extent of the defeat in an action in which they admitted over 3,000 troops had been employed with at least a ten to one superiority over the "Viet Cong" in terrain favorable to them. The Ap Bac battle was presented as a "shattering defeat." Duyen said he had been informed at 7 PM on the evening of January 1, that the attack was to be made, so regular troops were rushed to the spot and all preparations were completed by 2 AM next morning.

"The result was of great importance to us," he said, "because it showed we could defeat the helicopter tactics. And it showed that even when we employ a small force we can defend ourselves against vastly superior enemy forces."

The Ap Bac battle was a turning point in the war. It showed the Front forces had "grown up" and was followed by a series of shattering defeats inflicted on the Saigon troops that led to a serious decline in their morale, and eventually to the overthrow of the Diemist regime. After Ap Bac, American commentators began speculating for the first time whether the war in South Vietnam could ever be won.

After a thorough discussion on the lessons of the Ap Bac

battle, a new tactic was developed which the Saigon command had the utmost difficult in countering. It was tested first at the battle of Loc Ninh, in Chuong Thien province in the Mekong Delta. The official American version was that, acting on perfect intelligence information, they had trapped a 300-strong battalion of "Viet Cong," but were beaten back with heavy losses in an attempt to wipe them out. In fact, the Front forces deliberately invited battle in what is known as the "wipe-out-enemy-posts-and-annihilate-enemy-reinforcements" tactic, which has been repeated time and again since.

On October 17, 1963, guerillas attacked and wiped out one of half a dozen posts surrounding Loc Ninh village, after the garrison had refused to surrender. The following day helicopter-borne forces arrived, but finding themselves surrounded by guerillas, they withdrew. That night, two more of the posts were attacked and a bridge destroyed.

"Once we had wiped out so many posts, we were fairly sure how the enemy would react. It was inevitable that they would come in force and this is what we wanted," a lean, hollow-cheeked veteran company commander who took part in the action told me later. "We planned to receive them at the deserted hamlet of Ba Ai, near Loc Ninh village and we did not hide the fact." Local guerillas were stiffened by some regular NFL troops, well dug in along a strip of land almost a mile long by about 100 yards wide. They were less than 300 troops in all, but dug into well-camouflaged positions in ridges and clumps of bamboo, interlaced with communication." After a heavy air attack at dawn next morning, 17 helicopters started unloading troops. After that, developments were similar to those in the Ap Bac battle. The NFL troops came out to their positions after the bombing finished and the attacking troops were allowed to come within 15 to 20 yards before a blistering fire of automatic weapons cut them down in the rice-field mud. Assaults and retreats were interspersed with bombings and strafing throughout the day. "The Diemist troops simply refused to move forward, however, once we started firing and they started getting casualties," continued the officer. "The Americans exhorted them to advance but the troops refused to budge."

The result of the Loc Ninh battle was another stinging defeat for the U.S.-Saigon command. U.S. reports admitted that the U.S.-Diemist troops had at least a seven to one superiority. They put their own casualties as 42 Diemist troops killed and 85 wounded, plus 15 Americans wounded, but the Liberation army commander insisted the figures were much higher and included at least one U.S. officer and seven Diemist officers among the killed. U.S. press reports said that because of bad light, helicopters had been unable to come in for the wounded on the evening of the battle and they had been left all night in the rice-field mud where they had fallen. There was no attempt to conceal that this was another demoralizing defeat.

"Our forces slipped away during the night," the company commander said, "leaving a few guerillas behind as observers. The Americans did not know we had withdrawn, and early next morning opened up an artillery barrage against our positions. But they didn't try another attack, it was only a cover to pick up their wounded."

In the weeks that followed, these tactics were used time and again. The U.S. command had only two alternatives: either to abandon the military posts completely or "send good money after bad" and suffer endless defeats as reinforcements fell into the sort of traps set at Ap Bac and Loc Ninh.

WAR OF MOVEMENT

On the evening of March 16, I marched with a battalion of the regiment referred to earlier—together with the regimental commander—to a point about four miles northwest of Tay Ninh. We marched in single columns, the troops adorned with bits of greenery, until sundown when there was no further danger of planes. They were all smiles and confidence; some of them marched in pairs with bazookas slung between two pair of shoulders; others with base plates and barrels of mortars divided between them, and a surprisingly high proportion of automatic arms. Uniforms were nondescript, according to the color of the cloth that had been made available to the tailoring unit. But the Front's military leaders do not think it essential that their troops should be clad exactly the same; the main thing is that their aims and ideas about the enemy should be uniform. At around 10 PM, I was left swinging in a hammock in a safe position, with an interpreter and a couple of guards; troops and command post moved on, with lamps out and no cigarettes. The target was a post guarding a "strategic hamlet" at Cai Xuyen, three miles from Tai Ninh city. For my own safety, I was not permitted to get any closer to the scene of action.

Zero hour was 11:30 PM and a few minutes later, I heard some bursts of rifle and automatic fire which ended surprisingly quickly. Around midnight, however, there was a terrific series of explosions and flashes all around and we took to the slit trenches. Artillery and mortar shells were bursting everywhere and it seemed the battalion had run into far more serious opposition than expected. A relatively small force was being used to attack the post while a much larger one was ready to deal with the reinforcements. By the noise, it seemed a full-scale battle was raging. It kept up for about an hour, then died away. But in the small hours of the morning, the commander turned up full of smiles and said: "There was no fight. We started to cut through the barbed wire with shears, but as there was no reaction, we hacked through the wooden poles and toppled over big sections of the fence. When we fired a few rounds at the post and started the assault, the garrison fled into the houses; some of them hid in the wells. It took us nearly two hours to round up 31 of them. They never fired a single shot."

"But what was all that artillery and mortar fire?"

"Ah, that always happens. If other posts know that one is being attacked, they fire their artillery all over the place. They don't aim at anything in particular but they figure if they keep on firing at least their post won't be attacked that night."

Next morning we waited for the counter-attack with reinforcements, but nothing happened. It had been expected that there would be a fair-sized battle during the day and the battalion would withdraw during the night. But apart from a few *mesdemoiselles* there was nothing. The commander decided to attack another post the second night, though this was not in the program. After dusk, we moved off again, this time to the

south of Tay Ninh. I was left in a dugout on the banks of the
Cam Co Long river. The target this time was Thanh Dong, less
than three miles southwest of the city. "The enemy has some
gunboats downstream," said the commander, "and he is bound
to come out this time." There were almost the same noises
as the previous night, starting around midnight. The commander turned up around 8 AM with a disgusted look on his
face. "Nothing," he said. "The garrison fled without firing a
shot. And if they haven't sent reinforcements by now, it means
they're not coming at all." He decided on something really
audacious—to attack in broad daylight a post at Thanh Trung,
only one and one-half miles from the city.

"They'll have to send reinforcements from Tay Ninh this
time," he said, and after downing a few bowls of rice, he strode
off again. But, incredible as it seems, at the sight of the "Viet
Cong" moving towards them in broad daylight, the Thanh Trung
garrison fled into Tay Ninh city, and again there was no reaction. In the actions, including the night bombardments, the
battalion had not a single casualty. Each of the three posts
controlled a "strategic hamlet" and, once the garrison had been
dealt with or fled, the people turned out to help the troops
demolish the barbed wire fences and post fortifications. The
20-odd weapons captured at Cai Xuyen, were turned over to a
self-defense corps set up on the spot and the battalion detached
a few men at each hamlet to help them organize their defenses.

The commander regarded the operations as a "non-success."
"The main thing now is to destroy the enemy forces in this
area," he said. "We don't have any transport to get at their
main forces quickly. It is much better for us to take advantage
of their helicopters and trucks to bring their forces to us, where
it is convenient to deal with them. But on this occasion it
failed—they didn't come out."

To celebrate, however, on the way back to a base area the
battalion's hunting unit shot two elephants and two wild boars;
as one elephant provides plenty of excellent meat for several
days for a whole battalion, everyone was in high spirits. For
several days afterwards, I dined off wild boar soup and elephant
steaks which one could easily mistake for good "filet mignon."

The "wipe-out-enemy-posts-and-annihilate-reinforcements" tactic remained the main Liberation Army counter to the superior mobility of the Saigon forces. The *New York Times* international edition of May 16-17, 1964, for instance, reported on a battle 25 miles north of Saigon in which half of two Ranger companies were wiped out, with at least 54 killed. "Reliable sources said the ambush was set by four to eight Vietcong companies numbering at least 300 men. They baited the trap shortly after midnight with simultaneous attacks on five outposts clustered near a provincial highway.... The defenders fought in the eerie light of parachute flares dropped by U.S. Air Force C-123's to illuminate the battlefield.

"Ranger relief companies set off on foot at dawn, marching directly into the Vietcong trap. The Vietcong then opened fire from all sides of the road....

"An American source described the fighting as one of the bloodiest encounters of the year. 'We make the same mistakes all the time,' an American adviser commented. There is an average of one major Vietcong ambush every week. American advisers are concentrating much of their effort on making the South Vietnamese ambush-conscious." And this gloomy account is capped as usual by the wishful-thinking estimate of "Viet Cong" casualties. "Only three rebel bodies were found, but a Vietnamese officer estimated that 100 were killed, mainly by artillery."

The Ranger companies are regarded as the "elite," "most combat-ready" troops among the Saigon forces. They are the pride of U.S. instructors, specially trained in guerilla tactics. In the "Special Warfare" manual captured with the four U.S. prisoners* at the Hiep Hoa "Special Forces" training camp, the Rangers are always depicted as on the giving and not the receiving end of ambushes. In fact, the Liberation Army has wiped out a large proportion of them either in their beds or in operations such as the *New York Times* reported. By the first half of 1964, as the Rangers were in fact the most combative troops, the Front was concentrating its attention on them.

* See next chapter.

The only counter the U.S. command has yet found to the new tactic, is to abandon posts without waiting for a fight. Thus after the overthrow of Ng Dinh Diem, General Harkins ordered the abandonment of all posts garrisoned by less than 150 men, a total of around 300 posts, mainly in the rich Ca Mau peninsula area of the Mekong Delta, creating a vacuum which was immediately filled by the Front forces. But no matter how "planned withdrawals" are presented they in fact spell out "retreat" and "defeat."

One other development in Liberation Army tactics was to be noted in the wiping out of Saigon's notorious "Black Tiger" battalion in a battle which lasted four days starting from New Year's Eve, 1963, with two Liberation Army battalions and one company engaged against two regiments plus two battalions of Saigon troops, the "Black Tiger" and a marine battalion. It was a surprise engagement which upset the plans of both sides for other operations and it involved the Liberation Army troops for the first time in the elements of a war of movement. Their companies were maneuvered with great skill; while the main body moved swiftly to pin down the main force of the adversary, two companies used a pincer movement to encircle the "Black Tiger" battalion, notorious for its cruelty in the region, with a black record of massacre, rape and pillage. While the other companies blocked attempts by the two regiments and the marine battalion to cut their way through to the rescue, the Liberation forces started to wipe out the "Tigers." Ten tons of supplies parachuted to the latter fell into Front hands. The answer to radioed appeals for help by the desperate battalion commander was that further help and reinforcements were "useless" and he was told "do the best you can." The battalion was completely wiped out, its commander captured. One helicopter was shot down and three damaged.

Just as Ap Bac marked a new phase for the new year of 1963, so did the "Black Tiger" battle for 1964. It marked another step forward in tactics from the night attack plus daylight battle from fixed positions which is the essence of the "wipe-out . . . and annihilate" tactics. The battle took place in Long An province, the one which General Harkins announced was to be "pacified" within 12 months in a more modest variant of "pacifying" the whole of South Vietnam in 18 months, as the original Staley-Taylor plan provided. Long An, which stretches from the Cambodian border to very close to Saigon, is one of 43 provinces of South Vietnam.

Chapter 7

PATRIOTS AND MERCENARIES

A Terrorist Squad

My journalist-interpreter friend excused himself for having awakened me. My watch showed 10:44 PM; I had been dead to the world in my hammock for a good two hours. "Three compatriots have arrived with a very interesting story," he said. "Can't it wait till morning?" I asked, and he replied that it was really an "exceptionally interesting story," and the three were only resting for an hour before they took off again.

So I swung out of the hammock and was guided to a little clearing where the tiny bottle lamps had been set up on tree stumps, the flickering flames lighting up the faces of three exhausted looking, but triumphant men. Almost exactly three hours previously, they had exploded a 25-pound bomb inside Saigon's "U.S. Only" Capitol cinema. According to the official account of the results, as I heard it over the "Voice of America" next morning, three U.S. servicemen were killed and 57 wounded.

Two of the three before me were former peasants from the Saigon outskirts, the third a former factory worker, and I shall refer to them as No. 1, 2 and 3. No. 1, the worker, was the master planner and also organized the escape: "We had previously blown up the MAAG (Military Aid and Advisory Group) headquarters," he said. "That was in July 1963. Another group had tried to blow up this cinema but failed because they tried to attack it from the rear. And still another group had exploded a bomb in a U.S. baseball stadium the week before. Our task was to succeed where the others had failed at the Capitol. We had decided to do this after the Lunar New Year ceasefire period, but when American planes napalm-bombed a big meeting in Cu Chi district on New Year's day, we decided to teach them a lesson. Also we thought they should be punished for the coup they had just made in putting Nguyen Khanh in power. By that they wanted to show that they were the real masters in Saigon; we wanted to show that the people are still there too. So we decided to attack within the ceasefire period which they had violated."

As they described it, while Nos. 1 and 2 created a diversion at the side entrance, No. 3, the second peasant with the rather exalted face of a poet, walked through the main entrance with the explosive. "Because of the shooting outside, the Americans inside were alerted," No. 3 said. "Two jumped on me as I entered and started to strangle me. Because I had the explosive in my arms, I could not defend myself. But I managed to pull the detonator and as it spluttered the Americans were stupified with fear, and ran up some stairs. There is just ten seconds after pulling the detonator before it explodes. I had time to put it down between the aisles and walk out, closing the grenade-proof steel doors after me just as the explosion took place."

"You intended to blow yourself up with the two Americans?" I asked, and he eyed me calmly and said, "Of course." Looking at him, I thought of the descriptions in 19th century Russian literature of the poets and intellectuals who sacrificed their energies and talents, and often enough their lives, in trying to blow up the tsars. No. 3 was of that category. What pushes people to such deeds, I wondered, scanning as much of their tense faces as the bottle lamps would permit, their profiles etched against the impenetrable black of jungle night on which a newly born moon made no impression at all. There was silence for a moment, except for the monotonous cry of an intensely boring night bird which never ceased its metallic two-note cry between dusk and dawn.

"There are thousands of militants like us in Saigon," said No. 2, "ready to sacrifice ourselves at any moment, but we want to kill five or ten Americans for every one of us."

"Were there women and children in the cinema?" I asked.

"We don't make war against women and children," blazed forth No. 2. "But what do they care for our women and children? In that cinema are only the pilots that go out day after day in their planes and blindly bomb and strafe our villages. Do they ask if there are women and children inside the houses they napalm? They bomb and fire on every living thing they see."

No. 1 explained that a 12-year-old sister of the one who had planted the explosive had been killed with 15 other children in the strafing of a school in Cau Xe.

I was interested in knowing enough about their lives to understand what impelled people into such desperate ventures. No. 1 had spent five of the preceding nine years in Diemist prisons: "In front of my eyes, I saw my comrades, the finest men that ever lived, tortured to death for no other reason than that they had been patriots in the struggle for independence," he said. The hamlet of No. 2 had been bulldozed out of existence to make way for airfield extensions north of the city. After that he had worked as a coolie on an American military base. "I will never forgive them for what they did to our women," he said. "I saw things that no human being should see. As long as they remain on my soil while I live, I shall take my revenge. For my own sister and my own compatriots, our young women violated, comrades tortured and massacred."

It was time for them to move on. As they swung their small packs on their shoulders, I asked where they were heading. "We are going to a rest area," said No. 1, "and there we have to work out something special to mark May 1. In Saigon we have a tradition of celebrating May Day." I thought of them later when the radio reported an audacious coup in which a 14,000-ton U.S. aircraft-transport was sunk in Saigon harbor in the small hours of May 1 and a second bomb exploded killing and wounding Americans who came to investigate salvage possibilities. This happened despite exceptionally strict security precautions and mixed U.S.-Vietnamese anti-sabotage patrols set up following the Capitol cinema incident.

Hatred of the Invaders

Huynh Tan Phat had earlier explained to me that terrorist attacks against Americans were part of Front policy. "We have the spontaneous support of the population for such actions," he said. "We attack only cabarets, cinemas, sports grounds, restaurants reserved exclusively for U.S. military personnel. They have to put up barbed wire and anti-grenade grilles, as the French did in their time. This helps to expose their real situation—that they live in mortal fear of the population. Of course it would be impossible to carry out such actions with a handful of isolated, individual terrorists, but it is possible with the support of the whole population who always find means of sheltering them. It has happened several times when someone has been hurrying away after such an action, before the police got on his trail, that an unknown person has pushed him inside his house or shop and hidden him; or pressed money in his hand and said: 'Take this for a taxi.'"

A couple of weeks after the Capitol cinema incident, the Front broadcast a warning for Americans in Saigon not to take their wives and children to public places reserved for Americans. The terrorist attacks were for "men only."

In the days when France was involved in her "dirty war" in Indo-China, there was no lack of American leaders who saw things in a realistic light. The late President Kennedy's remarks on April 6, 1954, when he was still the "Senator from Massachusetts" were realistic enough: "To pour money, material and men into the jungles of Indo-China without at least a remote prospect of victory would be dangerously futile and destructive. ... No amount of American assistance in Indo-China can conquer an enemy which is everywhere, and at the same time nowhere; an 'enemy of the people' which has the sympathy and support of the people." This quote has become rather famous today when it is truer than when it was uttered ten years ago. But there was an observation equally apt made a year earlier by Adlai Stevenson, published in Paris (*l'Intransigeant*, May 21, 1953) after his visit to Indo-China. Following some correctly gloomy appraisals of the situation, Stevenson, now chief U.S. delegate at the United Nations, commented:

"One sees here in a startling way one of the major difficulties the French are up against. How to persuade the peasants in their rags that these Germans, these French, these Senegalese and these Moroccans are fighting *for them* against the Vietminh, who after all are of their race and their country?"

It was a good question then and a good question for Adlai
Stevenson, Dean Rusk and President Johnson to ponder over
today. How to persuade the peasants in their rags that these
Americans, these Kuomintang Chinese, these Filipino and Australian and other troops are fighting *for them* against the "Viet
Cong" who after all are of their own race and country? It
would still be a good question even if there were Vietnamese
from north of the 17th parallel fighting side by side with their
southern compatriots. The point is that the peasants in their
rags have long ago answered this question in their own hearts
and the acts of the young terrorist group only underlines this.
They regard the Americans as interventionists and aggressors,
no less odious than other invaders in Vietnamese history.

I came across a grim story while I was in the Tay Nguyen
which illustrates the point. It was related by H'Blong, a young
tribeswoman from the Rhade minority, now a Liberation Front
cadre responsible for information in her village, in Lac Lac
district of Dak Lak province. "There had been many enemy
raids," she said, "lots of people had been killed, livestock
slaughtered and stolen. American advisers were many in this
area. Our people were very angry and we started resisting, first
by traps and spikes to stop them plundering our houses. But
still the enemy persisted and our young men set up self-defense
units. We had no guns, only crossbows and poisoned arrows.

"Once when a surprise raid was made against our village, all
but two lads, who were too young to be in the self-defense
team, were away in the fields. They saw a column of enemy
troops approaching and hid themselves on the village side of
a river which the enemy troops had to wade across. When they
were in the middle of the stream, the two fired their arrows
and hit two Americans and four Diemists. They died immediately from the poison arrows. The rest went back and opened
fire with their machine guns from across the river. The boys kept
their heads down and waited. The enemy troops started to
cross again and when they got to the same spot, our boys fired
and more of the enemy fell. The enemy thought this was a
large-scale ambush and fled. They greatly fear poisonous arrows.
The dead were left behind, so the lads went and dragged them

on to the bank and collected the weapons. On the Americans were two daggers. Then they raced off to the fields and told what had happened. Our people had heard the shooting but they could not believe that these two lads, who were not considered old enough to be in the self-defense corps, could have defeated such an enemy force. Everyone came down to the river.

"There, sure enough, were the dead bodies. But the two Americans had been stabbed through the heart. 'Why did you stab the Americans when they were already dead?' we asked. 'And why only the Americans?'

" 'Because the Vietnamese are our people. They do wrong because they are misled,' replied one of the boys. 'But the two Americans are foreigners. They have come from far away, crossed the ocean with the clear aim of harming us. It is these big noses that put the Diemists up to doing so much harm. So, we stabbed them with their own daggers, even though they were dead.' The two boys are now members of our self-defense unit," concluded H'Blong, "and the enemy never attacked our village again."

I accept this as the grass-roots feeling that even what may seem to be the most primitive of minds recognize the primary source of their miseries and act accordingly. When planes are shot down and it is bits of blond-haired skulls that are plastered over the fields, when American "special forces" experts direct the slaughter of buffalo and chickens, things become crystal clear—as Adlai Stevenson recognized, when it was the French and not the American presence involved.

AMERICAN POW's

Quite another view of the situation, both as concerns morale and an appreciation of what the war is all about, came from four American war prisoners whom I met in what was doubtless the beginnings of the first camp for U.S. POW's to be established in Southeast Asia. They were all sergeants - first class, and were captured at the Hiep Hoa "Special Forces" training camp on the night of November 23-24, 1963, when guerillas overran the camp, destroyed all its installations and made off with enough arms to equip an over-size Liberation Front battalion.

Considering that these are the men especially selected to train Vietnamese in anti-guerilla or "counter-insurgency" operations, as their textbooks spell it out, it was interesting that all four had been captured without arms in their hands; that not a single shot seemed to have been fired in defense of this key training center; that of 12 Americans allotted to the camp only five were there when the attack took place, the rest "whooping it up" in Saigon.

Kenneth Roraback, a veteran of the Korean war with 15 years' service in the U.S. army, was the only one of the four awake at the time of the attack, around midnight; he was writing a letter to his wife. "What actually happened?" I asked. "They called our place a training camp," said Roraback, a dour-faced person with thinning hair and bushy eyebrows. "In reality, like a lot more, it was just a sitting target to be wiped out at any time. It was a well planned, well executed night attack, all over in about 15 minutes." To my question as to what action he personally took, he replied: "I ran for the trenches."

"Did you take a weapon?" I asked.

"There was no time."

"Was any resistance organized?"

"It was impossible. Everything was burning, there were 'Viet Cong' all over the place, streaming in over the ramparts, around all the buildings."

The other three—Camacho, a swarthy Texan; McClure, a Negro specialist on demolition; and Smith, a medical assistant and radio operator—were all in bed and all gave about the same account as Roraback. "A perfectly organized night attack," said Smith. "I was awakened by explosions right behind the barracks. There was a mortar barrage. I think they were using white phosphorous. Everything was ablaze within minutes. There were explosions in the bunkers. I raced for the trenches. Within a few minutes the 'Viet Cong' were there, too. They tied up my arms and led me out over the ramparts."

None of the four had taken weapons with them. I could no

more imagine a guerilla rushing for the trenches without a weapon in his hands than I could imagine an elephant flying. Their arms are set up right alongside their nylon hammocks in which they sleep and they would automatically grab their weapons even if they fell out of their hammocks. The four POW's had been on the move for months after capture, sometimes in sampans, mostly on foot, zig-zagging around, heading in all points of the compass until they had little idea where they were. They were now in a safe rear area.

I asked Roraback if air raids had bothered them much in their travels. "Planes were over for a strike soon after the attack. Whether they did any good or not, I don't know. The main thing, thank God, I was not touched. A couple of days later a B-26 came over and made 12 strafing runs. Whether anyone was hit or not, I don't know. In any case, like I said before, the main thing, thank God, I was not touched." My thoughts went back to the three that had attacked the Capitol cinema: "thousands of us ready to sacrifice our lives at any moment, but we want to kill five or ten Americans for every one of us."

Each of the four sergeants assured me, in separate conversations, that they had been well treated and each expressed surprise at this. "My captors were considerate from the moment I was taken," said Roraback. "I expected to be shot right away and I guess this showed in my face. When it didn't happen at once, nor the second day, I figured they were taking us a bit further away to shoot us."

"Why did you expect to be shot?" I asked, and Roraback looked a little confused. "Well, I considered it normal," he said after a pause. "Guerillas don't have conditions to look after prisoners. But they saw I was afraid and did everything to calm my fears."

"How were you able to communicate? Did you have a common language?"

"No, but they patted my back, waved their hands in a sort of friendly way in front of my face, stroked my arms and generally made signs that I shouldn't worry."

One could guess why Roraback and the others were worried, because they knew very well that any guerilla captured is almost

invariably tortured to death immediately, and the "Special
Forces" to which they were attached were amongst the most
savage in their behavior. One only has to look at photos published on the front pages of American newspapers of "Viet Cong"
prisoners to know why these men were worried. On the front page
of the May 24, 1964, international edition of the *New York
Times,* for instance, there is a photo of an almost nude Vietnamese, lying on the ground, his hands tied together over his
head and attached by a long cord to a U.S. tank.The caption
laconically informs the readers that the "Viet Cong" is about to
be dragged around by the tank, including through a river, as a
preliminary to "making him talk."

McClure was wounded in the attack by mortar fragments.
"I had first-aid treatment next day and the fragments were removed four days later," he said. "They treat us real well—that's
the main thing. No rough stuff of any kind. I never thought to be
treated like that, a real surprise."

"The treatment has been fair," said Smith, "considering guerillas don't have proper facilities for taking care of POW's. They
do the best they can under the conditions." And Camacho ob-
served: "They treat us very well, but it's difficult for them to
supply us with the food we're used to." I was surprised to find
that U.S. soldiers still seemed to be convinced that a white man
cannot live on rice instead of bread as the basic diet, but this
was the main problem for the four prisoners. Following the high
death rate among U.S. POW's in Korea, compared with virtually
none among British, French, Turkish and other nationalities,
much publicity had been given to the fact that all U.S. soldiers
destined for Asian service were to be conditioned to eating rice.
One would have thought that, especially for guerilla "specialists,"
a pre-requisite would be the ability to "live off the country."

Liberation Front policy in the past had been to give captured
Americans a few weeks of "explanations" as to what the struggle
is about and then set them free. Judging by the way the little
camp, where I met the four sergeants, is organized, it seems
many more American POW's are to be catered for, and release in
future may be a matter of negotiations. The uniforms of the four
had been taken away and replaced by two sets of tailored black

shirts and trousers. They had been given soap and toothbrushes, were able to take a bath once a week and "when they want us to shave, they bring us a shaving kit," as Camacho expressed it. Each hut has an air-raid shelter and a high bamboo palisade surrounding it. They sleep on the standard Vietnamese bamboo bed. Camp authorities told me that although "with the best will in the world we can't set up a bread factory in the jungle," they would try and vary the diet in deference to the American stomach.

Their surprise at seeing me coming out of the jungle could not have been greater than if I had dropped down from Mars. As they had been out of touch with the outside world for months, I asked each if they had any special questions. I was astonished at their lack of interest. Camacho assumed a dead serious, almost tragic air when he asked if he could put one question. "Do you by any chance happen to know who won the world heavyweight boxing championship?" By chance I had heard the result over the radio: "Yes, Clay beat Sonny Liston in the 7th round with a technical knockout." A smile spread over his face as he thanked me and marched off with an almost beatific expression.

I asked Roraback what he thought about the war, now that he had had several months to think about it. After explaining that as a military man he had no right to discuss "political" matters, he said: "It's all a mystery to me. I've no idea what it's all about. Of course, as a legally constituted government, Saigon has the right to put down the guerillas and ask us to help them. But there are two sides to every question and the guerillas also have the right to try and overthrow the government if they don't like it. But as to who is right and who is wrong, who will win or lose or what the whole thing is about, I have no idea." The others replied similarly. They had "no idea" what the war was about or why they were really there. They all insisted on their purely "advisory" role.

Very different were the interests of the young soldiers and cadres of the Liberation forces. Questions ranged over the whole world and discussions lasted far into the night. They were especially interested to know what the outside world knew and thought about their own struggle and to know about national liberation movements in other parts of the world. They may often have been hazy about geography and the status of many of the countries they named, but they knew what they were interested in, and it was not the world heavyweight boxing championship that was on the top of the list.

When I asked Roraback how he occupied his thoughts—the POW's had nothing to do except keep their individual, tiny bamboo huts clean—he said: "I think of all the things I'll do when I get home. I've built, in my imagination, a barbecue pit; put shelves in the kitchen; made six model planes for the kids and three radios. It's the only way I can keep my mind occupied."

It was typical of the way things are in South Vietnam that both Smith and Roraback had been wounded, in an action at Can Cho, a few days after they had landed in South Vietnam. "My wife was mad with anxiety when I left," said Roraback. "So many friends and acquaintances of ours had been killed, badly wounded, or just missing, once they left for South Vietnam. The first word she got about me was that I'm wounded. And four months later that I'm captured."

The question arises why do people who have no ideological interest in, or knowledge of, what this war is about, volunteer for such dangerous, unpleasant duty? For that, one has to look at their pay. Roraback's basic pay of $335.00 per month, jumped up to $858.40 a month while he is in South Vietnam and the other three each received from $450 to $500 per month extra for the South Vietnam service, which must make them about the highest paid mercenaries ever, in relation to their rank. Their Liberation Front opposite numbers, from rank and file troops to regimental commander get 40 piastres per month—a little over one dollar at the official rate and about 40 cents at the real, black market rate. But the difference between patriots and mercenaries on the field of battle reminds one of the dog explaining why he had failed in a hard race to catch a hare. "That hare was running for its life, I only for my dinner." The Vietnamese are fighting for their lives, the Americans for their dinners, and that means the difference between victory and defeat in the type of struggle being waged in South Vietnam.

PART II

RISE OF THE LIBERATION FRONT

Chapter 8

HOW DID THE WAR START?

MOTHER CARBINE AND HER CHILDREN

"We call her our Mother Carbine," said the guerilla leader with a grin, holding out a battered U.S. army carbine. "It was our first weapon but in four years of constant labor she has produced many others." He was a short, nuggety man with a cocky smile, beautiful teeth, a brush of stiff black hair and bulging muscles under his black shorts. We were sitting outside a thatch-roofed peasant hut under the shade of a frame from which dangled festoons of curling cucumbers and some gourd-shaped squashes. At the surging roar of approaching helicopters, he went to lean against a corner post, watching a pair of the ungainly craft with a speculative eye, chewing on a toothpick. "HU-IA's," he said. "Flying high, heading northeast. There's an action going on there and it seems they're taking casualties. When they fly in pairs like that it's usually to pick up wounded." After they had roared and clattered overhead, showing no interest in our little corner, he sat down again, performing that Vietnamese miracle of accomodating his behind and his feet on six square inches of wooden stool. He poured a few thimblefuls of bitter, yellow tea into two miniscule cups.

"Until this arrived," he said, fondling the carbine, "we had not a single firearm in our district, nor even in the whole of Gia Dinh. There was a big action at Tua Hai in Tay Ninh province, early in 1960. Lots of arms were captured; of these, six were sent to Gia Dinh, one for each of the six districts. That's how we got 'Mother.' With her we captured our first post and she presented us with her first litter."

The conversation was taking place less than 12 miles from Saigon. I was speaking to a district leader of what the West calls the "Viet Cong," abbreviation for Vietnamese Communists, and what he and his fellows call the Giai Phong Quan, the military arm of the South Vietnam National Front of Liberation.

"How was it possible to capture a post with a single carbine?" I asked.

"First of all, life had become so desperate, the oppression was so ferocious, with arrests, torture, executions a daily occurrence in our district, that people were ready to move. The young men, constantly on the run from the Diemist press-gangs were clamoring for action. A few of us who had been guerillas in the war against the French got together and made many wooden dummy copies of 'Mother' here. One moonlight night we staged a march past the post, firing a few shots and warning the garrison through megaphones that if they did not behave better they would be dealt with by the 'People's Armed Forces.' They were too scared to come out and we went back to the village by a roundabout route and hid our weapons. Next morning the post commander and a few of his trusties came to the village market and started questioning people. We had made sure the market women would have the right answers. It went something like this:

" 'Who were all those armed men around here last night?'

" 'I don't know,' replied an old market woman, 'but there were a whole lot of them. It took nearly an hour for them to march through the village. I suppose it must be those "Viet Cong" the papers have been talking about.'

" 'What sort of arms did they have?'

" 'They had a lot of arms. Mainly rifles, but some others that it took two or three men to carry. Weapons we never saw before, like big tubes. And a lot that had two or three legs.'

"These replies made the post commander shake like a leaf. He had visions of a big force equipped with bazookas and heavy machine guns and the word soon spread to the rank and file troops in the post. The market women made sure of that. The enemy sent some reinforcements from district headquarters for a few days, but nothing happened; they couldn't find any 'Viet Cong', so they went back. A couple of nights later we moved.

We had bought a lot of carbide for bicycle lamps and prepared dozens of giant bamboo tube sections filled with carbide and water. We surrounded the post around midnight and started exploding the carbide bombs—bamboo bursts with a terrific noise and in between the explosions there were a few shots from 'Mother.' With the megaphones we called on the garrison to surrender or they would be 'wiped out to the last man.' They were terrified at the explosions all round their barracks and meekly filed out and laid down their weapons. We kept our dummies well out of sight and had one of our men with the real carbine check them as they came out. By the time the last surrendered, we were really well armed with their weapons. And that is how we took out the post at Phu My Hung, about nine miles from Saigon, in Cu Chi district."

"Wasn't there any resistance at all?" I asked.

"They never fired a shot," he replied. "They were thoroughly demoralized. But I forgot to mention one detail. After we got 'Mother' we started sending warnings to the local despots, the cruellest of the Diemist officials. We ordered them to quit their jobs and that if they did not do so after repeated warnings, they would be punished. And in fact we did execute one of them, the chief of Cu Chi district. He had been a terrible brute and apart from all the other deaths he had caused, he had personally tortured to death or simply killed over 80 of our comrades who had taken part in the anti-French resistance war. We sent him several warnings and as he continued his terrorist activities we captured him one night, read out the list of his crimes, the names of his victims and then executed him. We left a copy of the indictment and execution order with his body and posted some others up around the district center. He is the only one to have been executed in Cu Chi, but it had a terrific effect on the smaller fry. They quit their jobs in all the surrounding villages and the worst of the terroristic activities ceased almost overnight. Of course this had a big effect on the post commander and the garrison at Phu My Hung, especially as we had sent propaganda teams there at night warning of the terrible consequences if they opposed the 'People's Armed Forces.' "

BATTLE OF TUA HAI

If "Mother Carbine" was the first weapon in Gia Dinh, it seemed to me that the battle of Tua Hai, must be the "Mother Battle" which provided the clue for one of the constant objects of my visit—to find out how, where and when did this war in South Vietnam start. The guerilla leader only had the vaguest details, that a "great number" of arms had been captured. Later I was able to seek out the very man who had commanded the action, Quyet Thanh, a big, raw-boned peasant who is now a regimental commander in the Liberation Army's regular forces. He had been a guerilla leader in a small village in Tay Ninh province during the anti-French war or, as the guerillas call it, the first resistance war.

Tua Hai is a Vietnamese corruption of the French "Tour 2," as the French designated this fortress, about three miles north of Tay Ninh, capital of the province of the same name, and about fifty-five miles Northwest of Saigon. It was, and still is, a solidly-built, rectangular fortress, and at the time the action took place, it was the base headquarters for the 32nd regiment plus one battalion of the Diemist 21st division, about 2,000 men in all.

"We had lots of worries and many discussions before we launched that action," said Quyet Thang, "and even immediately afterwards. The 'line' up till the end of 1959 had been exclusively a legal, political, non-violent form of struggle, but faced with the wholesale wiping out of all former resistance cadres, it changed at the end of 1959 to permit the use of arms but in self-defense only." I asked who set the 'line' and who changed it. He gave me that quizzical look which I was used to by then when I put that sort of question to any former resistance worker. But his reply was fuller and made more sense than any I had received before.

"We had an organization, the Viet Minh, which carried on the first resistance war. There was nothing in the Geneva Agree-

ments* which said this organization was to be dissolved once
the Ceasefire Agreements went into effect; or that all Viet Minh
members should withdraw north of the 17th parallel with the
troops of the regular army. A big part of the population would
have had to leave their homes and villages in that case. Although
the Diemists have done their best to hound down and extermin-
inate all former Viet Minh members and in fact anyone who
played any role, no matter how small, in the first resistance,
there are still plenty of us around. We find means of keeping
in contact despite the dangers and difficulties.

"As for the 'line,' this was set by our leadership the moment
the Geneva Ceasefire Agreements were signed for the whole
of Vietnam. Absolute strict respect for the Geneva Agreements
was spelt out into detailed instructions to observe discipline;
not to go beyond the bounds of legal, political struggle. We
are revolutionaries. That was an instruction which our sense
of revolutionary discipline does not permit us to violate. It cost
us the lives of many of the finest of our comrades in the period 1954-59. We are used to having a 'line' set for a considerable
period. In the first resistance war, it sometimes took a whole
year just to get the 'line' communicated to all regions. A delegate from the extreme south would have to travel for six months
to attend a key conference, then walk back again to report on
the new 'line.' And in the conditions under which we worked
then, and to a lesser extent now, we were used to working in isolated, autonomous groups, making our own decisions for months,

* The Ceasefire Agreements on Indo-China, concluded after three months
of negotiations at the Geneva Conference, were signed in July 1954 by all
the great powers, except the United States. Although refusing to sign,
the United States pledged to respect the Agreements. The key provisions
included the withdrawal of the Viet Minh forces north of the 17th parallel,
regrouping of the French armies to the South; a general election in July
1956 to unify the country, to be preceded a year earlier by preliminary
consultations between the two sides. The Agreements also forbid any
form of reprisal or discrimination against participants in the war, and set
up an International Control Commission (India, Poland and Canada) to
check on application of the agreements. For further background and
details see Burchett, *The Furtive War*, International Publishers, 1963.

years on end, but always within the framework of the 'line.' That line was non-violence till towards the end of 1959, and 'violence for self-defense' after that."

As to my question as to who changed the line at the end of 1959, he gave me another of those long, quizzical looks and said: "There is still enough of our former leadership around to take a decision like that and there are enough former Viet Minh, patriots, communists, former resistance workers, new recruits from youth who have fled to the forests from the Diemist press-gangs, to implement such decisions.

"Our big worry was whether an attack on the Tua Hai fortress went beyond the decision on violence for 'self-defense only.' In the end, after long discussions, we decided that even for self-defense we had to have weapons; that our proposed attack was in fact a 'self-defense' action to get arms and was not a formal violation of the 'line.' We decided to make the attack just prior to the Lunar Year (around the end of February), 1960. The enemy's terrorist campaign had reached its climax in the previous weeks. The Tua Hai regiment had just returned from a big military campaign in which hundreds of peasants in the Tay Ninh region had been massacred. The commanders filmed massacres and tortures and forced people to attend screen shows, to terrorize them more completely. The mobile guillotines had been at work, trundling across the countryside with the special tribunals set up under Law 10/59. A leading former resistance cadre, Ut Lep, for instance, was guillotined at the Chau Thanh district center. His wife was forced to display the head in the market place while Diemist cameramen filmed the scene.

"The biggest operation was launched at the end of January, not only to round up any former resistance members they could lay hands on, but to grab young able-bodied men for their armed forces. They fled in the thousands to the forests. Enemy troops then pillaged their homes, stealing all the food and presents laid in for the Lunar New Year. On this occasion, the enemy had with them the most degenerate of the commando groups who took a delight in gouging out eyes, slitting nostrils, hacking off the ears of victims right in the market place, drinking their blood and carrying out in the extremist degree possible their instructions to drive black terror into the hearts of the people. People were unnerved, demoralized by all this but underneath they were boiling with pent-up fury.

"It was clear to us that the new 'line' was right. There were only two courses: take to arms and defend ourselves or die like chickens. We could not count on any outside force coming to the rescue. We had to stand up or be wiped out. A few of us, old resistance cadres, held the fateful meeting where we took the decision to attack Tua Hai. We got together 260 men—former resisters, young men who had fled the press-gangs, some deserters from the Diemist army who had a few precious guns and some remnants from the armed religious sects. These were particularly valuable. As they [the Hoa Hao, Cao Dai and Binh Xuyen sects] had been part of the French armed forces, they of course had not been required to withdraw with their weapons to the North as our troops had been. Later when Diem turned against the French, he turned against them too and almost wiped them out. But some fled to the western parts of the country and carried on local guerrilla actions. A few joined our group of 260 and others gave us their arms. Altogether we had 170 firearms, most of them archaic and with a strictly limited number of cartridges."

"Our maximum aim," continued Quyet Thang, in his quiet voice, "was to seize 300 arms and corresponding ammunition to arm our own unit with modern weapons, to distribute leaflets prepared in the name of the 'People's Self-Defense Forces' and to explain to the enemy troops why we were going over to armed action. Apart from our fighting force, we also organized another 500 people from remote villages—to avoid any reprisals on nearby ones—to arrive towards the end of the action to carry off our booty and any casualties."

The attack was planned for Lunar New Year's Eve, when they knew vigilance would be relaxed. Tua Hai is a substantial fortress a thousand yards long by eight hundred wide, surrounded by seven-foot high earthen ramparts with machine gun towers at each corner, and smaller sentry posts around all the main installations. Thanks to the former resistance fighters, Quyet

Thang had been able to get scouts in for days beforehand to study the disposition of installations, the layout of fire postions, the time of changing the sentries and other essential data. There were two companies of troops on permanent guard duty; the rest of the 2,000 slept unarmed in the barracks, their arms locked up in an arms depot.

The scouts inside had set mines around some of the key buildings, this explosion being the signal for the attack. When the mines exploded with a terrific noise, setting on fire radio installations, command post and other buildings, 120 guerrillas poured in over the ramparts from the south and 80 from the north, the rest setting up an ambush on the road leading from Tay Ninh, in case reinforcements were sent. The men quickly armed themselves with new weapons, and stormed the guard towers. Troops poured out of the blazing barracks, some surrendered, others rushed into the trenches, but most of them raced over the ramparts and fired from outside, but never dared to make an assault.

"In that No. 1 arms depot," said Quyet Thang with something like tears in his eyes at the memory of it, four years later, "there were arms everywhere, unopened cases of new weapons, far more than we could possibly carry away. There were arms I had never seen before, 57mm recoilless rifles, for instance. I had no idea what they were for, but decided to take five of them anyway. They were very effective later against the enemy's M-113 tanks and blockhouses. It was a terrible thing to leave all those precious weapons there. But the maximum we could carry, even with some of the enemy soldiers who had come over to us and offered to help, were about 1,000 arms, including 800 rifles and a good selection of automatic weapons. The 500 porters had turned up safely and within an hour and forty-five minutes of the attack, our convoy was moving back into the jungle again, everyone doubled under the weight of weapons and ammunition. We could have had uniforms, cloth and a host of other stuff had we had the transport means."

I asked if the Diemist forces made no attempt to track them down and recover the weapons. After all, to locate them they would only have to draw a circle of some ten miles around

Tua Hai, the maximum that could be covered by dawn with such burdens as the guerillas were carrying.

"They sent two battalions after us, but they dared not enter the jungle, We were resting all next day, but we had set up solid defense positions. Our men were very tired but were ready for battle, the porters too with all those lovely new arms. This attack had terrific repercussions. A couple of days later over 100 puppet troops from Tua Hai deserted. Badly scarced local officials started contacting us. The local puppet bullies started being very tame, became almost human when they knew we were around with a thousand-odd new weapons. Diemist agents started talking politely to the same people they had been terrorizing only a few days previously.

"We kept enough arms for the battalion we set up immediately as a result of the battle, others were distributed to all other provinces, where they were most needed. The enemy's repressive machine started to disintegrate. With even a few arms in their hands, the people started moving everywhere and enemy prestige suffered a deadly blow. 'Mother' carbines turned up all over the place and soon started producing children. A completely new stage in the struggle was ushered in."

As to whether the leaders considered the "line" had been violated, Quyet Thang replied with a broad grin: "Actually we were still worried for some weeks after the battle; but then the word came back, not only approving but bringing the warmest congratulations. The situation changed almost overnight, in fact. Prior to this action, when we got letters from other provinces, they made depressing reading; full of pessimism, telling of the arrest or the beheading of this or that comrade. But after the action which we started, the tone of the letters changed. Of course there were occasional losses but nothing to the same extent; the letters became almost exultant as they brought news of successes everywhere, the heightened morale of the people now that they had weapons in their hands and an open resistance struggle had started. 1960 was the first time since the Ceasefire Agreements went into effect that we could really say 'Happy New Year' during Têt [Lunar New Year].

"From this battle," concluded Quyet Thang, "we drew the conclusion that it is not numerical strength or arms that count, but morale and determination. The way the action was planned and executed was used later to illustrate the necessity of a political-military struggle to handle the special situation in South Vietnam, with emphasis on the political. It was clear that the high morale of our men which alone made such an action possible was due to the thorough political discussions we had beforehand and also to the political work we had been able to do on some of the troops inside Tua Hai."

Among the weapons seized were $81mm$ and $60mm$ mortars—favorite guerrilla weapons and ones which they use, from a hundred or so yards range, with deadly efficiency.

The Tua Hai action set the pattern for many that followed, the political softening up beforehand, contact with the troops inside the target area, enlisting the support of the local population to carry off casualties and booty so that the small striking force was always a 100-per cent combat unit; more men than arms at the outset of every action, more arms than men at the finish; the sudden, speedy night attack and quick getaway, which followed Tua Hai. With direct U.S. participation from the end of 1961 onwards and the massive use of helicopters, other tactics were developed.

Perhaps historians will later settle on the Tua Hai battle as the time and place at which the war in South Vietnam started. I think they would be wrong for reasons soon to be developed. But it did mark the beginning of large-scale, organized armed resistance to the dictatorial regime of Ngo Dinh Diem that U.S. policy-makers had installed and maintained in power in Saigon.

Later when I met the leaders of the Liberation Journalists Association, I found the Tua Hai battle marked a "first" in something else. The first issue of *Chien Thang* (Victory) now the weekly organ of the Armed Forces of East Nam Bo (Cochin-China) appeared on the Tua Hai battlefield. The present editor, Trung Thang, a slim young man with a skin stained walnut brown from years of living in the open, told me how he and a tiny staff produced their first issue especially for the Tua

Hai battle. They used paper torn from notebooks and wrote the "newspaper" by hand, using a process of rice flour for duplicating up to 20 copies after which they had to rewrite. "We distributed the first copies as the troops were moving up for the attack," he said, "and it greatly encouraged them. I was with the Command Post, and as soon as we moved inside, we started distributing to the captured enemy troops lying face down on the ground. Some of my colleagues had to drop the work and join in the battle for a while. At the Tua Hai battle, we started the tradition of soldier-journalists who fight and write at the same time." He went on to explain how the paper had gradually developed, from handwritten to typewritten form, then stereotyped, and from 1963 onwards in its present printed form.

"Distribution at first was exclusively among soldiers, passed on from hand to hand," explained Trung Thang. "Now it gets down to village level and is very popular among the peasants and in the local self-defense units."

As to why "Mother" carbines, Tua Hai battles and handwritten newspapers were considered necessary, this is a matter that diplomats and historians will wrangle over for generations. I can only set out what I was able to gather on the spot, fill in the details of a picture, the outlines of which have been etched fairly sharply by events in South Vietnam in recent years.

DIEM TAKES OVER

Normally one can pinpoint a war, even a civil war, with precision; the firing of the first shots are recorded in time and place. To my ceaseless probing as to how and when this war in South Vietnam started, I got as many differing replies as questions put. Replies always related to the firing in the particular village, district or province of the person questioned. The most authoritative person to whom I put this question was Nguyen Huu Tho, president of the National Front of Liberation.

He himself was not regarded as a leftist when he practiced law in Saigon and he did not take part in the anti-French war. But in March 1950, he did walk at the head of a demonstration protesting against the arrival of three U.S. warships in Saigon as a display of solidarity with France's "dirty war." Tho and a few hundred thousand Saigon residents were very angry at this and he headed a group of intellectuals who took part in the protest. The following day the warships pulled up their anchors and left. Nguyen Huu Tho was arrested by the French authorities and imprisoned in Lai Chau, a remote town north of Dien Bien Phu. He was released a couple of years later by Viet Minh troops. When the Geneva Agreements were signed he resumed his law practice in Saigon. So it was to him that I put as one of my first questions: "How did it all start? When and where were the first shots fired?"

"As far as Saigon is concerned, we had our first great shock on August 1, 1954, twelve days after the Ceasefire Agreements were signed. I can tell you that people in Saigon were overjoyed when the word was flashed through that the Geneva Conference had succeeded. There were mixed feelings about the two years' delay over reunification but the general sentiment was that this was a small price to pay for a return to peace and a normal life, free of foreign rule. On August 1, there was a monster demonstration of gay, cheering people in Saigon, mainly to hail and celebrate the signing of the Geneva Agreements, but resolutions were also passed asking for the immediate release of political and military prisoners, as provided for in the Agreements. The reply came in a volley of rifle fire. Several people were wounded and a pregnant woman was shot through the stomach. That this, the first demonstration in peace and freedom, as we thought, should be brutally suppressed, acted as a cold douche on the most ardent spirits. The same day we set up a Committee of Defense of Peace and the Geneva Agreements, and I was elected president." It became better known in the West as the Saigon-Cholon Peace Committee and included among its leaders the cream of Saigon's intellectual life.

"For us," continued Nguyen Huu Tho, "this was a sign that the new regime of Ngo Dinh Diem was only a puppet government, like that of Bao Dai*, and was out to suppress the people

* The puppet emperor under the French who was replaced as Chief of State by Ngo Dinh Diem, who had U.S. support.

from the first days of its power. We had not expected this and we had many bitter reflections on that night of August 1 and the days that followed. In Saigon the first shots of repression were fired 12 days after the Ceasefire Agreements were signed." The committee aimed at acting as a sort of watchdog to see the Agreements were strictly applied and to bring to the notice of the International Control Commission (comprised of India, as chairman, Poland and Canada) any violations.

Reports started trickling in and soon flooding in from the countryside telling of wholesale arrests and massacres in areas from which the Viet Minh troops were withdrawing to regroup north of the 17th parallel, in accordance with the Geneva Agreements. "Within a couple of months of setting up of our committee," Nguyen Huu Tho said, "we started getting delegations from the provinces, begging us to set up similar committees all over the countryside. We started organizing them when—on November 11, four months after Geneva—the police suddenly swooped down, dissolved our committee and arrested a number of leading members, including myself."*

"We had no idea at that time," President Tho continued, "but in forming the Saigon Committee and its various branches we had created the embryo for the National Front of Liberation, set up more than six years later."

TERROR ON THE COUNTRYSIDE

As for what was happening on the countryside, some faint glimpses appeared through the cautious reports of the International Commission. I remembered one early reference to the Cho Duoc incident, so when I was in Central Vietnam—fief of the medieval monster Ngo Dinh Can (a brother of Ngo Dinh Diem), I sought out the full details from Dinh Chau, a member of the Liberation Front's executive committee of Quang Nam province. A former middle peasant, with a cheerful face hewn from granite, he had lost a leg in one of his first military

---

* I visited Saigon about a week after this and watched the Diemist police arresting people as they came to the International Commission Headquarters to report the arrest of friends and relatives.

actions, but continued to direct activities from a secret mountain base. Chau, like most of the cadres I met in the provinces, had been more skeptical from the start than those in Saigon, as to how the Agreements would be applied.

"We received news of them with very mixed feelings here. Of course there was relief that peace would be established over the whole country and we resistance workers pledged ourselves as an act of discipline to do everything to respect the Agreements and do everything possible to prevent violations by friend or foe. But we doubted that our opponents would really respect them.

"The Cho Duoc incident proved our skepticism justified. Most of Quang Nam, except for the Tourane naval base, had been a liberated area in the latter years of the resistance. But in September 1954, a regiment commanded by Le Van Kim [later a leading member of the military junta which overthrew Diem] came to the area. A unit was sent to Cho Duoc in the central part of the province and without a word to anyone, the troops started cutting down fruit trees and bamboos in private gardens to build their barracks. People gathered together and protested about this. There was no violence, not as much as a stick in anyone's hands. People demanded only one thing, that their property be respected. The unit commander rapped out an order and before anyone could grasp what was happening, the troops started firing repeatedly into the crowd. Terrible cries and screams mingled with the crashing volleys of rifle fire; when the firing stopped the ground was covered with the dead and dying and groaning wounded. There were 40 killed, almost all women and children because most of the men were away in the fields. But the survivors closed in on the soldiers like a great human wave and they ran.

"What first-aid was available was given to the wounded; those that could be moved were placed on rough stretchers, the dead also, and a grim procession set out for the battalion headquarters. Word spread to neighboring villagers and long before the stretcher-bearers arrived a great crowd had assembled around battalion headquarters. People swept in and with their bare hands, disarmed the soldiers and poured sand down their rifle barrels and into the artillery pieces. The stretcher-bearers arrived and the bodies were laid out in the barracks square, friends of the victims demanding punishment for those responsible, medical help for the wounded, compensation for bereaved families. The crowd continually built up, completely surrounding the barracks and preventing any troops leaving.

"For three days there was a permanent crowd of about 15,000 camped around the barracks, some leaving and others coming in a sort of spontaneous relay system; those from nearby villages bringing rice and cooking it for the others. Banners and slogans were rigged up, connected with the specific outrage, ranging from demands of punishment to denunciations of the U.S.–Diem regime for an outrageous violation of the Geneva Agreements. The battalion could not link up or even communicate with the other two battalions of the regiment. People discussed things with the soldiers, especially those who had not taken part in the shooting, and a number deserted on the spot. The 15,000 were disciplined, elected their spokesmen, divided the food up equally and showed that they were prepared to keep up the protest indefinitely.

"Eventually the battalion commander had to agree with the demands; to bury the dead at government expense, free medical treatment for the wounded, compensation for the bereaved, an end to destruction of people's property and an International Commission investigation. An ICC team actually came but they were very passive and the authorities managed to prevent them having any contact with the people. Three months later, there were two similar incidents with troops from the same regiment, in which 30 people were killed at Chien Dan and 40 at Cam Coc. People's hopes that peace had come began to disappear altogether."

By all I could find out from provinces widely separated, the Cho Duoc incident was typical for most areas which had been completely controlled by the Viet Minh during the war, "liberated areas" as they designated them. The idea seems to have been to paralyze the population by deliberate terror within the first weeks or months of the Ceasefire, as soon, in fact as the Vietnam People's Army forces and cadres had withdrawn. In compliance with the Geneva Agreements, 140,000 troops and cadres, includ-

ing a handful of wives and families, had regrouped to the North
under International Commission control, taking their arms with
them. Repression intensified in proportion to the agitation for
the Consultative Conference and the July 1956 elections, which
people still hoped would take place and relieve their immediate
suffering.

In another area, distinct from that where I had met Dinh
Chau, I was able to talk with Huynh Thanh, also a member of
the Quang Nam provincial committee of the Front, a doctor with
a sensitive acquiline face who had left his practice in Tourane
to take part in the anti-French war and, after a few weeks of
peace, had fled back into the mountains again. He spoke of conditions in the mainly mountainous district of Tam Ky which
includes part of the Annamite mountain chain and borders on
Quang Ngai province to the south.

"We consider that the repression was even worse in Tam Ky
than in other districts, because it had been a completely liberated
area," Huynh Tanh said. "First order of the day for the Saigon
command was to eliminate anyone who had taken part in the
resistance administration and to install the Diemist one. Violence
was used to effect this and was stepped up as soon as the new
administration was in office. Puppet troops who had been defeated in the anti-French war now came as victors, occupied
homes and temples, threw the inmates out into the streets.

"Once the administration was set up, next thing was to try
and list the population according to their roles in the resistance. At first they wanted to list all those who had taken any
part at all. But this was impossible because every able-bodied
man and woman had taken part and also any child big enough to
carry a parcel or message. So they started listing everyone according to what they considered their importance. Cadres who were
exposed—those still in the administration when they arrived—
were imprisoned without any hope of ever coming out again.
None of them have ever been seen since. Others had to pack
enough food for three or six months or more, and take off for
'anti-Communist indoctrination courses.' Each family on the
average had to put in eight months of unpaid corvée in that
first year, building roads, barracks and other military installations.

"In the villages, barracks were set up and the young men and women were herded into separate huts where they had to spend the night, subject to endless harangues against the Viet Minh, Ho Chi Minh and everything to do with the North. The main idea was to root out every bit of patriotism, any memories of the resistance period or even political thinking. Nothing must be left to hang on to."

Huynh Thanh produced some records which he insisted were based on incomplete figures. Of the 180,000 population of Tam Ky district—now a liberated zone of the second resistance war—13,000 have "disappeared" and another 7,000 are held in various prisons. The overwhelming majority of the "disappeared" are known to have been killed and a proportion of the 7,000 have certainly died in jail. One in nine of the population killed, or in prison for an indefinite period. It is worth noting that Article 14c of the Geneva Convention stipulates that:

"Each party undertakes to refrain from any reprisals or discrimination against persons or organizations on account of their activities during the hostilities and to guarantee their democratic liberties."

During the first year of its activities, the International Commission investigated 40 violations of this article in the South, a tiny fraction of those that occurred. Some of the violations involved massacres of hundreds of people. Of these, 16 violations had been confirmed by the end of the first year, 13 had been investigated but the findings had not been published, eight cases were still under investigation and in three cases, the evidence was considered insufficient to bring in a finding. No evidence was ever found of violation of this article in the North. The International Commission's Mobile Team No. 24, sent to Quang Nam and Quang Ngai, was able to work a total of 15 days in the eight months it stayed before being withdrawn. A second team, No. 61, sent to help the first was immobilized for 100 days without being able even to start work. It was also withdrawn and the massacres continued. The ICC Report No. 4 stated:

"In cases where enquiries were possible, we have verified 319 cases involving the loss of human lives. . . . The Commission was unable to determine that, apart from the cases cited, there have not been other reprisals and discriminations." A part of the balance sheet in the first year of peace!

Of course no Consultative Conference took place in July 1955; the French had already packed up their bags and had withdrawn from Vietnam—and from their Geneva Agreement obligations—in order to indulge in another desperate military adventure in Algeria. Diem, with lavish U.S. aid, had largely evicted French interests and had capped this by smashing the armed religious sects. July 1956, came—and there were no elections. Nobody but the most naive by that time believed there would be. The campaign of terror was stepped up after July 1956, as Diem expected a severe popular reaction to the frustrated election hopes.

In 1957, the "denounce-Communists" campaign started. And by this time Diem had informed the International Commission that he would no longer tolerate any investigations under Article 14c. In its Report dated November 4, 1957, the ICC informed the Co-Presidents of the Geneva Conference that: "The Government of the Vietnam Republic has decided not to reply further to complaints relative to this clause and not to permit any activities by enquiry groups provided for in the Geneva Agreements to carry out enquiries relative to these complaints."

It was Le Quang Binh, a veteran resistance worker, and a member of the Front's Quang Ngai provincial committee, with iron grey hair and skin so tightly stretched over his face that one felt the bones might poke through any moment, who gave me a graphic account of the "denounce-Communists" campaign. "It started just because we had given no pretext for repression during the earlier provocations in our area. It was a long drawn-out campaign that cut down many of our best resistance cadres and their families. Children of former resistance workers were banned from going to school; wives of those regrouped to the North were forced to divorce and then remarry to prove they were 'sincere.' Land which had been distributed under the resistance administration's reform project was taken back and given to former landlords if they were still around, or to some

of Ngo Can's cronies if they were not. Mutual-aid teams set up
to help those families which were short of manpower were dissolved. Thousands of former resistance members and peasants
who were now dispossessed were rounded up and sent off to the
so-called 'agricultural settlements' in the mountains; irrigation
projects built by the peasants during the war years were either
destroyed or enormous taxes were levied for the right to use the
water. As most of the people had taken part in resistance activities the repression touched a large proportion of the population. At Quang Ngai provincial capital, 6,000 were held per-
manently, many being shipped off to Poulo Condor and other
prisons; there were new jails set up at district and village levels.
Every arrest was synonymous with barbarous tortures—this was
an absolute rule. Even if an arrested person was ready to turn
traitor, to cooperate from the first moment, he could not escape
the preliminary torture.

"Economically things went to pot. Even within a year of the
Diemists arriving, there was starvation and famine, especially
in the coastal areas where people actually died from hunger
in 1955. With manpower gone, land confiscated, irrigation systems destroyed, what could you expect? People ate wild pineapples and roots instead of rice. Sugar cane and silk production
was also finished because the Diemists maintained it was cheaper
to import American sugar and nylon cloth."

If things were bad for the Vietnamese they were ten times
worse for the minority peoples. There are—or were—about 80,000
in Quang Ngai, mostly Hre, but with smaller tribes of B'Nam,
K'Dong and Kor.

"We have fairly accurate round figures for that period,"
continued Le Quang Binh, "because the four mountainous
districts are now liberated, solidly this time. In one year, from
around mid-1955 to mid-1956, 2,000 tribal people died of epidemics without a finger raised by the Diemists to help them; 600
were killed in mass slaughters, usually buried alive, or hands and
feet tied and hurled into rivers or ravines; 450 died in prisons, 500 were either secretly liquidated by agents or disappeared
without a trace after arrests, and another 500 died of starvation.
In many hamlets one in every ten died."

This was only the beginning of the agony of the minority peoples and I had it described by chiefs and ordinary tribespeople of a score of different minorities—a story of unrelieved horror that recalls the wholesale wiping out of the Red Indians in the USA and of the Australian aborigines in the first years of white settlement there.

As for that first question I had put to Nguyen Huu Tho, I knew the answer long before I met him—but it was interesting to have confirmation from Saigon, too. The war in South Vietnam has no starting point in time and space because it never started. It never started because it never stopped. All that happened was that after the withdrawal of the 140,000 Viet Minh and cadres to the north, a one-sided war continued against an unarmed people. A large part of the same military machine built up to serve the French with U.S. arms and dollars, was turned loose over vast areas of South Vietnam to wipe out the political resistance the French had never been able to crush and thus suppress at birth any potential resistance to the reactionary policies Diem was committed to pursue.

Chapter 9

SPARKS ON A MOUNTAINSIDE

REVOLT OF THE KOR

Half a dozen men, their deep bronze-colored bodies naked but for skimpy loin cloths, squatted on their haunches around the frail old man on the low-slung, woven hammock, listening to his slow-spoken but impassioned words. They then turned to another, not of their race, clad in the loose black cottons of the Kinh, or Vietnamese from the plains. The old man's fine white hair was drawn into a tight bun on the back of his head, a sparse white beard reached far down his chest, his skin over the wasted frame was the hue and texture of a shrivelled orange. What remained of his teeth, filed down almost to the stumps as tribal custom demanded, were black from betel-chewing; his ears had large holes from which adornments had been removed; around his wrist was a copper bracelet. After he finished speaking, he turned his sightless eyes towards the Kinh and listened attentively to every word. For hours it had gone on like this, only the two speaking and the tribal elders giving an occasional grunt of approval or disapproval.

The old man was Pho Muc Gia, chief of the tiny Kor tribe which numbered about 4,700 at that time and lived on the mountain slopes of Tra Bong district of Quang Ngai province in Trung Bo (Annam). In his day, Pho Muc Gia had been a mighty warrior and had led his tribespeople against the French even before the first resistance war started. Now he was half paralyzed and his age, calculated by the number of times the tribe had changed their "ray" (the clearings hacked out of the mountainside and used for a strictly limited number of years for cultivation) was over 90 years. But he was still the unchallenged leader of his people. Like most of the tribal peoples, the Kor are passionately devoted to the free life of their forests and mountains and fiercely resent any interference in their customs.

A condensed version of the conversation, with the same points endlessly repeated in different variants was something like this, according to Sao Nam, the Vietnamese from the plains who had lived with the Quang Ngai tribespeople for years previously and spoke Kor among several of the tribal languages.

"Our tribe will be wiped out like fish in a drying pond. Our people are being killed faster than new ones are born. Over 500 since the Diemist savages came."

"My heart bleeds with yours at your people's sufferings."

"They violate our women, steal our buffalo and pigs, take our young men as slaves to work in the plains. It is not life but living death."

"We have protested together many times at their black deeds."

"They insult us every time they see us or come to our villages; defile our customs, show no respect for the old or our women. They treat us like animals. They intend that no Kor people shall hold up their heads again."

"Still we must be patient. I know and my comrades know full well of your terrible sufferings. That is why we believe you should move to another district, further away from these evil beasts."

"Never do our people move without a battle. It would be to insult the graves of our ancestors. And you and your friends who were such brave warriors in the fight against the French, why do you not join us and fight together again? Either we fight together or we are struck down together like buffalo tied to trees."

"If we fight back, the sufferings will be still greater. Why don't you move? The mountains and forest are the same there as here; the fish in the rivers, the animals in the jungle are plentiful. But it is more difficult for the enemy to oppress and insult you."

"Did we weaken when they tortured us to betray your hiding places? Did we shrink from their blows and tortures when they wanted us to insult you?"

"We will never forget how brave and true were you and your people."

"Then don't ask us to run away like a craven antelope without a fight. Never will I ask my Kor people to do that. Never till the forests die out and the mountains crumble and the sky falls in. Never! Never! Never!"

"And at that point," Sao Nam told me, "the other elders joined in with very decided grunts of approval, repeating 'Never, Never, Never' in voices that rose to shouts, bringing people all over the village outside their hut."

"Before you were real warriors," the old man continued. "We fought as one. Now we see you are no longer resistance fighters. If you were, you would support us and not ask us to run away."

"You are too few, the enemy is too many. The sufferings will be still greater."

"We will never run away without a fight."

"And so it went on," said Sao Nam, "and this was by no means the first time. The Kor people had been brave as tigers in protecting those of us who had fled from the plains. At first the Diemists had tried to buy up Pho Muc Gia because they knew of his great prestige. But he spat at them when he saw they wanted him to betray his comrades of the resistance. The whole tribe was solid about this and some suffered severe tortures rather than betray the fact that former resistance cadres were hiding in the area. We felt terribly bad at their sufferings and at a meeting shortly before this conversation, we had decided to propose that they move. We had chosen a spot where we felt they would be relatively safe and where the living conditions would be even better than where they were. I was deputized to try and persuade the old man."

On the night of the day which followed this conversation, there was a meeting of the Kor men folk and a few days later, a big feast was organized in the village nearest the Teo-Reo post which was the immediate source of their troubles. All but one of the Saigon garrison came swaggering over, when they learned that food and "shum shum"—the fierce mountain alcohol made from glutinous rice—were plentiful. The Kor people are traditionally hospitable, and this time more so than ever. After the "shum shum" had had its effect, at a signal from the old chief, who had been carried to the spot, the young men of the tribe fell on the garrison, 54 in all, and slaughtered them to a man. Some of the tribesmen raced back to the post, but the lone sentry had already fled. The arms, however, were there. The Kor tribe was now in possession of 54 firearms and a plentiful stock of ammunition. This action took place around the end of January 1959, and as far as I could discover it was the first act of violence from the "other" side in all of Central Vietnam and one of the very first in South Vietnam as a whole.

"We were appalled when we heard of it," said Sao Nam. "First, it was a clear violation of the 'line' and, secondly, we knew that this uprising would be repressed with terrible ferocity and the Kor and other tribes perhaps completely exterminated."

The reaction was swift and terrible. The No. 2 Diemist division, plus 23 companies, was sent to Tra Bong district to wipe out the Kor. To get to Tra Bong, the punitive expedition had to pass through two other districts of Tra Mi and Son Ha, burning villages and slaughtering the inhabitants as they went, building up a store of hatred—and accounts to be settled. The Kor were not caught unawares. Skillful hunters, they were used to protecting their homes and fields from wild animals and they set series of terrible man traps along and around all tracks leading to their villages. These were very rudimentary compared to the elaborate integrated systems of traps developed later as a result of exchanges of experience between the tribes, but they were still very effective. What seems to be solid ground suddenly gives way under the feet of one or more troops and they fall several feet to be impaled by needle-sharp, steel-hard bamboo spikes. It does not take too many cases of impaled troops to dampen the ardor of the rest. There are special traps the Kor had developed against elephant marauders trying to get at the "ray" maize crops, which are released with such force that they drive a bamboo spear deep into the elephant's stomach; trip wires that release an avalanche of stones while one is tapping the ground for a suspected trench trap.

Like all the tribespeople they are natural masters of the art of ambush and the silent fade-out. In addition to the arms they seized, they also had home-made "praying mantis" guns, fearsome bell-mouthed affairs which discharge a load of grape-shot accurately enough for the few yards range at which they operated. Set up to cover a jungle path, they are released when a guerilla jerks a string from a respectable distance as the enemy reaches a pre-selected point. A single shot has been known to put a dozen troops out of action. The weapon the Diemist troops feared most, however, was the crossbow and poisoned arrows; the slightest scratch from the latter causes immediate paralysis, and death follows absolutely inevitably within three to five minutes. The faint click of the crossbow trigger makes it impossible to locate from where it was fired.

The Diemist troops began running into traps and ambushes long before they reached the Kor villages, but they rarely caught sight of a Kor tribesman. After many days of slugging through the jungle with losses every day from an invisible enemy, the punitive expedition arrived at the Kor villages and found them empty and silent. Old man Pho Muc Gia, honor satisfied because his tribe had given battle, had led his people to a remote area where they made new homes in grottos, carved out of the sides of ravines, and set up intricate permanent systems of traps at all approaches to the new site, around their homes and cultivation patches.

The first punitive expedition was a failure as far as punishing the Kor was concerned. Within three months of the Teo-Reo incident, 65 operations, from battalion size upwards, had been launched against them. Diem fully understood the need for stamping out completely these first sparks in the Quang Ngai mountains. But his troops never got to the new Kor villages. Other tribespeople, emboldened by the success of the Kor and enraged by the savagery of reprisals against villages that had nothing to do with the uprising, on top of years of unbearable repression, started hitting back. Diemist troops returning through remnants of villages they had burned out without opposition on their way forward would suddenly find themselves under fire from all sides.

During that first three months, the Kor leaders claim they inflicted about 1,200 casualties on their enemies: "We preferred to wound and not to kill," one young tribesman told me. "Their dead they just threw into ravines or into the jungle, but their wounded they had to carry. Along those mountain trails, it took four men to carry one wounded and his equipment. So if we wounded one, we put five men out of action. You only had to wound a dozen troops in a company and it was no longer a combat force."

This in fact was not always correct, because later the Diemists, in Central Vietnam at least, shot their own wounded if they were unable to march. I heard of this on innumerable occasions and met some former Diemist wounded, shot and abandoned as dead by their own officers, but found still alive and nursed back to life by the guerillas.

As they could not wipe out the Kor by military action, the Diemists clamped down an economic blockade, the most serious effect of which was to cut off the vital salt supplies.

"We former resistance cadres felt terrible about what was going on but we marveled that the heroic Kor were still holding out," said Sao Nam. "We held a meeting of all former cadres we could collect in the province and decided we must organize at least economic help for them. Normally the Kor exchanged cinnamon and tea for salt and medicines from the plains. We decided to help them move their products out through other districts and bring back what they needed from the plains. Soon there were human caravans moving at night between mountains and plains and the supply situation for the Kor people improved radically. We also collected various types of medicinal plants and planted them around the new Kor villages. We showed them how to burn bamboo and the roots of certain reeds to obtain a sort of salt and introduced them to the bark of a certain tree which contains lots of tannin which also helps replace salt. We procured seed manioc and persuaded them to cultivate this valuable tuber to eke out their rice supplies, since rice cultivation was difficult in the rocky area they had chosen. Old man Pho Muc Gia was deeply touched with all this support and regained his confidence in us."

PHO NIA'S WEAPONS

Meanwhile there was a new, unexpected development among the Hre minority, a tribe in which the French had raised a puppet battalion in the past and which was taken over by Diem. One of the most respected leaders of the Hre was Pho Nia, a deputy canton chief under the French but who retired to his native village in Son Ha district as an "elder," once the first resistance war started. After the Diemist administration was set up, Pho Nia had to go into hiding because of the repression. In his own village the usual savagery was employed in seeking out former resistance members. Many tribesmen were killed, women were violated, livestock stolen. When Pho Nia heard of the Kor uprising, he sent a delegate over to check what was happening. Then he decided the Hre should also move.

Most of their troubles came from the Hre puppet battalion under Dinh Ngo and Dinh Enh. People like Pho Nia had tried to reason with them, to awaken some feelings of national solidarity, but as Sao Nam expressed it, "They had been too long corrupted by the colonialists; they had become too used to killing and plundering and the Diemists maintained the specially high privileges and rewards for treachery that the French had introduced."

Pho Nia, a diminutive, sedate figure with a head like a Red Indian warrior chief, decided to deal with them. He made thorough preparations, taught his tribesmen how to make a wide variety of traps and also the *sung van nang*, "ten-thousand-purpose" gun, a primitive firearm with a firing pin triggered by rubber thongs and which could fire any small arms bullet likely to be picked up on the battlefield. Like the "praying mantis" it was sufficiently accurate from the sort of range the tribesmen would be using it. The barrel was made of metal from plane or automobile remnants, heated in local smithies and beaten around a perfectly straight, slim stick of appropriate caliber, the stick being burned out later. Soon virtually every tribesman had one of these.

From July 1959, Pho Nia started his ambushes and night attacks, using fire arrows shot from crossbows which lodged in the thatch roofs of the puppet battalion's barracks in the first attack. Within three months the puppet battalion had suffered severe losses. Later it was wiped out completely. Within six months of his first action, the Diemist forces launched 102 "mopping up"

operations in Son Ha district, according to the careful statistics
of the Liberation Front cadres who now control the area, but
Pho Nia dealt with these in well planned guerilla operations.
His men went into action under the slogan: "Let the enemy return the blood, the bones and property they have stolen." Pho
Nia was and still is a natural military and political leader who
now heads the Son Ha district committee of the National Liberation Front.

"His very name struck terror in the heart of the Diemist
troops," Sao Nam said, "and later on when some other Hre
leaders followed his example they always operated under the
name of Pho Nia. The legend spread that he had some sort
of magic medicine that protected his men from bullets. In fact
the 'magic' was his very careful preparations for every engagement and the superb morale of his people fighting to defend
their own villages and avenge themselves for the previous five
years of unparalleled oppression."

Pho Nia continued to develop rudimentary weapons and by
mid-1960 there had already been exchanges of experience with
tribal weapons experts from neighboring provinces. I have already mentioned the "praying mantis" and the "ten-thousand-
purpose" gun which fired any caliber from a Sten gun bullet
down, with adjustable grips for those that did not fit the barrel
exactly. Its added advantage was it could easily be built into a
hoe or plough handle, ready for any emergency. A jerk at the
plough handle if an enemy suddenly appeared, and there was
a deadly weapon. It was used by everyone, men, women and
children, and local smithies turned them out in serial production. If bullets were short, they filled empty cartridge cases with
home-made powder, prepared by roasting bats' dung, rich in
saltpeter, and mixing it with ash from a certain type of bark.
Anything from bicycle ball bearings upwards were used for shot.

There was also the *bay da,* a sort of stone-age "Honest John,"
very much used in the rough sort of mountain area to which the
Kor had withdrawn. Boulders "big as buffaloes," as one old
tribesman expressed it, were maneuvered on to stout bamboo
racks, disposed along the length of an ambush area, depending
on the size of the enemy unit expected. As many traps as possible

were fitted in over the chosen area, the racks controlled by an inter-connected trip wire system. When the lead troops come to the farthermost trap, so that the whole column is in position behind, the first trap is tripped, discharging its own boulders and automatically all those behind.

I inspected only small-scale models to demonstrate the principle, but I believe the old tribesman's words that "there is a thunderous noise which strikes panic in the hearts of the enemy as the boulders crush down." The drawback is that after the *bay da* is used, there is no booty. Because of the height, weight and speed, everything is crushed out of recognition, bodies as well as weapons.

The *ten lua* or fire-arrows are shot by special crossbows with a range of up to 200 yards. They look like ordinary arrows but have a hollowed-out section in which sulphur and a bit of gasoline-soaked cotton and a wick are placed in lightly separated sections. A special haft set behind the arrowhead prevents it penetrating too deeply into the target, usually a thatch or palm-leaf roof. The wick, leading to the sulplur, is lit before firing and at about the moment of impact the sluphur explodes, the gasoline-soaked cotton ignites and the thatch is a blazing mass within seconds. It is the guerilla's answer to napalm, but infinitely more selective and accurate. The *ten lua* are used mainly against enemy garrison buildings.

When enemy troops tried to cross a stream to "mop up" at a Ngao village in Son Ha district in March 1960, the first troops in the line suddenly fell, screaming. They would have drowned had not others come to their aid—but they too were soon writhing around, trying to prop each other up and there was a terrific melee going on in midstream, at the only place where a crossing could be effected by wading. They had run into the *chong giay* or "spiked rope"—a brand new invention of Pho Nia. Made of long pieces of stout jungle creeper, they were studded with eight or nine-inch spikes of razor-sharp bamboo, and set in series of threes, one end of each anchored to the bed of the stream. When they were stepped on, with the action of the current, they coiled around the legs of the troops like snakes and the more the latter struggled to get free, the more

the *chong giay* stabbed and slashed and tended to bring the victim down to his knees. This was a natural setup for an ambush.
The Diemist troops had 46 casualties and had to abandon the
attempt to cross the stream.

A major arm of the Diemists in trying to subdue the minority
villages was the destruction of food crops. Regular expeditions
were sent to slash down rice before it was ripe for harvesting
or even to tear out new plants by the roots. Pho Nia developed
the "spiked rod" as an answer to this, similar to the *chong giay*,
but the spikes are set in rigid lengths of bamboo and planted
deep in the rice-field slush in series of three all around the
perimeter of the fields. Wounds inflicted in the rice-field slush
were particularly serious because of the human and pig excrement lavishly used as manure. After a few lessons from the
"spiked rods," rice fields in Pho Nia's villages were left alone.
Amputations were almost the only answer to infections from
such wounds. A rough way of fighting, one may well comment,
but so was the attempt to starve out the tribal people by destroying their food crops. And the Hre and Kor were only defending their own fields and villages; if the Diemists kept away
there would be no trouble.

The Vietnamese jungle abounds in scores of varieties of plants
with formidable spikes. I have seen trees with six-inch spikes,
larger than the diameter of the trunks, set almost as thick as a
porcupine's needles up the 30 or 40 feet of the trunks; one constantly runs into thickets of shrubs, palms and even spiked
bamboo impossible to traverse. These were selectively used by
the tribespeople and set in camouflaged positions at different
levels for feet, calves, thighs, stomachs, chests, along all the
tracks leading to their villages. While a marauder was treading
carefully to avoid one in the feet, he was liable to be run
through the stomach, and while trying to avoid one in his chest,
his foot was liable to be spiked. Casualties were so frequent
from these that troops just refused to advance on such villages.
American experts devised metal sheaths to be fitted down onto
heavily soled boots so legs would be protected at least. These
naturally impeded the soldier's movements, especially in just
those moments when he needed to move at lightning speed.

The first time they were used in Quang Ngai by a column advancing into Hre territory, after a heavy toll had been taken by crossbow and "ten-thousand-purpose" guns on troops stumbling on their "metal legs," the sheaths were flung away and "lots of useful metal fell into our hands," as Sao Nam expressed it.

Later when I visted the areas of the M'Nong (famed as elephant hunters), the Rhade and Jarai minorities, I came across even more terrible rudimentary weapons, including one of the most fearsome I have ever seen. I have dubbed it the "flying mace," as it bears some resemblance to this medieval weapon. They are made in various sizes, 50, 100, 200 or even 500 pounds of clay packed into a woven basket. Running right through the basket and set at all angles, are long bamboo spears, sharpened to razor-blade standards at both ends and hardened by fire. According to the overall size, anything up to a yard of spear projects from each side of the basket. Series of these are suspended from stout overhead cables, jungle creepers, which are concealed in the impenetrable mass of leafy branches that form a roof over most jungle tracks, even wide ones. The baskets are swung back out of sight. When a trip wire is released, either by the advancing troops or by a guerilla behind a tree, the "flying maces" swoop down with great force, the whole thing spinning and sweeping back and forth across the track about eight inches above ground level at its lowest point. It is impossible for anyone within its range to escape; if he throws himself on the ground, his back will be slashed to pieces; if he throws himself off the track at the point where the "flying mace" is operating, he will fall into spiked trenches.

Combined with this is an integrated series of traps that may cover anything from a couple of hundred yards to a half mile. Half a squad can operate a two-hundred-yard section, a platoon controls the larger area. I inspected multiple spear-launchers which might be called "jungle katyushas," after the Soviet multiple rocket-launchers. A young sapling, cut and trimmed, is firmly pegged down at one end by two or three of the strongest of the tribesmen, and bent back until the bowstring—also of jungle creeper, which the tribespeople prefer to any cord—reaches the required standard of tautness. A delicate triggering mechanism

is set and anything up to a dozen bamboo spears are put in place,
their hafts fitted into the bowstring, their heads resting on the
sapling. The latter is almost, but not perfectly, parallel to the
ground, so the spears are in a slightly tilted position to ensure
that each flies at a different height—from around eight inches to
seven feet. These are set at spaced intervals each side of a track,
interspersed with the "flying maces," "honest Johns" and jungle
"bombs." The latter are made of six-inch-diameter sections of
tree trunks to which short dagger-like bits of bamboo have been
attached. To increase the "caliber" and weight, usually three
sections of trunk are bound together for this weapon. They drop
from trees only when the target touches a trip wire which in-
dicates he is in the precise position to be hit.

Those described above are only a few of the more spectacular
rudimentary arms I saw, but they exist in infinite variety, especially of the automatic type which require no one to watch
them. "Hundreds of thousands, millions of faithful sentries on
guard day and night, wet season and dry, who don't need rice or
salt or cloth," as Ybih Aleo, the great Rhade chief, was to ex-
press it later. One of the impressive things was the contrast between the clumsy, primitive aspect of most of the traps with
roughly trimmed saplings, jungle creepers, boulders, etc., and
the delicate release mechanism in which fine nylon fishing tackle
usually played a role, in trip wires as well. In general, the traps
were adaptations from those used by hunters for everything
from quail, partridges and monkeys up to tigers and elephants,
but the nature of Diemist repression, as Ybih Aleo said, "forced
us to make adaptations for human tigers as well."

One stalwart young Vietnamese peasant who had started fighting the French at the age of 15, after noting my rather horrified
reactions at the first really comprehensive series of traps I had
seen, made a valid point: "You see, our weapons don't have much
range. Some of them none at all. They're not intended for aggression against the Americans or anyone else. The enemy elimi-
nates the need for range in our weapons when he commits aggression against us. We place them around our hamlets and
homes, around cultivation patches, fruit trees and poultry yards.
If the enemy keeps away he won't be hurt. But when he comes

into our backyards to kill and steal, he will be hurt plenty. We warn him of this."

The balance sheet for Quang Ngai was somber enough if measured in material destruction. In the operations launched in the last six months of 1959, according to Le Quang Binh, member of the provincial NFL committee, an equivalent of two army divisions was used in an area of 125 square miles in "kill all, burn all, destroy all" campaigns. Over 200 hamlets were burned down and in Pho Muc Gia's district of Tra Bong, 3,000 families were made homeless, another 13,000 in the other three mountain districts of Son Ha, Minh Long and Ba To. In Tra Bong this meant that virtually every house was razed to the ground, people had to flee to the forests and eat wild roots, living in caves and temporary shelters. Most of their livestock was wiped out but "human losses were relatively small," according to Le Quang Binh. "From that moment, the mountain people prepared to wage a violent struggle with rudimentary weapons to protect lives and property in a new life which they started to organize further back in the mountains and forest. Meanwhile we started to back them up by activities in the plains."

Chapter 10

BREAKING THE GRIP

ARMED ACTION ON THE PLAINS

On the night of May 18, 1960, a group of army officers and their bodyguard entered a Chinese soup restaurant in Mô Duc district center on the coastal plains of Quang Ngai province. They brushed past the diners gulping down their noodle soup and passed through to the apartment in the rear. After a few exchanges in low voices with an attendant and the production of a document, they were ushered into a spacious office which seemed to have little in common with the needs of a Chinese restaurant. Seated at a desk was a ponderous Vietnamese with a thin line of moustache that continued over his upper lip, down the sides of his mouth to the chin. Respectful salutes from the officers, a grunted greeting in reply.

In ten minutes, the group moved out by an elaborate rear entrance to the road leading out of the town. With them was the man behind the desk. After they had walked in silence for a while, one officer pulled out a revolver and pointed it at the "restaurant proprietor." "In the name of patriotic officers of the Government's armed forces," said the officer, in a voice tinged with steel, "you, Chau, have been sentenced to death for crimes against the people of Vietnam. Sentence will be executed immediately." And before another word could be spoken, he fired a bullet into the fat man's head. The body slumped to the road and was pulled away to the side, while someone affixed to it a slip of paper.

The officer and a small group hurried back to the restaurant, this time entering from the back entrance. With keys taken from the body, they opened a large, black safe, filled with documents, which they glanced at and stuffed into a nylon bag. There was a momentary gasp of horror when they pulled out one large drawer and found it full of human ears, in each case the left ear only, and stapled to each a paper with a name and a receipt for 5,000 piastres.

"They were the ears of 432 of our comrades," said Sao Nam, the "officer" who conducted the operation. "Chau, the tyrant we executed, was Ngo Dinh Can's special agent in charge of secret police in the provinces of Quang Ngai, Quang Nam and Binh Dinh. The restaurant was a blind for his activities. For each of our comrades killed, he received 5,000 piastres after forwarding the right ear as proof.

"We had a rich haul that night, all the names of those marked down for arrest and killing and the names of a whole network of agents working under Chau. We were able to warn all those on his lists and arrest his agents or frighten them into inactivity."

Execution of agents like Chau had become policy after the decision was taken to support the tribespeople by starting resistance by "armed propaganda groups" in the plains. The form of "armed propaganda groups" had been started in 1944 by Vo Nguyen Giap, the "Tiger" of Dien Bien Phu, and Pham Van Dong, now prime minister of the Democratic Republic of Vietnam (North Vietnam). The first unit of 34 men then grew into the powerful army which Giap used with such success ten years later to defeat the French. It was this form that was adopted as the main weapon in the politico-military struggle to which Sao Nam and his group, and an increasing number of similar groups in other provinces, were now committed, as armed resistance became general.

It was not easy to start armed resistance on the plains, where enemy control was almost complete. Only a handful of the resistance cadre had survived the Diem terror, by fleeing to the mountains. But as word spread on the plains of the extermination campaign against the tribespeople on the mountainsides, the people's anger and hatred rose. Sao Nam told me of how the Vietnamese cadre in the province of Quang Ngai came to adopt the new policy of armed resistance. At first, in the latter part of 1959, they decided to launch a movement of "non-cooperation" against the Diemist administration to take some heat off the tribespeople. Towards the end of the year, the Diemists planned a new all-out campaign to crush the uprising of the mountain people once and for all, bringing in troops and militia from the neighboring provinces; they could do this because Quang Ngai was the only place in Central Vietnam where there was any armed resistance.

"We had another meeting, a very serious one this time," continued Sao Nam. "Due to the repression aimed primarily at crushing the Kor, other tribes and districts had taken to arms, all the mountain districts in fact. The policy of peaceful struggle had crumbled in Quang Ngai because the enemy had consistently applied non-provoked violence. We had done our best to keep to the line and many of us felt we should still stick to strictly legal struggle. But we could do nothing to halt what the people themselves had started spontaneously. If the Vietnamese in the plains did not come in with their support, the tribespeople might well be exterminated. Should we continue this line when the enemy was preparing for a wholesale massacre before our very eyes?

"We took the extremely serious decision to constitute ourselves as a 'resistance committee'; to support the armed action already started by the tribespeople; to base ourselves in the mountains but also to try and penetrate the plains from our mountain bases. We realized this was against the line as we had last known it, but we hoped our decision would be understood in the light of our special situation. If we did not support the tribespeople, who had helped us so magnificently in the first resistance and protected us later in our bitterest moments, our prestige and that of the revolution would be lost forever. We sent delegates to contact comrades hiding out in the neighboring provinces to inform them of our decisions."

An historian could pick on this decision of Sao Nam and his comrades as a starting point of the "two-sided war." As far as I could discover, it was the first such decision taken at that sort of level, and it had widespread repercussions. The example of the Kor tribespeople and the support it finally received from Vietnamese cadres was later used as a decisive argument in changing the "line" at the highest level and generalizing armed resistance throughout South Vietnam. Pho

Muc Gia made his stand just about 12 months before the heart-searching decisions of Quyet Thanh and his band when they launched the Tua Hai attack mentioned earlier.

Quang Ngai, home province of Pham Van Dong, has long revolutionary traditions; the people do not bow their heads easily, but the Vietnamese in the plains at least seemed to have been in black despair by the end of 1959. I heard of one incident, however, that illustrates the spirit of some of them. October 26, 1959, was celebrated by the Diemists as "National Day." A military parade was organized, troops in their best spit-and-polish uniforms, tanks, artillery and planes overhead. The local military chief made a big speech comparing the splendidly equipped troops of President Ngo Dinh Diem to the ragged groups of "Viet Cong" guerillas. An old man walked up to the tribune, and in front of the beaming military chief said:

"The governor is quite right. I agree with him. The 'Viet Cong' are miserably off compared with the 'Nationalists.' They have nothing to eat even, only potatoes and manioc; the 'nationalists' have plenty of rice, bread and meat. The 'Viet Cong' are dressed in rags. Look at the splendid uniforms of the 'nationalists.' The 'Viet Cong' don't even have decent weapons. Look at the weapons here, all the splendid American guns, tanks and planes. The only thing in which the 'nationalists' are not better is that they serve in a foreign army, while the 'Viet Cong' fight against the foreigners who invade our country. After a battle, the 'Viet Cong' help the population, but the 'nationalists' only burn and steal."

The military chief had shut him up at this stage, trying to laugh; and shouting, "The old man is mad," pushed him off the tribune. Police shoved forward to arrest him but the crowd closed in and managed to smuggle him away.

Later he made his way to the mountains. "Why on earth did you do that?" asked one of the Vietnamese cadres. "I saw everyone was depressed, demoralized with all those tanks and guns," the old fellow replied, "so I thought I'd put a few facts straight for them. I'm old now. If anything happens to me it is of no importance. But we should keep people's spirits up."

The Kor, in the meantime, had not remained on the defensive.

The support that started up in other areas heartened them. In late November the younger men decided to attack a post which the Diemists had set up as a key point to enforce the economic blockade, at Eo-Chiem. The old man, Pho Muc Gia, whose advice was sought, proposed extensive "sound support." The first time I had heard the term was in connection with this action, but since then I have learned that it is now a standard "weapon" in the guerilla arsenal. He insisted on being carried to the scene to direct operations. Around midnight, the whole tribe assembled with gongs, drums, trumpets, pieces of giant bamboo, encircled the post and started a tremendous din. After this psychological warfare, the attack was launched and demoralized troops surrendered after a few shots were fired. The post was completely destroyed; more arms passed into the hands of the Kor and some were shared with the Vietnamese cadres; the salt-for-tea caravans had their route shortened by many hours.

SENTENCE AND EXECUTION

People on the plains had been so terrorized that at first they trusted no one. "When we started, we lost some cadres," Sao Nam told me, "and it was almost impossible to make contact with the population. While such a terrorist machine continued to control their daily activities it would be impossible to do anything. We decided it was necessary to break the grip of the enemy; to wipe out the worst of the Diemist agents and to make strong attacks against selected posts. Once we started doing this, a new light came into people's eyes, confidence returned. It was clear whom we represented when we struck down the worst of the tyrants, always posting up explanations as to why. Until the National Front of Liberation was set up at the end of 1960, we operated under the name of Armed Propaganda Groups of the People's Self-Defense Forces."

To my question as to what was the actual form of sentence and execution, Sao Nam explained that the situation in every village was first carefully studied; the activities of the local agents, the extent of their crimes. "You could be certain that the hand-picked chief agents were always responsible for

multiple murders, but we did not mark them down for execution
if there was the slightest chance they might mend their ways.
The agents, chiefs of village, police and security chiefs, etc.,
usually all lived in the same building. We would send a group
at night with loudspeakers to explain the policy of the new
resistance movement, to expose the crimes of the Diemist regime
and tell the people how to struggle against it. Finally we would
give a stern warning to the local agents, our megaphones directed
specifically at their homes. Usually we fired a few shots in the
air to impress them.

"At first, the agents took little notice, actually stepped up
their terror. Our group would pay another visit, usually with
two variants of hand-written leaflets. On one was written the
biography and crimes of the local agents and the death sentence by the local organ of the People's Self-Defense Force; the
other was similar except it contained a pardon with a warning
not to commit any more crimes. If we found the chief agent
at home, we executed him, leaving the execution slip with the
body and posting up a few copies. For the others, and for the
chief agent in case he happened to be away, we posted up the
pardon and warnings.

"Many of those 'pardoned' found ways of contacting us,
thanking us on their knees for the pardon. Many offered to
serve us while pretending to serve the enemy. In fact, we knew
in most cases they would continue to serve the enemy as well.
But we counted on the people exercizing strict control over
them in the future so we could accept this. Unrepentant sinners,
after such a visit, would leave the village and operate from
the nearest military post, visiting the village only in day-time.
If we learned that several were in a specific post we would
attack it; to exploit the fact that we were attacking only because
the terrorist agents were there was very important—for the
troops inside as well as for the population. Our main motive
in the beginning was to win the support of the population,
raise their morale.

"Before we attacked a post, our megaphones went into action.
We explained to the troops that we were only out to punish
the agents for their crimes against the people. 'If you don't shoot,

we won't we said. 'If you do, we will and we'll wipe you out.'
Often enough they shoved the agents out, shouting, 'Go and
answer for your crimes against the people.' All this had a marked
effect on people's morale and the smaller fry among the agents
became very polite. Once we had dealt with a handful of
agents in any one district we could go in and out of the villages
as we wished and the old resistance type of relations were
established again with the people."

Sao Nam, by any standards, is a remarkable person. At the
time I met him, he was a leading staff officer of the NFL forces
in Quang Ngai province, a former landless peasant, educated,
as he expresses it, "by the revolution." He is extraordinary, but
also typical of many I met at that sort of level, from company
and battalion commanders upwards. Everything about him reflects vigor, resource, confidence—a man in whom one would
have unlimited confidence in the worst of situations. His face
is deep chestnut, polished by years of wind and sun and open
air. He took part in the first resistance from the age of 17 and
has been caught up in the revolution ever since. Two of his
brothers died in the first resistance, another is a company commander with the NFL forces, a sister is a school teacher in the
Front-controlled zones. His father is serving a ten-year sentence
for former resistance activities. His wife, if still alive, is in prison.

"We had just one week of marred life," he said with a rare
sigh. "That was during the last year of the war against the
French. Then she was rounded up by the Diemists and tortured
until she put her thumb print on a divorce document. I don't
know whether she is still alive; practically I can't remember her
face, try as hard as I can. I remember how soft and gentle she
was with me but made of steel when it concerned the enemy.
Life can be bitter at times. But compared to many of my comrades, I consider myself lucky. I knew the beauty of a woman's
love for a week. Many of my comrades, men of 40 and more, have
never known this beauty."

Sao Nam learned to read and write in the Viet Minh forces
where he had risen to the rank of company commander by the
time of Dien Bien Phu. He had all the bearing of a first-class
military commander and although I doubt if he had ever studied

anything about psychological warfare, like so many of his comrades-in-arms he applied it in a natural and supremely effective way in day-to-day activities. It was natural to them, because they are of the people among whom they work and fight, know profoundly their sentiments and what moves them to love, hate and fear; what will instill confidence or arouse suspicions. Despite the skimpy formal education he had received in gaps between resistance activities, Sao Nam is a cultured person with a deep knowledge of the lives and customs of the minority peoples. Night after night, we sat around a camp fire, chewing at roasted manioc roots and slapping at mosquitos, while he told stories to awaken my interest in the nobility, the courage and dignity of the tribal peoples whom he regarded as his closest brothers. My own contacts with them would have been impossible had it not been for their confidence in cadres like Sao Nam who had shared their lives for a dozen years and more.

By the end of 1960, word had gone out to overthrow Diemist rule wherever possible. Once his own district was rid of Diemist rule, Pho Nia went looking for enemy troops on the plains. By now, no matter who carried out military operations in Quang Ngai, even if orders and leaflets were signed by the NFL or local resistance organs, Diemist troops always credited them to the redoubtable Pho Nia. The Diemist reply, in late 1960, was to start hedging in all the villages in the plains, razing all bamboo clumps, fruit trees and patches of forest, to provide wood and bamboo ramparts for what were embryo "strategic hamlets," and to deny any natural cover for the guerillas. But, in the words of Sao Nam, the "grip of the enemy had already been broken" and the influence of the FNL easily penetrated the bamboo hedges and the barbed wire that was added later.

During 1960, the Diemists launched over 200 operations against Pho Nia's area alone, but the more they tried to "mop up," the wider the resistance spread. There seemed to be a set pattern in such a struggle that operated according to fairly set laws, confirmed in many areas where I was able to check. By 1961, the Diemists could no longer even try to launch raids into Son Ha, the home district of Pho Nia. Starting from his own village of Son Tinh, which he had moved back to the crest

of a mountain and which the Diemists tried six times in vain
to reach, Pho Nia gradually carved out a zone entirely free of
Diemist rule and into which their armed forces could not penetrate. Diemist agents were cleaned out of village after village
until Son Ha district became a solidly liberated zone and this
quickly expanded into neighboring districts.

"The Diemists were dead scared of what had happened in
the western mountain districts and now concentrated all their
forces in the plains," said Le Quang Binh, quoted earlier, "but
this forced the plainsmen also to take to guerilla warfare. One
of their first acts incidentally had been to protest at the massacres
of the tribespeople and to try and educate the Diemist troops
to halt such atrocities. They did a splendid job in organizing
supplies of salt, cloth, agricultural implements and other badly
needed goods for the mountain areas and this forged new ties
of solidarity between Vietnamese and tribespeople. They even
sent teachers up from the plains to organize schools and introduce some rudiments of public health."

ARMED ACTION SPREADS

To the south of Quang Ngai lies Binh Dinh province. It was
the commander of the provincial troops of the Liberation Army,
Nguyen Van Hao, a 46-year-old veteran of the first resistance
war, who filled in details of how the sparks kindled at Quang
Ngai flew across the provincial border and fell among tinder,
ripe for the kindling. The developments there until 1959 were
similar to those of other Central Vietnam provinces. "In early
1959, there was a slight change in the situation," he said. "Till
then the struggle had been passive, people trying to delay as
long as possible summons to present themselves to the authorities for investigation. But early in 1959 the minority people in
the mountains flatly refused to come down to the plains for the
police 'convocations.' Word had come that the Kor people over
the border were in revolt. So the Bahnar and Hre, who are the
main minorities in our province, said in effect: 'Come up and
get us. We're not coming down to be beaten and tortured like
the Vietnamese.'

"In the lowlands a certain number of Vietnamese had been press-ganged into military service; we understood they had no choice and this influenced our attitude later when we met them with arms in our hands. But the minority peoples refused to present themselves for military service. 'We can't live without our families, our ray, our mountains,' they said. By mid-1959, the Diemists were sending units of platoon strength, then company strength to enforce their orders, but with no success. They could never lay their hands on anyone of military age. They tried to round up whole communities and concentrate them in the plains, but this failed too; villages faded out into the jungle. Any whom the Diemists succeeded in capturing they tortured in a most bestial way and when word spread of this, people started sharpening their knives and looking to their crossbows.

"In September and October, there were some incidents. These were harvest months and the enemy came to Tao Loc and Tu Lec, villages of the Bahnar tribe in Vinh Thanh district, to destroy the ripening crops because the men had failed to report for military service. By then everyone knew of the successful uprising and resistance of the Kor people. The Bahnar tribespeople withdrew from the villages into the forest, killed three Diemist soldiers with poisoned arrows and wounded eight more with the traps they had left around their ray. The Diemists sent aircraft to bomb the village to cover the withdrawal of their troops. This was the first spark in Binh Dinh. It seemed to stop at that. But the example impressed on other villages what could be done and, although all seemed quiet, passions were seething underneath the surface. In the meantime, we former resistance cadres had received word from our comrades in Quang Ngai and this gave us plenty to think about. After long discussions we decided it was shameful to let the enemy concentrate all his forces in Quang Ngai because of inactivity in the neighboring provinces.

"Just as the Diemists started their big action in Quang Ngai, we attacked one of their posts at Hoaui Ton in An Lao district, near the border with Quang Ngai. We did not kill anyone, just tied up the troops while we relieved them of their weapons. We captured 26 rifles, 30 grenades and over 1,000 cartridges.

That is small stuff these days," he said with the sort of grin that indicated "these days" one thought in terms of hundreds of rifles and tens of thousands of cartridges, "but it was a tremendous thing for us then. It also helped to take the heat off our compatriots over the border. The Diemists realized it was dangerous to leave Binh Dinh unguarded."

There were similar actions in Quang Nam and Thua Thien provinces to the north, so before the big action against Quang Ngai could be completed, the Diemist command had to withdraw some of the troops and militia they had brought from outside. These were rushed back to their own bases to try and stamp out sparks that were already spluttering there. The latter were soon fanned into forest fires when word got round that the line had changed and the use of arms in self-defense was the general order of the day.

The setting up of the National Front of Liberation on December 20, 1960, following by five weeks an unsuccessful anti-Diemist officers' coup in Saigon,* was a major event which put the sporadic uprisings on an organized basis and provided the political framework within which the general military struggle was now waged.

* See Burchett, *The Furtive War*, pp. 80-83.

IN THE WESTERN HIGHLANDS

Struggle Around B. M. Thuot

Ban Mé Thuot is a strategic center in Dak Lak province, a key area of the Tay Nguyen (Western Highlands) or *Hauts Plateaux,* as the French call the area. Militarily, the Tay Nguyen for South Vietnam could perhaps be compared with the Plain of Jars in Laos, a vast area with plateaux suitable for airfields. Ban Mé Thuot is near enough to the borders of Cambodia and Laos to make it of vital importance, a fact that U.S. military men in Saigon had not overlooked. After Saigon, in fact Ban Mé Thuot, is perhaps the second most important military center. It is also a center for the biggest concentration of ethnic minorities in South Vietnam, mainly the Rhade, Jarai and M'Nong tribespeople.

Tran Dinh Minh was a Vietnamese but had lived in the Tay Nguyen for 14 years, since the age of 14, having volunteered for service there because he was too young and small to bear arms in the anti-French war, though he had served as a "liaison agent" from the age of 13. He had completely adopted the tribespeoples' customs, their food, language and dress, having practiced the three "withs" policy of "work with, live with, eat with," as advocated by President Ho Chi Minh. He knew the general area, knew the people and was trusted by them. Like Sao Nam, he was a "child of the revolution." His whole family

Chapter II

was wiped out in Quang Nam province in the early stages of the anti-French war. After volunteering for work in Dak Lak, he learned five of the tribal languages and was adopted as a "son" by several of the tribes. His fiancée was arrested and killed by the Diemists; several of the tribes, when I met him, were competing to find him a suitable mate. He was the ideal man for the task in hand—but it was a tall order to be sent alone, with one pistol, to encircle Ban Mé Thuot with NFL

153

bases. That was in December 1960, in the same month the
National Front was formed.

B. M. Thuot, as the name is usually written on maps, was
the headquarters base for the 4th Diemist army corps, a division
plus one regiment. Within a few days, Tranh Dinh Minh had
recruited some old friends, three Vietnamese and four tribesmen,
each of whom had a sheath knife.

"Our main job," he told me, "was to establish ourselves in
the hearts of the people. That is the only way we recognize of
establishing a base. But it was difficult to do anything at all
without arms. One day, we ambushed a Diemist lorry; but
there were no arms, only uniforms. We carried off as many as
we could, although at first I was very disappointed. Then I had
an idea. B. M. Thuot was encircled by 'agricultural settlements'
to which Vietnamese 'suspects' from the plains had been exiled
to carve out rubber and coffee plantations for the Diem family.
Each of these was controlled by a military post set up within
the 'settlement' itself. Why not try and use the Diemist uniforms
to infiltrate and capture the arms from a post?"

Just after dusk one evening, clad in Diemist officer's uniforms,
they stopped a truck which had just emerged from one of the
"agricultural settlements" and was heading towards B. M. Thuot.
The driver proved to be friendly, told them the exact layout
of the post and agreed to drive them back in. Since they were
in Diemist uniform, the sentry at the gate let them through.
"We drove straight to the captain's quarters," Tran Dinh Minh
related, "and found him sitting on a bed, playing a guitar, some
of his soldiers dancing western style to the music. Their guns
were piled up in a corner and we grabbed them and the captain
simultaneously. We explained that we were from the NFL,
ordered the captain to assemble his men, get them to lay down
their arms immediately and then listen to a statement on Front
policy. Otherwise he would be killed on the spot. The rest of
the platoon came out of their barracks, piled up their arms
and assembled in the garrison square. Our men seized the arms
and took up appropriate positions, while I talked to them. Long
before I had finished the soldiers were with us."

The garrison troops were peasant conscripts, like most of the

Diemist troops, and every word of Tranh Dinh Minh found
its echo in their own experiences. All 29 joined up, and offered
to help organize a meeting of the settlement inmates, although
there was another military post only about a mile away. Altogether 2,700 people gathered. "They could hardly believe their
eyes and ears when they saw and heard us," Minh told me.
"People actually wept for joy when we explained who we were.
Over 400 young men begged to be taken into our ranks, but as
we only had the 30 weapons just captured and had no real base
or supply system, I accepted only 75 of the toughest and most
decided. I promoted my seven raw recruits to squad leaders on
the spot and put the new men under them. We had driven
into the settlement, a force of eight with one pistol and seven
knives, we moved out with 112 men, a submachine gun and
28 rifles."

Around B. M. Thuot, forest and plantations alternate in
checkerboard fashion. At the time Minh started operating,
around the city were 11 French plantations with 5,000 Vietnamese workers and six "agricultural settlements" with 25,000
Vietnamese from the plains. Minh succeeded in setting up bases
in all of them.

The "agricultural settlements," incidentally, were part of a
crazy plan worked out by Diem and his U.S. "advisers." They
were aimed at killing a number of birds with one stone: first
to exile "suspects" or potential "trouble-makers" from the plains;
second, to set Vietnamese and the tribespeople at each other's
throats as the "agricultural settlements" were formed by bull-
dozing minority villages out of existence and driving the tribespeople off their hunting grounds; third, to provide cheap labor
to transform the fertile Tay Nguyen lands into coffee, tea and
rubber plantations; and fourth, especially in the case of B. M.
Thuot, to fill in the gaps of the protective human hedge around
that strategic center. But it did not take long for a skilled
propagandist like Minh to prove to the Vietnamese exiles and
the minority peoples, had they not seen it themselves, that their
miseries came from one central origin, the U.S.-Diemist regime
in Saigon. Minh and the "armed propaganda teams" he formed,
soon developed united action between Vietnamese and tribes-

people against a common oppressor. And it was no more difficult to organize the plantation workers than it was the exiles
and tribespeople; Minh being far too good a tactician, however,
to use his control over the rubber workers to the detriment
of the French plantation owners and managers. Certainly it was
he, and not Saigon, who now, on behalf of the NFL, collected
their taxes with the tacit understanding that if the French behaved correctly, there would be no labor troubles. By the end
of 1961, Diemist control had been removed from the "agricultural settlements" and the military posts were eliminated.
The inmates, now affiliated to the Front, had elected self-
administration committees. The rubber workers, through their
trade unions, were also affiliated to the Front.

The Americans by this time were very concerned with the
situation; they still had big plans for B. M. Thuot. In documents captured by the guerillas there were even hints that it
should be developed as a last-ditch bastion in the event of a
threat to Saigon. Great efforts had been put into building underground arms depots and a complex of installations and fortifications. The new plan was to complete the circle of human armor
by concentrating as many of the tribal people as they could in
"strategic hamlets," another wall to take the "first shock" of "Viet
Cong" attacks, as it was put in the captured documents. According to the plan, the "agricultural settlements" were to be brought
under control again and the inmates as well as the tribespeople
in the "strategic hamlets" would be armed to defend themselves
against the "Viet Cong." These were the new instructions which
came with direct U.S. intervention at the end of 1961.

'NEW' AMERICANS

Buon Ea Nao, a village less than two miles from B. M. Thuot,
was selected as the main camp for concentrating the minorities
and instructing them in the use of U.S. weapons. Every village
was supposed to send its elders for political indoctrination and
ten able-bodied men for military training to protect themselves
against "wild beasts." Ybih Aleo, the most authoritative leader
of the 37 minority groups in the Tay Nguyen and himself from

"BLOSSOM" and LISSOM"
— *they helped beat off
an enemy attack at
company strength from
their fortified village.*

*Jungle uniform factory
— the workers brought
their Singer sewing-
machines with them
from Saigon.*

(Left) CHI *(Sister)* KINH, *of the Bahnar minority people, is president of her provincial Liberation Women's Association.*

(Below) In small schools, children like these M'Nong kids learn their ABC's; written scripts for the tribal peoples have been invented by the NFL.

B. M. Thuot district, a grizzled and grey French-trained military veteran and vice president of the NFL, told me that the Diemists, under specific U.S. advice, avoided saying they were to be armed against the Liberation Front or "Viet Cong" because they knew any derogatory remarks would have alienated the tribespeople. "It was above all a U.S. officer in priest's clothing who spoke and said the weapons were against 'intruders' who came to steal their pigs or chickens, even if these were 'Diemist troops.' It was a clever line," Ybih Aleo said, "and it took into account the fact that the Diemist troops were completely discredited because of their atrocities against the people."

I heard a more detailed account from an elder of one of the villages; neither name nor village can be revealed because he is still there and his village is now under Saigon control. A fine dignified figure, he chose his words with great deliberation.

"This American spoke Rhade and called himself Eay (Father) Teo. He said he was a 'new' American and that the 'new' Americans were against the 'old' Americans who helped the Diemists hurt our people. 'We will help you become really independent,' he said. 'But you must not help either the Diemists or the "Viet Cong." We will give you everything you need and you will come into new homes we will help build. Cloth, rice, salt, bicycles, and arms to defend yourselves against any evildoer —we will give you all these.' We were confused. We knew the Americans help Diem; now others come and say they oppose him. This 'new' American looked just like the 'old' ones. He seemed to be a military man but was dressed like a French priest. But he said he was not a priest. 'I am sent by Christ to help you but mine is the 'new' religion of the 'new' Americans.'

" 'You see,' said this Eay Teo, 'it is this way. The "old" Americans and the "Diemists" behave like cats. The "Viet Cong" is the mouse. If the mouse smuggles itself into your paddy, the cats come to kill the mouse. But in doing this they also harm your paddy. But if you block the mouse coming into your paddy, you can block the cat also. Then no harm will be done by cat or mouse. We will give you weapons to deal with both.'

"Our people talked this over but we were all suspicious. We

did not want to be concentrated; we did not want their weapons. So we said, no concentration and no weapons. We have always defended ourselves till now in the old way. Eay Teo was very angry. 'If you refuse to take arms and the "old" Americans and Diemists come to kill you, it is your own fault,' he said. In a few days more than a thousand troops came to our area. Five villages were burned and 20 people, mainly children and old people, were killed. Our tribespeople were ordered to go to B. M. Thuot again and to be ready to accept concentration. We were over a thousand who assembled and our hearts were heavy. Diemist troops surrounded us with their arms pointed at our backs. Eay Teo was there, the governor of the province and the chiefs of all the districts. 'Either you agree to concentrate immediately or the troops will be sent against all your villages tomorrow,' said Eay Teo.

"We were all sad. Everyone looked at the ground for there seemed no hope. But then the old man, I Bru of Buon Dju village, climbed onto the platform of a hut and started to speak. He was old, nearly 70, but everyone knew him: 'We tribespeople,' he said, 'always lived with our ray, our forests and brooks and trees. Now you want to lock us up, away from our trees and forests. In that case we will slowly die. Now you have your troops and guns around us. Better pull the triggers now so we die all together.' The district chief strode up to him: 'If you disagree with the government, the Americans, you old fool, you *will* all be killed. And if *you* continue to speak like that you will be killed first, now.'

" 'If you are killed,' shouted old man I Bru, 'you lose your villa, your plantation, your fine car, your beautiful women. If I am killed, I lose this only,' and he snatched off his loin cloth, threw it in the face of the district chief and stood there naked, his chest thrust out to receive the bullets. There was tremendous excitement. Everyone rushed forward to save the old man, shouting, 'No concentration! No concentration!' Officials were swept off their feet and the soldiers made their guns ready. Then Eay Teo spoke up again, trying to smile but his lips were twisted. 'Why all the noise? Why all the excitement?' he said. 'We invited you to hear your opinions. Now you may go home.' "

That night, troops came from a nearby post, dragged the old man off and killed him. Next day people from 20 villages met to honor the old man. The tribespeople took a pledge that they would carry on the fight as the old man had done and it was agreed that only when there is no more forest and the brooks have dried up will the Rhade people allow themselves to be concentrated. But some of the villages near B. M. Thuot were fenced around and turned into strategic hamlets. "Though they could fence in our villages, they could not fence in our hearts," the elder concluded. "They belong to the revolution."

LIFE ON THE RESERVATION

The incident with I Bru took place at the end of 1961 and by February 1962 a partial economic blockade had been clamped down, with the stopping of salt supplies as the first step. Local officials ordered the tribespeople to halt rice-growing and cultivate jute instead, the Americans could supply rice more cheaply. About this time, according to Ybih Aleo, the Diemists started planting "Gibbs" and "fountain pen" bombs in the minority villages, apparently as a reprisal for the traps with which the tribespeople were defending their homes and cultivation patches. The first was a tiny flat pressure mine, about the size and shape of Gibbs' toothpowder tins. The second were shaped like Parker fountain pens. Raiding parties, which found hamlets empty when they arrived, would conceal Gibbs bombs everywhere, under a bed or table or a cooking pot or the bamboo strips which served as a floor in the tribespeople's huts. The "fountain pen" bombs were strewn around in the grass and a child picking one up would have his or her hands blown off. "After an enemy raid and the people returned to their homes, there were explosions, cries and groans until late at night," Ybih Aleo said. From that period, February-March 1962, it was also forbidden to beat gongs or drums, because the Diemists suspected these were signals to the "Viet Cong."

Tran Dinh Minh told me that during that period many of the younger men came to their base area and enlisted in the NFL forces. "Whole villages came to settle near us," he said, "but it was difficult to accept too many because of our own supply problems. The struggle became difficult; once they had fenced in the villages, the Diemists then started setting up military posts to 'protect' them. We were not prepared at that time to lead the tribespeople in a general armed struggle. They would have been exposed then to merciless reprisals from which we could offer no protection. Unlike most minority areas, there were no mountains to retire to and the enemy's military strength there was many times greater than ours. We concentrated on political consolidation."

Life for the tribespeople gradually took on the pattern of that of the Red Indians in the "reservations" the Americans devised for those that survived the wholesale massacres of a century ago. As they were only allowed to move out from their enclosed villages in daylight, it was useless trying to work their ray and in fact they were only permitted to work land within a radius of one kilometer of the village. Normally the tribespeople leave the village in time to get in a full day's work at the ray between sunrise and sunset. The new regime was imposed to prevent contacts with the "Viet Cong" in the forest. There was no place to keep cattle within the barbed wire perimeter, so these were abandoned to the tigers. Intervillage visits to celebrate each others feasts, the most popular form of social intercourse among the tribespeople, were banned. Even though the men only wore loincloths and the women only ankle-length skirts, they were submitted to the indignity of being searched as they left and entered the stockades. Hunting was finished; what could you hope to hunt within a kilometer of the village?

The parallel with the American Indians is too painfully obvious. The Diemists had started the old-type extermination campaign—and now the reservations for the latter stage. With tribal lands gone, hunting finished, customs trampled on, their way of life turned upside down, they would die out anyway! But the tribespeople are not so resigned to their fate. As the tribal elder, mentioned earlier expressed it: "What you would see of our life if you could come to our village now, would be like ash. But underneath the ash are glowing coals. We await the day when the wind will come and blow away the ash and fan the coals into life."

Control in the stockades is exercised in daytime by Rhade nationals, selected long ago and trained in the Philippines and introduced as representatives of the "new" religion of the "new" Americans. From what I have learned about religious services among the Rhade people, they are Catholic-trained, but the pastor-priests insist they are not Catholic; "that was the religion of the French colonialists," they said. "We represent the 'new' religion." They combine political with their religious functions, but dare not stay overnight in the stockades, returning to B. M. Thuot. "The most cruel of these agents," I was told by the tribal elder, "have accidents on the road. It appears they are taken by tigers because the body is never found."

After a major effort by the Diemist regime in 1962, the area immediately surrounding B. M. Thuot, including the "agricultural settlements," was brought back under Saigon's nominal control, but it was obvious from all I could see and hear, that the "glowing coal" situation was the real one.

By the end of 1963, the Diemist had pulled back again to a perimeter in an approximate radius of six miles from B. M. Thuot, and the city itself had been converted into a sort of medieval fortress, surrounded by a series of three nine-foot high palisades, 20 yards between the outer and second wall, ten yards between the second and third. Inside, the town is divided up into scores of sub-sections, each of which is also walled off. Between the palisades are moats filled with spiked obstacles and even individual houses are surrounded by spike-filled ditches with a plank leading to the entrance which must be taken up at night. The main victims are the people themselves, their children, dogs and pigs. The spikes must be uncovered after sunset and can be covered again only when the gongs sound at 6 AM.

At least, this was part of a detailed account given me of life in B. M. Thuot by a journalist who smuggled himself out of the city especially to contact me. "It is a town of fear and terror," he said. "The authorities are terrified because they know the NFL have their armed forces all around the town and bases inside as well, despite all the precautions; the people are terrorized because the place is crawling with police and agents who are empowered to arrest or kill any 'Viet Cong' suspect on the spot. Once a person is arrested, there is never any further news. Things have come to this. If someone walking in the street recognizes another who is NFL, even though he may not give the slightest sign of recognition, that night, if he has not already been arrested, he will flee with his family to the liberated zone. Why? Because, with pimps and agents around everywhere, he runs the risk of being arrested and killed for having seen but not denounced his acquaintance. Suspects are all killed now. Before you were tortured, then thrown into jail for a while. Now they torture you to get what they can, then kill you. It is an absolute rule; it reflects the state of mind of the enemy, his fear and weakness."

Tran Dinh Minh can presumably consider that, although he overreached himself in the first year, he carried out his task. About 90 per cent of the territory of Dak Lak and 70 to 80 per cent of the population are now controlled by the NFL. He succeeded in setting up bases around Ban Mé Thuot itself and by all one could see and hear had succeeded in the more important task of "establishing bases in the hearts of the population."

THE JARAI REVOLT

The great centers of the tribespeople of the Western Highlands are, in addition to B. M. Thuot, the town of Pleiku in Gia Lai province, and Kontum in the province of the same name. As far as I could find out, the first act of rebellion in the Tay Nguyen took place in November 1960, among the Jarai in Gia Lai province. I heard about it from Rachem H'Ban, a Jarai girl who was 17 years old at the time of the action. She is slight and rather sickly-looking, with a round olive-skinned face and large holes in her ears from which ornaments had been removed. She wore an ankle-length skirt of black homespun with a six-inch hem of red and white embroidery. Her native village is Sung So, in Le Thanh district, and her name is now famous throughout South Vietnam.

"The trouble started," she said, "when the Diemists came to install a new chief of canton in our hamlet. They wanted to use our village as the center for a 'strategic hamlet,' to group other hamlets in our canton around ours and then fence the whole thing in. We had been objecting to this. The Diemists then started a terror campaign not only against us but against all the Jarai in our district. First they came and took away four of our young men. One they killed, a second they kept in prison, the other two they released. When they came back we hardly recognized them; they had been badly tortured. We all met in the 'roong' [community meeting hall] that night to talk things over. Life was becoming impossible. From other villages came news of our tribespeople being killed, women raped, houses burned, pigs and buffalo stolen. We decided that to live, we must fight back."

Two days later, a unit of 11 Diemist troops came very late at night. They forbade anyone to leave the village; they went into every house, collecting knives and crossbows, and then ordered all the young men to present themselves. When they came out, eight were arrested and tied up. The people fought back for hours; the whole hamlet had turned out and formed a circle around the troops. The people had no weapons. The unit chief, a big brute of a man, fired into the leg of one of the captured young men and he fell, blood trickling down his leg. At the sight of blood everyone was furious. Rachem called out instructions in Jarai and the women, who had armed themselves with pieces of firewood from under the huts, jumped at the soldiers. Rachem and two others went for the unit chief, with the first blow knocking his automatic out of his hands, and then they strangled him. Five others had already been clubbed to death, while the rest fled. The tribespeople now had five carbines, a light machine gun, a pistol and lots of cartridges.

By midday the whole hamlet had fled into the jungle. They took everything they could carry—rice, clothes, cooking pots—and also pigs and chickens, but had to leave the cattle. Soon afterwards an enemy force of about 200 came and burned down the village, killing all the buffalo and cattle. They had big guns and fired shells into the forest, but no one was hurt. Within ten days the Jarai had built a new village.

In the new village, first thoughts were obviously for protection. Like the Kor and Hre people nearly 18 months previously in Quang Ngai, they had moved back into a fairly inaccessible area, but obviously the Diemists would soon learn where. The young men set up a "self-defense" corps, armed with crossbows, and spent most of their time preparing defenses; digging ditches for spikes and preparing all sorts of other traps along the approaches to the village. The older people were responsible for production. Everyone spent their spare time sharpening spikes and the young people gradually spread out the traps to cover all approaches. Although the village only comprised 45 houses with a total population of about 300, the Diemists were never able to subdue it. Enough were killed with poisoned arrows or wounded in the spiked traps out of any column moving to the attack to dampen the ardor of the others. But the main thing was that, following this example, there was a general uprising of the Jarai people in Le Thanh and neighboring districts. It was another illustration of the fact that when repression in any area reached a certain degree of intensity, it only needed a spark to touch off a raging fire.

Those which had previously been Diemist-controlled "strategic hamlets" now were transformed into "resistance" hamlets like that of Rachem H'Ban. Rachem is now a member of the Le Thanh district committee of the NFL, a heroine of the Jarai people and of the whole liberation movement for having struck off such important sparks with her billets of firewood.

'SELF-MANAGEMENT'

A heroine in another field is Chi (Sister) Kinh, a plumpish, very feminine girl of the Bahnar minority, with a soft mouth and broadish nose, hair clipped straight at the shoulders and an ingenué smile which lends her otherwise serious face a very gentle expression. She is president of the Gia Lai provincial committee of the Liberation Women's Association. The Bahnar and Jarai are the main minorities in Gia Lai province and Chi Kinh is a living illustraton of the capacty of the tribespeople to move swiftly forward once they have a minimum of education,

support and guidance. Her answers to questions, her clear ex-
posés were those of an efficient committeewoman anywhere in
the world. A few years ago she was an illiterate tribesgirl whose
experiences in life had been limited to the primitive agricultural
work in the ray.

I had been told that despite her 24 years, she was a top-rate
organizer and knew a great deal about the history of her people
and region. I wanted to hear her own account of how administration functioned in practice in the Front-controlled tribal
areas. She started by explaining that prior to August 1945, when
the Viet Minh seized power from the Japanese, there were in
fact parallel administrative systems in that part of the Tay
Nguyen, "one appointed by the French, the other secretly elected
by the people." In places close to the cities, it was the French-
appointed that was on top, further away it was the one elected
by the people.

Most of Gia Lai was a Viet Minh-controlled area at the time of
the 1954 ceasefire. When the Diemist administration arrived, it was
the usual story of wiping out the elected administrations still
in office, hounding down former resistance workers with the
extra brutality reserved for the minority "savages." But the
resistance started moving into the enemy organizations, changing
their character, capturing them from within, from under the
very noses of the enemy. Before they knew what was happening,
everything had slipped away from under their fingers. The
NFL in this area was only set up at provincial level in December
1961, but within a year, Diemist control was limited to the
provincial capital of Pleiku and a few walled-in strategic hamlets
along the major military highways Nos. 14 and 19. The rest
of this large province and about 70 per cent of the population
was under Liberation Front control by the end of 1962. This
was the period of which Chi Kinh was now speaking.

How did they actually get the administrations running in the
villages? I had heard that her mother was president of the "self-
management committee" in Chi Kinh's native hamlet. How
did that happen?

"Yes, that's correct," she said. "A simple tribal woman who
knew nothing but looking after livestock and cooking before.

Now she administers the village and has the confidence of the whole people. She is also vice chairman of the local Liberation Women's Association. While the men are mainly responsible for military affairs now, it is the women who keep production going and run most branches of village activity. My mother is an energetic woman; people liked her attitude to work and so they elected her. Once a village is liberated and the Diemist agents kicked out, all our secret organizations, for the youth, women, peasants and others, come out into the open. They take the initiative in organizing elections, in which everyone takes part, to set up a self-management committee. This appoints teams and groups for self-defense, public security, public health, education, information and culture, agricultural production and economic affairs. The self-management committee directs and coordinates the activities of the teams and groups."

I asked about education because a few days previously I had visited a school in a M'Nong village—just a roof supported by woven bamboo walls on three sides, the fourth opening out towards an open-air easel blackboard. The pretty young teacher was vague about who provides textbooks and whether what she taught was in line with some general program. My questions were academic, as the rows of round-faced, bare-foot children on their log benches were struggling with the M'Nong variant of the ABC, using pointed bamboo for pens and charcoal mixed with water for ink, copying what the teacher was laboriously writing with a piece of dried manioc for chalk on the blackboard.

Chi Kinh explained the question of textbooks and program was not yet important in her province, and the main drive was to teach adults at evening courses to read and write in the Bahnar and Jarai scripts and provide primary education in day schools to children from six years old to teen-agers. "We have no material facilities for higher schools yet," she explained, "and almost no children that qualify. Don't forget that almost everyone was illiterate when we started only a little over two years ago. But at the provincial level, we have a teachers' training school." Textbooks there are provided by the provincial education committee of the NFL. I asked if this was an autonomous body which had worked out a general program for the province and she explained that it was based on a program worked out for the Tay Nguyen area—with variations for the different tribal groupings—by the NFL's sub-committee for education, a department of the central Committee for Information, Education and Cultural Affairs. This latter body laid down overall educational policies for all Front-controlled areas, but in the case of the Tay Nguyen, these were developed in consultation with Ybih Aleo's Movement for Tay Nguyen Autonomy.

The central organ also printed basic textbooks, while provincial committees did the best they could to provide duplicated, type-written or even handcopied supplementary material. "Paper in some of our areas is a great problem," said Chi Kinh, "we have to use the flattened-out skin from giant bamboo."

Public health teams worked in the same way; within a framework of overall policy laid down by the central Committee for Public Health, as passed on down through provincial and district public health committees. "But many organizations are run by the people themselves," this remarkable young tribeswoman explained further. "We don't have to wait for higher instructions to organize educational courses. Anyone who knows a few letters of the alphabet can start teaching those who know none at all, and learning from those who know a few more. And anyone who has some notions of hygiene, the need for keeping houses and clothes clean, of boiling water before drinking and keeping toilets back from the houses, can start doing something about public health without waiting for word from the district or provincial public health committees. Later, when things get a bit organized we send someone from every hamlet to district and provincial centers to get training in public health and education. But it is the same with public security, self-defense, improving agricultural production. These are things that work on their own and that is why our committees are called 'self-management.' With the time it takes to move on foot or even on horseback from a distant village to a district center, any other way of doing things would be very stupid. There will be time for that," she added with another of her charming smiles, "when we have all the towns and highways in our hands. Our women's association, for instance, plays a big part in such things as public health, economic affairs, planning agricultural production and marketing—we have to do that because the men are often away on military affairs—as well as child welfare and purely women's affairs."

Chi Kinh, who only learned to read and write in her late teens—she had taught herself—is not often in her own village. She is constantly on the move, setting up other women's committees all over the province, including inside the walled strategic hamlets which she penetrates at the risk of her life. When I met her, she was touring the countryside on foot as chairwoman of a campaign committee to organize elections at provincial level for the permanent committee of the Liberation Women's Association. "At present ours is only a provisional committee at province level," she explained, "but up to district level they are all elected committees."

Economic Planning

Another remarkable young tribeswoman was Chi Bar, from the Jeh minority in Kontum province, one of the twelve minority groups in Kontum. Chi Bar is a very important personality, combining the functions of member of the NFL executive committee for Kontum province, chairwoman of the provincial committee of the Liberation Women's Association and member of the executive committee of the Movement for Tay Nguyen Autonomy. The latter to some degree fulfills already the functions of an autonomous administration for the Tay Nguyen region, the Front already having taken the decision to set up an autonomous zone there. Much of what Chi Bar had to say of the struggle in Kontum was similar to other accounts already quoted. At the time I met her, five of the six districts in the province were already under Front control, with Saigon control limited to Kontum town itself and highways Nos. 13 and 5, the latter linking Kontum with Attopeu in Laos.

Chi Bar, a stocky young woman with a serious, intelligent face, was also well versed in the history of her people and started by telling me about the 60-year war between the Jeh in Kontum and the K'Tun over the borders in Quang Nam. "It continued

in feud form till 1952," she said. "Our people used to put knots
in creepers to keep toll of the accounts that had to be settled.
It was only when the Viet Minh cadres came and organized
solidarity meetings between the tribes and we saw that only the
colonialists gained from such feuds, that they were stopped. Till
then hundreds of our tribespeople were killed every year for nothing."

The Diem regime, it transpired, had never been able to establish its rule over most of Kontum and life continued in those
areas under the previous resistance administration as if the
Diemist regime in Saigon never existed. "For instance," said
Chi Bar, "in my village of Nong Con, north of Kontum city,
we decided to imitate North Vietnam and go in for economic
planning. Everybody greatly admired 'Uncle Ho' and when we
heard over Hanoi radio what was going on up there, our people
—especially the young ones—wanted to do the same thing." Incredible as it seems, while the Diemist military and police
machine was rolling over the rest of the land, an experiment in
socialist planned economy was set up in what had been one
of the most backward parts of the country. The Sedang minority,
one of the biggest groups, had started to emerge from stone age
society only a generation ago.

"We had a total labor force of 250 to work the ray and living
standards had been very low. In general we only grew enough
rice for four months of the year, between November and April.
For the rest of the year we grubbed in the jungle for edible
roots and leaves. So, in 1956 we set up a cooperative; all the
ray became the common property of the village to be worked
under an elected management committee, the harvest to be divided up equally among the labor force. The first year things
went well; there was a much bigger harvest than ever before
because the ray were much better looked after. But the second
year, the work was bad, because we had nobody used to giving
orders and directing such a big labor force. The weather didn't
help; the harvest was really bad.

"The older people wanted to go back to the traditional ways,
but the younger ones objected. There were some fierce inter-
family arguments. We younger people held a meeting and we

compared our life with before. Even though the harvest had been bad, life was much better. We felt freer, life was gayer; it was more fun working together, people had got friendlier. The harvest was bad, we decided, because the management was weak. So we decided to divide the labor force up into five groups of 50 each. Each group should elect a head and the five group heads would be the management committee for the whole cooperative. Our parents grumbled and said the old way was best but we insisted in sticking to group work. The older people had to give way. We adopted the slogan, 'Work quickly, work hard, work thriftily.' We set up a control system to decide what should be distributed among members, what should be sent to market. The 1956 harvest was a bumper one and we continued like this till 1961, with never a bad harvest. The older people were all on our side by then.

"In 1961, the harvest was especially good, but we younger people thought, why bother to divide it up? We work together, why not eat together? So we stored the grain in huge common bins and set up three big kitchens, for 60, 120 and 150 persons, corresponding to how the houses and ray were grouped; our total population was 350, including children. The five work groups were reorganized into three, each with its own kitchen-restaurant. This works splendidly till today, the whole village like one—well, like three—families. Harvests have gone up every year, till the last one, because of drought. But still we can contribute 848 kilograms of rice to the Front. We shall eat rice mixed with manioc, but even then this is far better than the best harvest year even the oldest can remember. We are sure of food all the year round. Our young men have learned to become blacksmiths and they now make iron and steel implements for production."

"Where does the raw material come from?" I asked, knowing that lack of iron and steel and agricultural implements of any sort is the biggest problem in the minority areas, apart from the salt shortage.

"Of course the village has its guerilla force and when they ambush a truck or blow up a bridge, they bring back as much of the metal as they can carry. Road No. 5 for instance has been put out of action, so there is plenty of metal there from the bridges; bridge railings are very good for plowshares. What we don't need ourselves, we sell at reasonable prices to villages further back in the mountains.

"The example of our Nong Con cooperative caused many more to be set up," she continued, "and although there are few so well organized, economic planning has become widespread, even over our borders into Quang Nam.

I suspected that many times she used "we," Chi Bar could well have used "I," as I knew that she was the driving force in the latter phases of this movement, spreading it far beyond Nong Con village, as also the fight against illiteracy, for better public hygiene and everything that was new and progressive. This is why she had such a high position in Front organizations and will doubtless emerge as an outstanding leader of the tribal peoples. She had made her first contact with "the revolution," as she expressed it, by looking after babes in a co-op crêche; taught herself to read and write, then took charge of the education of older girls and so on to more responsible tasks. We talked till late into the night in a thatch-roof hut, set high up on piles with pigs and buffalo snuffling and snoring underneath.

The smoky lamp, fuelled with some sort of unprocessed tree oil illumined the fine, sensitive faces of Chi Bar and some of her friends, dignified, reflective faces strong as steel, but with something of compassion in them as well; faces of people who have suffered for generations and pondered long over the causes and remedies for their sufferings. They were faces one never tired of studying because essential truths were engraved there; human qualities which we prize in theory in the West, but which have been preserved by the tribespeople in purer, elemental form. When napalm burned their ripening crops and poisoned chemicals were dropped by planes into their streams, one began to alter conceptions about savages and savagery.

ETHNIC GROUP POLICY

There were many things to learn and know about the customs and mores of the tribespeople and I wondered whether people with the mentality of the Saigon regime could ever win their confidence; whether they were capable of such detailed, understanding studies as the Vietnamese liberation cadres had made. I believe it is impossible, and that goes for the U.S. advisers, too. They would have to recast their thinking, adopt other political and social yardsticks. The Americans relied on winning over a few chiefs with baubles of material goods or offers of power. But the tribespeople are sensitive, with a sound instinct for what is bogus and what is real. It was only after years of living and working together that they started opening their hearts even to those Vietnamese they trusted most.

It was a tremendous advantage for the NFL that Ho Chi Minh had asked for volunteers in 1945-46 among young people of the caliber of Tran Dinh Minh, Nguyen Han Chung and others I met, to go to the Tay Nguyen area prepared to spend the rest of their lives there. Not only had they sunk their roots deep down into the minds and hearts of the tribespeople, but they had compiled registers of all clan names and inter-clan relationships. Later, these were of vital importance in extending NFL influence in the Tay Nguyen.

A new era in relations between Vietnamese proper and the minority peoples started during the anti-French resistance war because for the first time the tribespeople met outsiders who treated them as equals, under the policy laid down by the Viet Minh. They had always been treated as "savages" before and indeed the only term I heard applied to them by Westerners was "Moi," which I took to be a common term for all the tribes. Later I discovered it was Vietnamese for "savage."

"In general," I was told by Nguyen Han Chung, a Vietnamese who had spent his adult life among the tribespeople, "we still do not interfere in customs at all, but the minorities are influenced by the way we live; they ask many searching questions. Gradually many of the more damaging customs are dying out. Our slogan for them is 'anti-puppet, anti-imperialist' and in these they support us with all their hearts. If we have been accepted as brothers, this is because those of us who have lived amongst them for years have tried to grasp and understand their customs and never, never to violate them.

"The only thing is that, as occasion offers, we try and show them why they are unhappy, why their life is miserable. At first they answer that 'it is the will of God.' Bit by bit we showed them that it was not that. They argued that 'God created the tribespeople and ordained that they should be unhappy, that they should be slaves.' So they are liable to eat up all their rice in feasts after the harvest, slaughter their cattle for some ritual and starve for the rest of the year. 'It may appease the Gods,' they would say, 'and in any case the tax collector would get it.'

"We explained that it was not God, but in the old days it was the French who made them give up all the fruits of their labor in taxes, or took them away for unpaid labor for months on end and that now it is the U.S. puppets. Maybe after some weeks they come back, having thought it all over. They ask many more questions and the day comes when they will shout: 'It's true, it's true what you say. Our land is good, the soil is rich, the forest is full of elephants. There are riches all round but we wear old, torn loincloths. We could live much better.' When the truth dawns on them, they start to weep a lot at first and then they get angry. 'Look how they cheat us. For a cup of salt, we must pay 30 or 40 kilograms of rice; for a brass gong we must give a buffalo or even an elephant; for a month's work on the plantation the French used to give us an old shirt or a worn-out pair of pants, and the U.S.-Diemists may give us a bottle of perfume or a bit of soap for a hard day's work. They give our women a few beads and bits of nylon cloth and take so many pigs and buffalo in return.' "

A major reason for their miseries for generations past has been the almost complete lack of any medical or public health work. Smallpox and dysentery, their two greatest scourges, have wiped out whole communities in the past. Vietnamese cadres told of many instances of coming across abandoned villages where no one was left to bury the dead. The few survivors had set fire to the houses and fled into the forest. I have talked with Jarai, Rhade and M'Nong tribesmen who have wept as they told of such calamities which they put down to the "gods" in the past. Their enemies exploited these superstitions and did everything to encourage them. At first the French, later the Diemists, used planes to drop napalm on dissident villages. Local agents said these were Kim Phiar, the firebird, dropping his excrement because God had been displeased by the tribe's disobedience. They believed it till the NFL troops started shooting down some of these planes and they found not "firebirds" but U.S. and Vietnamese pilots inside. But customs and superstitions die hard and it was impressive to see the careful way such things were being tackled by the Vietnamese cadres. The meticulous briefings on behavior that I received while traveling in these areas were an illustration of this.

"We feel very moved when talking with the tribespeople," said one veteran Vietnamese cadre who had been sheltered by them for many years. "They are so straightforward, so pure in their thoughts and expressions. Once they have given their word, it is for life. They are generous and honest and prefer to die or endure the most terrible tortures rather than ever betray a friend."

"Our Kinh brothers brought us life and light in our darkness," one dignified chief of the Hre people told me. "We will never abandon them." These were typical observations, variants of which I was to hear time and again in the Tay Nguyen area. The sending, in 1945-46, of cadres to live and work in the Tay Nguyen was not only because of the strategic importance of having guerilla bases in this natural paradise for guerilla warfare, with its common frontiers with Cambodia and Laos. Otherwise it would have been on a short-time basis. It was in accordance with a policy of "revolutionary humanism," as my Vietnamese friends expressed it, to let a few rays of life into the backward lives of the tribespeople. Cadres were selected from tough peasant stock, with stomachs, as well as nerves and revolutionary ardor, strong as steel. For years and perhaps forever, they elected to live and work with the tribespeople, to adopt their customs, which meant in some cases even filing their teeth down to the gums, dressing in loincloths, letting their hair grow long to be coiled in buns, having their ears pierced for massive ear ornaments, adopting a diet which was fairly sure to ruin stomachs after a few years.

Among their early activities was the holding of inter-tribal "solidarity meetings" at which, with the cadres presiding and often acting as interpreters, the tribespeople were encouraged to speak of their lives and sorrows. Tribes which had been at war for generations attended and as each recounted their troubles it was easy to see they originated from the same source—not from the tribe on the other side of the river, but a common oppressor who bled them white with taxes, raided their villages for manpower and set the tribes at each other's throats. Gradually solidarity was forged among the tribes, the feuds died a natural death. The next step was to hold "solidarity meetings" between the tribespeople and the Vietnamese majority people to forge unity on a still broader basis.

Bit by bit the cadres were able to introduce elements of public health and education, improved methods of cultivation and cattle-breeding and a more rational way of husbanding the fruits of the soil and the hunt to avoid the periodic famines which plagued the minority areas. With the formation of the NFL, the process was speeded up, written scripts developed for the first time for the main tribal languages; young people from each hamlet attended courses in public health and education at the Front provincial centers and returned as education and public health workers.

In the latter years of the independence struggle, the ethnic minorities, with a few unimportant exceptions, were unwavering allies of the resistance forces. This explains why in the blackest period of Diemist repression, when thousands of former resistance workers fled from the plains to the forest and mountains, they were received as brothers and allies by the minority peoples, who with their own tremendous attachment to their families and villages sensed that only some monstrous calamity could force people into such exile. Many of the plainspeople who had had no previous contact with tribespeople were greatly astonished at their hospitable, compassionate reception. It is no exaggeration to state that at the peak period of the repression, virtually all revolutionary forces, all the future activists of the Liberation Front in Central Vietnam, were concentrated in the minority areas, fed, protected, hidden when necessary by the tribespeople. I never heard of a single case of betrayal.

My own observations, based often on conversations conducted through a whole string of interpreters, could be wide of the mark in some respects. But the deep, mutual respect and affection between Vietnamese cadres and the tribespeople was something very real. No aid or barrier of language could falsify this. Had this not been true, despite the charms given me by tribal chiefs and the involved briefings on behavior, I would have been killed in a score of different areas. Because the Vietnamese of the resistance have "bases in the hearts" of the tribespeople, I was received everywhere as a brother.

Chapter 12

FRONTAL ASSAULT

LAND PROBLEM IN DELTA

For a short answer as to who formed the National Front of Liberation, one would have to say Diem and Dulles. They pushed the most varied forces into each other's arms in desperate search of a means of survival. In a remarkably short time, Ngo Dinh Diem had succeeded in alienating the main religious, social, political, national and economic forces in the country. With total U.S. support for every move he made, he violated all the rules. A Catholic in a country overwhelmingly Buddhist, he insisted on installing co-religionists in all key posts down to provincial and district level. Power, it is usually acknowledged, is based on a class, but Diem based it on a faction of a class; on dispossessed landlords who had fled from North Vietnam and his own landlord cronies from the Center, plus what was left of the old mandarinate.

All political parties, even the most reactionary, were driven underground and only the personal creations of Diem and his more diabolical brother Nhu, were permitted. The national minorities, whom the French in their time had made considerable efforts to win to their side because they occupied vital strategic areas of the country, were treated by Diem as savages of racial excrescence to be liquidated as soon as possible. Local industry and commerce were despised and crushed in favor of goods imported with U.S. dollar aid and which passed through the hands of the Ngo family.

The class, in other words, on which Diem based his power, was outside the country. All real forces inside the country were driven into opposition. One error, more fatal than all the others, was to try and undo land reform, to seize back from the peasants the land distributed to them during the first resistance war. Even in doing this, Diem did not base himself on an established class. In the rich Mekong Delta area, for instance, the land taken back was not given to the old, southern landlords but to landowners from Central Vietnam or to Diem's cronies as a reward for political, military and police "services rendered." That the U.S. government—at his elbow all the time —supported and applauded every move, when it did not actually initiate them, is only evidence of the naïveté of their whole approach to Asian problems. The Dollar and the Bomb for Diem and Dulles were a sufficient substitute for the classical forms of support governments hitherto had needed.

"Although the Front was formed officially on December 20, 1960, it existed in fact before," said Nguyen Huu Tho, when I asked him about the actual setting up of the NFL. "But at the end of 1960, it assumed a concrete form with statutes and a program. The Front as an idea existed from 1954 when the broadest sections of the population were delighted with the Geneva Agreements and our Saigon-Cholon Committee was formed as a sort of watchdog to ensure the strict application of the Agreements.

"When Diem set out to crush the religious sects and large areas of the Saigon suburbs were burned out in the battle against the Binh Xuyen,* committees were set up to give relief to the victims. These represented the broadest section of the population, but were immediately suppressed by Diem, and leading members were arrested and tortured. Once Diem had consolidated his power, he lashed out at all sections of the population, at all the political parties, the religious sects, the minorities and the peasantry. The latter were the most dynamic in resisting, and in return received the heaviest blows at the beginning. Of 500,000 hectares of land distributed during the first resistance, all but 15 per cent was taken back by Diem. Sects and political parties which had no mass basis were quickly eliminated. Major minor racial groups like the Chinese and Khmer (Cambodian) had to adopt Vietnamese language names and customs. Khmer schools were closed down. For the larger minority groups it

---

* One of the most important of the three armed religious sects and responsible for policing Saigon at the time Diem was put in power.

was a policy of brutal assimilation; for the lesser groups one of extermination. No class, no religious or racial grouping was spared."

The assault against the peasantry was the greatest blunder of U.S.-Diemist policy. What happened in Central Vietnam was multiplied on a much larger scale in the South, especially in the Mekong Delta, the richest and most densely populated region of South Vietnam. In the 13 provinces of the Delta area were concentrated 5,700,000 of South Vietnam's 14,000,000 population. If one adds approximately 2,000,000 for the Saigon-Cholon area, the Delta thus accounts for just over half the total, at a density of 16 per square kilometer.

The Delta was a region of big estates, with absentee landlords on the old European pattern, who lived in luxury in Saigon, with rents paid into their bank accounts by plantation managers, who travelled abroad and sent their children to study in France. This was very different from the Center where, up to the time of the war against the French, there were only eight families who owned over 100 hectares of land; landlords were considered "rich" if they owned 10 hectares (an hectare— 2.47 acres). They lived on their holdings and fought with the peasants for every pound of rice for land rent, for every day of unpaid labor.

In the Delta, a landowner was "rich" only if he held over 50 hectares; at the time of the first resistance, there were 2,700 owners of over 100 hectares, including 244 owners of over 500 hectares. At the other end of the scale there were 86,000 peasant families with less than a hectare and hundreds of thousands of others who had nothing at all. The Delta is the country's rice basket and used to feed itself and Saigon, supply rice to the North in exchange for coal, and provide an average of about a million tons a year for export abroad. It also had fruit, coconuts, fish and a valuable charcoal industry of a million tons a year, a major source of fuel for Saigon and other urban centers.

During the war against the French, the land of absentee landlords—many of whom had acquired French nationality, as was the fashion in those days—was taken over and distributed to poor or landless peasants. In cases where landlords stayed on and did not collaborate with the French, rents were substantially reduced and old debts were canceled. About 350,000 of a total of 1,684,000 hectares of rice fields were distributed. Of the big landowners, only about five per cent continued to draw rents.

Diem worked out a scheme with his American adviser on "land reform," Ladejinsky, to get this land back again. At a "landlords-peasants" conference in Saigon in September 1956, the landlords demanded reinstatement, with rents fixed at 33 per cent of crops. The plan, subsequently approved, was to force peasants on the distributed land to sign contracts under which they would pay amounts ranging from 15 to 25 per cent of their crops in rent, but as the pro-Diem Saigon paper *Tu Do* (Liberty) reported on March 3, 1960: "The contracts fixed rents at 25 per cent but in fact the landlords were levying 45 to 50 per cent as in the old days with no reduction even when the crops were bad." Moreover, they tried to squeeze out back payments for all those years when no rent had been paid and put the peasants back into debt for generations.

Naturally the peasants resisted this, refusing to put their thumbmarks on documents and even if they were forced into this, they refused to pay the exorbitant rents and taxes. So the tax and rent collectors were escorted by police and army units. Among other schemes adopted was one to force owners to sell land in excess of 100 hectares—which did not affect Diem's land-owning friends in Central Vietnam—to make a pool of land available for sale to the landless peasantry. But this was at exorbitant prices, entailing repayments at the rate of a ton of rice per year per hectare for six years, which no peasant could afford, whereas the landlords were paid out in cash and government bonds and encouraged to invest in industry. By July 1960, four years after the decree on forced sale of property over 100 hectares was signed, only 90,000 hectares of land had been purchased by 41,000 peasant families—and the Saigon press could announce that 18 big landlords had invested some seven million piastres in industrial shares.

For the peasants—whether the extortions were in the form of rents, part payments, interest payments or back debts—the

results were the same. The bad old days were there again, the
rent and tax collectors with the police and army at their beck
and call. The seeds for the classic form of a peasants' uprising,
resistance to the rent and tax collectors, were sown by the U.S.-
Diemist land policy and fertilized by the ferocious hunt to wipe
out any who had taken part in the resistance struggle. Diem
correctly estimated that those who had led the struggle against
the French colonialist and local landowners in the Delta would
probably lead a struggle against his own feudal land policies
and his U.S. backers.

Nguyen Tu Quang, now a member of the Liberation Front's
Executive Committee for An Xuyen province (formerly Ca Mau,
the extreme southern tip of the Mekong Delta) gave me some
details of how the Front was formed in his area. "People were
desperate by 1959. They had tried all forms of legal struggle,
individual petitions to the National Assembly as well as to provincial and district organs. Everything fell on deaf ears. As individual actions failed, they started collective struggle, deputations
of a whole hamlet or group of hamlets to local authorities, but
the more the protests the severer the repressions. It came to the
point where patriotic elements could no longer remain at home;
they fled to the forest to find other means of carrying on the
struggle. These included a real cross section of the population
—handicraft workers, small business people, schoolteachers and
other intellectuals, as well as peasants. There in the forests a
national front of patriots fleeing persecution came into being
spontaneously. We put our heads together as to how to fight
back."

Nguyen Tu Quang himself was a tailor and also had to flee
to the forest.

"At 3 A.M. on February 13, 1960," Quang continued, "junks
and sampans started converging on the market at the Cai Nouc
district center. They were laden not only with the usual pigs,
chickens and goats, but with people from all over the district.
Khue, the district commissioner, a real brute of a man, had his
offices overlooking the market, but he fled when he saw at dawn
the big crowd that had assembled. The police commissioner mo-
bilized all the police and with batons drawn, they ordered the

crowd to disperse. We refused—we were around 4,000 by then
—and locked arms when the police tried to lash out and arrest
people. A couple of hundred soldiers were called out and together with the police they started making arrests. The whole
crowd, together with the local market people, marched to the
jail with the arrested people, kicked in the doors and released
those arrested and others held from previous arrests. The troops
were ordered to fix bayonets and charge. They couldn't charge
because the crowd was too thick, but they stabbed at the legs
of the women in the front ranks; some were badly stabbed, but
they continued marching, blood streaming down their legs. The
police commissioner ordered the troops to fire on the crowd,
but the soldiers shouted to us: 'Keep your heads down and we'll
fire high.' So we lay down and they fired over our heads. There
was a stalemate for a while; Chinese merchants and restaurant
owners brought us tea and food. We kept shouting our demands
to see Khue and eventually he had to appear as the troops continued to refuse instructions to attack us. Furious as he was, Khue
had to promise in front of the whole crowd that he would forward our petition to the government.

"We doubted he would do it, but as a morale-builder for the
people it was highly successful. We had some wounded, but
we had freed people from the jail, humiliated Khue and staged
a demonstration which we knew would soon become known all
over the province. It had a big effect on the troops. A couple of
dozen deserted on the spot and went home in the boats with their
own people. It showed what could be done by a bit of mass action and some of us began to think what could be done if such
actions were on a provincial or a country-wide scale. The idea
of a big, national front was ripening not only in our minds
by that time but, as we knew later, in the minds of our compatriots all over the country.

"It was the beginning of political-military warfare. If troops
started to trespass, they were warned: 'The Viet Cong came and
planted traps around our homes and gardens. Stay away from
them.' That was a political act. If the enemy trespassed and
fell into a trap, that was a military action. 'Didn't we warn
you?' people would say. That was another political act. They

would then help bind up his wounds, give him tea, another political act. When the Front was formed, this political-military form of struggle was greatly developed."

THE RELIGIOUS SECTS

An important factor in the formation of the Front, especially its military arm, was the existence of remnants of the armed religious sects. After Diem drove the Binh Xuyen out of Saigon, he turned on the Cao Daists, using military pressures and U.S.-financed bribes to win over the military chiefs. Later he used the chief Cao Daist general, Tran Minh The, to make a treacherous attack on the Binh Xuyen in their jungle hide-out, having refused an offer to merge their forces with Diem's. During the action, Diemist agents shot The in the back of the head. The main Hoa Hao military leaders, Ba Cut and Nam Lua, after their forces had been defeated in battle, agreed to rally to Diem. On their way to a rendezvous to arrange this, they were captured by Diemist agents and beheaded. Diem thought he had been very clever, but for the rank and file in all the sects these were very sharp lessons. They were not very well up on politics, but treachery was something they understood, double-faced treachery of this kind, even more so. They had not been consulted about mergers with the Diem forces, but the manner in which their leaders had betrayed them and been betrayed themselves turned the rank and file of the sects against their traditional chiefs and Diem at the same time.

By now, the remnants of the armed sects were in the Mekong Delta; the Cao Daists and Binh Xuyen in the Plain of Reeds near the Cambodian frontier, the Hoa Hao further south. Former resistance cadres made contact with them. The sects often lived on semi-banditry; they had no money and supplies, only arms, and used these to pillage the peasantry. The resistance people started to help them with shelter and food, and later with clothes, and brought their dispersed forces together, always stressing the prime importance of being at one with the people and never opposed to them. The Liberation Army was eventually formed partly on the basis of a merger of the rank and file of the forces from the three sects under the leadership of reliable, proven cadres of the first resistance war.

An important step in forging a national Front, was the creation in early 1960 of the Association of Ex-Resistance Members, formed by those who had survived the Diemist extermination machine. The Association later developed into the People's Revolutionary Party. I was able to meet one of the founders of this Association, a burly, middle-aged veteran revolutionary, Tran Nam Trung, who is now vice president of the FNL, assistant general secretary of the PRP and represents the Liberation Army on the Front's presidium. He is, in fact, the Liberation Front's military chief.

"When we were not using force to resist the unrestrained violence of the enemy," said Tran Nam Trung, "the U.S.-puppets showed all their ferocity and inflicted enormous losses on us. But once we found, and used, a correct form of struggle we learned they were not as strong and invincible as they seemed. After we took the decision to form the National Front, to stand up and fight back, our losses were less. The enemy was really terrible when he could use unlimited violence against a passive, unarmed enemy.

"We realized we had to face up to something new, the 'special warfare' as laid down by the U.S. No. 1 military theoretician, General Maxwell Taylor, and we soon came to the conclusion that just as formerly we could not fight with political means alone, we could not now fight with military means alone. We needed a combined military-political form of struggle. The great majority of people by the end of 1959 were united in wanting to overthrow the U.S.-Diemist regime. And while the relation of forces did not permit us to try and overthrow power at the center, the peasants did rise up in 1960-61 and in armed struggle seized power from the reactionary representatives of central power in the countryside. There was in fact a local and partial peasants' uprising.

"We use the term 'armed struggle'," Trung said, a smile fleeting over his powerful, rather somber face, "but when the people rose up, they had no arms; they used hoes, knives, agricultural implements, jungle weapons, even billets of wood—but in the hands of people burning with hatred against the enemy, even these were powerful weapons. In 1960, counting what weapons the sects had, there were less than 1,000 firearms at our disposal in the whole of South Vietnam. But planes, tanks and artillery were powerless to suppress the uprising. Although it was the peasants who rose up, they had the support of other sections of the population.

"It is worth noting," he continued, "but probably strange for a westerner to grasp, that our peasants and workers, our rank and file people are politically very mature, more mature than our bourgeoisie. This is different in the West where the bourgeoisie is more experienced than the masses in political and organizational forms. In South Vietnam the bourgeoisie is not yet highly organized, with a definite political line. They are split into many groups. In ideology and organization they are on a much lower level than the ordinary people. This is specific not only for South Vietnam we think, but for other developing countries which have learned through suffering and have correct political leadership. I say this because it may seem strange to you that it was the peasants who were in the forefront of the struggle and the urban workers and intellectuals, plus a part of the bourgeoisie who supported them. Don't forget that for a long time in our country, there were only peasants and landlords and a mandarin ruling class formed, by and large, from the sons of landlords. As far as state power is concerned, this sort of situation in our days can be resolved in two ways. If a country is broadly democratic the people can come out on top. Otherwise it can degenerate into fascism. And if the colonialists or neo-colonialists intervene, it will always be in favor of the fascist solution, as we have seen here in South Vietnam.

"But the most outstanding feature of the struggle here," said Trung, concluding this part of our conversation, "is that the USA is employing a very special type of warfare and we are using a very special type of struggle to counter it. Perhaps it was unfortunate for the USA that they chose South Vietnam for their first such experiment. We have been fighting for 20 years; we know how to wage political struggles and also how to combine political-military struggles."

About the time the Association of Former Resistance Members was formed, a number of other organizations were also set up—peasants associations, workers associations and others representing youth, women, students, writers and theater workers, and so on. The Buddhists were suffering considerable persecution by that time, and also Catholic peasants and fishermen who had been tricked into leaving the North in 1954-55 under an impression created by Diem's psychological warfare advisers that the Virgin Mary had deserted North Vietnam for the South and the "infidels" that remained would be wiped out by nuclear bombs. The Catholic émigrés were being shot down and imprisoned for demanding either repatriation to the North again or fulfillment of pledges to provide them with homes and land or jobs. Buddhists and émigré Catholics were enthusiastic supporters of forming a broad front to fight for basic democratic rights, as were the religious sects, the Khmer and other ethnic minority groups, and the various associations which had mushroomed into existence.

NATURE OF THE FRONT

So a Front was formed and its composition reflected all the forces in South Vietnamese society that Diem and Dulles between them had alienated, including elements they could have had on their side had they shown a minimum of realism.

"The Front," said Nguyen Huu Tho, who was still in a Diemist jail when it was set up, "unites all political tendencies, all religions, all sections and classes of the population. Intellectuals are widely represented in the Central Committee. Saigon has its secret representatives and exiles abroad also." Among the leaders with him when we had our first meeting, were a Catholic priest and high dignitaries of the Buddhist and Cao Dai religions, an architect, a pharmaceutical chemist, a journalist, the commander-in-chief of the Binh Xuyen armed forces, and a peasant. Among those I met elsewhere were another lawyer—apart from Nguyen Huu Tho—a radio engineer, a writer and dramatist, a journalist, a woman schoolteacher, a professional revolutionary, and a chief of the Rhade ethnic minority who represented the tribespeople of the Tay Nguyen. I did not meet one of the vice presidents, a doctor of medicine who was ill, or two representatives of the Khmer community who were travelling in the Khmer minority areas, or a leading Buddhist dignitary who was outside the country. A high proportion of the Front leaders had been in the Saigon-Cholon Committee in Defense of Peace and the Geneva Agreements.

The common factor which united them was a determination to overthrow the regime in Saigon and to set up one which would end foreign intervention and guarantee a minimum of democratic liberties. The immediate task was to coordinate the various resistance activities which had started spontaneously and sporadically; to organize armed forces and place military activities under a centralized command; to stimulate and direct a national liberation movement. A more detailed program was worked out when the NFL held its first congress in February-March 1962. It provided for independence and neutrality in foreign affairs, diplomatic relations with all states, and foreign aid from all who would give it without strings, and moderate reform policies in internal affairs.*

"Our program reflects the broad nature of the Front and the forces represented in it," Nguyen Huu Tho said. "We are in favor of land to the peasants for instance, but not systematic confiscation; we are for reduction of rents but for the maintenance of present property rights except in the case of traitors. Landlords who have not supported the U.S. puppets have nothing to fear. We respect the economic liberty of industrial and economic enterprises, legitimate property rights of foreigners and to a certain extent we are not opposed to foreign investments. Above all, the Front stands for democratic liberties, freedom of speech, assembly and movement, and in our liberated areas these basic freedoms do really exist. People elect those in whom they have confidence and run their own affairs in a most democratic way. The Front had the immediate support from all patriotic forces from the moment it was formed."

* For detailed report of the congress and the program *see,* Burchett, *The Furtive War,* Chapter V.

The Front's armed forces were of three types: self-defense guerillas, regional guerillas and regular army. Self-defense guerillas are local village units, usually peasants by day and guerillas by night. Their primary task is to defend their own villages but also to carry out road destruction and neutralize enemy forces in the immediate vicinity of their villages. They usually rely a good deal on rudimentary arms, including a great variety of traps. Regional troops are on a more permanent basis, drawn from the region, perhaps a province or several provinces, which they are assigned to defend. Their job is to deal with enemy forces stationed in their region; to pin them down, harass or frustrate their operations. The regular army, based largely at first on the fusion of the remnants of the forces of the armed of this that the USA decided to intervene by launching "special new blood from the peasantry, was to deal with the enemy's mobile reserves and carry out military operations of their own, destruction of posts, counter "mopping up" operations, and so on.

As the Tua Hai and other operations showed by the time the Front was formed, it already had the nucleus of its armed forces and able leaders to direct them. Throughout 1961, there were peasant uprisings all over the country, mainly taking the form of cleaning the Diemist officials out of their villages and setting up local, elected bodies. "The great thing," said Tran Nam Trung, "was that the peasants rose up and became the real masters of the countryside; they could end for all time the type of repression suffered in the preceding years. The greater part of Saigon authority was disrupted. The peasants returned from the 'prosperity zones' [predecessors of the "strategic hamlets"] and started to till their old fields again and replant their orchards and this time they decided to defend their gains, arms in hand. Guerillas were organized in every village, constituting a vast, country-wide guerilla movement.

"In 1961," continued Trung, "before Diem started the 'strategic hamlets' scheme inside the liberated areas, we had approached Saigon and other urban centers; our forces were right alongside the strategic highways."

By that time, Diem was in very great danger. It was because sects but which grew rapidly later with generous infusions of

Laboratory in a
front-line hospital
of the NFL.

This portable X-Ray, "Made in USA,"
is used in a field hospital.

A training school for Liberation Front cadre at the Education Department
of the Commission for Culture, Information and Education,
an embryo ministry in fact.

(Above) In the printing shop of the Education Department.

(Left) The AUTHOR and a member of village self-defense corps. Note his shirt of parachute nylon.

Part of the Central Liberation Front Ensemble.

warfare" in South Vietnam within the framework of the Staley-Taylor plan. The principal points of the plan were:

(1) To create a no-man's land along the 17th parallel, and along the frontiers with Laos and Cambodia, by destroying all villages there and using air-sprayed chemicals to destroy the jungle, and thus isolate the liberated areas from the outside world.

(2) To set up 16,000 "strategic hamlets" into which two-thirds of the whole population of the South would be concentrated. By doing that, they calculated to isolate all the resistance forces from the population.

(3) Once the above two measures were completed there would be a general military offensive to wipe out all organized resistance forces.

The first part of the plan was to have been completed by the end of 1962, but things worked out somewhat differently, despite the setting up of a U.S. military command in Saigon under General Paul Harkins and the gradual build-up of some 25,000 U.S. military "advisers" and "instructors" in South Vietnam.

TUG OF WAR

If 1961 was a "Front year" in terms of territory and population gained, 1962 however must be largely credited to Saigon. With U.S. aid in men and materials pouring in from the end of 1961, a major effort was made to destroy and isolate the Front's armed forces, to push Front influence back from the gates of Saigon and other provincial capitals and to re-install Diemist power in the countryside. The use of helicopters and amphibious tanks to increase rapidity of movement and to avoid the devastating ambushes that the Diemist troops invariably fell into when they moved by road or river, caught the guerillas off balance at first. High mobility is something new in guerilla warfare—America's only "special warfare" tactical innovation. The drive to set up "strategic hamlets" was also a problem for NFL organizers and an additional hardship for the population.

Set up under the guns of military posts, swathed in several

rows of barbed wire or bamboo palisades with mine-filled moats
in between and a fantastic system of espionage and controls inside, the "strategic hamlet" represented Diem's maximum hope
of reimposing his control in the countryside. It was a scheme
which had total U.S. support and billions of dollars were spent.
It seemed an unequal and impossible struggle, with helicopter-
borne troops swooping down to encircle small groups of partisans
of whom only half or less usually had firearms; convoys of heavily armed troops in amphibious tanks or landing craft escorted
by gunboats along the rivers and canals of the Mekong Delta to
scoop people up like fish in a net and dump them into "strategic
hamlets"; setting up garrison posts every few kilometers to control them; planes overhead all the time seeking out targets for
their own bombs and machine guns, or groups of peasants who
had evaded the barbed wire and would be targets for helicoptered
troops.

The "strategic hamlet" scheme looked very efficient on paper,
as a means of preventing contact between villagers and resistance
leaders. One fatal weakness was that it turned even the most
passive and resigned among the population against Saigon. People were forced to abandon villages and soil they had tilled
for generations, abandon the graves of their ancestors—a very
serious thing in Asia. They had to watch while Diemist troops
hacked down their fruit trees, filled in their fish ponds and
burned their homes if they did not move voluntarily or quickly
enough into the concentration camp compounds. Freedom of
movement was ended; peasants could only move outside the
barbed wire to till fields immediately around the perimeter of
the compounds and only in daylight hours; controlled and
searched as they left the heavily guarded gateway, they were
always at the mercy of armed hoodlums.

Although it was difficult for Front organizers to penetrate
them, the "strategic hamlets" were rich soil in which to sow
resistance seeds once contact was made, a soil fertilized by the
total hatred of the inmates towards the Diemist regime and its
U.S. backers. Everywhere people fought against being concentrated and where they were concentrated they fought to break
out again.

By early 1962, the peasants all over South Vietnam were aware that large-scale armed resistance was well under way, and this was a business they understood. A tug-of-war struggle developed with the main Saigon effort directed at setting up the 16,000 "strategic hamlets" as called for by the Staley-Taylor plan, and the main Front effort aimed at frustrating this plan and helping the people dismantle those which Saigon succeeded in setting up.

One of the very first "strategic hamlets" in Central Vietnam was set up at Ky-Lô in Dong Xuan district of Phu Yen. Le Van Chien, a very high cadre of the NFL, member of a zonal executive committee for the whole of Central Vietnam, told me that the Front attached great importance to dismantling this particular hamlet because of the effect it would have on morale, "the enemy's and ours," as he put it.

"The difficulty was how to get in," said Chien, a stocky, grey-haired veteran in his early sixties, one of the oldest Front cadres I met. "We had no guerilla base in that district and it was exceptionally heavily fortified and guarded. Because it was a pilot project, the Diemists had also selected the toughest, roughest hoodlums to run it. We knew the gate opened at 7 AM and the buffalo were taken out first, boys on their backs in the traditional way. After taking the beasts to pasture, the boys returned to the compound for their early morning meal. We selected the youngest looking of our lads and when the buffalo boys came outside, we persuaded them to change clothes and it was our lads who went back in, in units of ten. The sleepy-eyed guards paid no attention; our lads went straight to the administrative headquarters, where the Diemist big-shots were still asleep and rounded them all up; we had a fairly complete dossier on every one of them. They were really a prize lot, 13 altogether. People started tumbling out of their houses and could hardly believe it when they saw their oppressors, looking very sorry for themselves, tied up and very meek and begging the chance to apologize to the people and ask their mercy.

"The people hugged and kissed us, tears streaming down their cheeks and a big meeting was arranged on the spot. First of all they started denouncing the crimes of the Diemists. They had lists of villagers who had been killed and tortured and the agents responsible, which coincided fairly exactly with our own dossiers. They wanted us to kill all 13, but in fact we executed four, another five we sentenced to prison terms and four who freely admitted their crimes on the spot and promised to repent, we set free. The local Diemist garrison, which had no stomach for a fight, surrendered and we took their arms. With the help of some nominated by the people at the public meeting, we drew up a land reform document, in the name of the NFL, and agreed on how many hectares were available for distribution. How it was to be distributed, we left them to decide, a special committee being elected for the purpose. But in the document it was stipulated that landless and poor peasants must have priority. In discussions between peasants and landlords, we established a fair scale of rents. Taxes and back debts were abolished. A self-defense unit was elected and we passed the captured arms over to them.

"Our calculations were correct and news of this soon spread. People in 13 other 'strategic hamlets' in the same district rose up without any help from us, dismantled the barbed wire and palisades, went back to their original villages and set up self-defense units. That was early in 1962. In March of that year, the Diemists launched their first famous Sea Swallow operation with a whole division and boasted they would wipe out the 'Viet Cong' within a month. They did succeed in herding people back into some of the hamlets. But the people destroyed them again as soon as they withdrew.

"In November 1963," he concluded with a broad grin, "the Saigon command launched campaign No. 55, the fifty-fifth since operation Sea Swallow. They got nowhere. And since they launched their first campaign, we have set up a solid guerilla base in the coastal area and others in every district throughout the province. All their north-south road and rail communications pass through our base. We can blow up their trains at will, but we attack only those carrying troops and war material."

The struggle could not develop everywhere as in Phu Yen. Although it had the most unfavorable conditions for guerilla warfare in Central Vietnam, it was a paradise as compared to the flat Mekong Delta, with no mountains at all and forest only in the unpopulated mangrove swamps bordering the coastal areas. During 1962, helicopter-borne troops took a fairly heavy toll of resistance fighters and there was a period when Front leadership almost decided the price was too high, that resistance in the Delta should cease and regular Front armed forces should withdraw to bases in the mountains. "But when we discussed this," one of the military leaders told me, "we realized in the bottom of our hearts that to withdraw from the Delta would mean never to return. It would mean to abandon the most revolutionary region, the foyer of the first uprising against the French in November 1940 and of the first resistance war in 1945. Millions of Delta peasants had vested their confidence in us: to desert them would be a terrible defeat."

It is clear that the situation at the end of 1962 was critical in one sense for the Front. Diem had not been able to set up his 16,000 strategic hamlets but he had set up many thousands and re-established some sort of nominal control in regions which a year previously had been solidly Front-controlled. Accurate figures are hard to obtain but it seems that Diem was able to establish about 8,000 strategic hamlets but never more than 4,000 were in being at any given moment. The "tug-of-war" struggle never ceased. Sometimes the outer fortifications were never completed, sometimes they were destroyed by the peasants themselves the very night on which they were completed, the blame always placed on the "Viet Cong" and with a complaint to the local Diemist authorities: "Why were you not here to protect us." I heard of cases in which hamlets had been destroyed ten or 15 times, the peasants working very slowly to rebuild the hedges and fortifications but working with lightning speed to destroy them and gain a few days or weeks of liberty. In terms of territory and population, Diem made a considerable comeback in 1962; in terms of winning popular support, he lost out heavily. In strictly military terms, the U.S.-Diemist forces registered a number of successes and held the strategic and tactical initiative. But this situation was dramatically reversed in the very first days of 1963.

In planning their "anti-insurgency" tactics, the American Saigon command was able to pool experiences from world-wide

anti-guerilla operations since World War II—from General Van
Fleet's experiences in Greece in 1946 to those of American advisers in the Philippines against the Hukbalahap; the British
in Kenya and Malaya; the Kuomintang in China, not to mention
those of the French in Indo-China and in Algeria, where helicopters were used in anti-guerilla operations for the first time.
But the Liberation Front, through the representatives it was able
to get abroad in a remarkably short time, was also able to draw
on experience from China and Korea to Cuba and Algeria. If
British experiments with concentration camp villages in Malaya
and the French use of *centres de regroupement* and helicopter-
borne troops in Algeria were valuable for the U.S. command,
the development of anti-helicopter tactics by the FLN in Algeria was no less precious for the Liberation Front. So a world
pooling of guerilla and anti-guerilla experiences went into operation in this very special war in South Vietnam.

If 1961 could be considered a "Front year" and 1962 was
"Diem's year," in the tug-of-war for power, the Ap Bac battle
was a good auger for the Front as to whose year 1963 was to be.
That battle, described in detail in Chapter 5, proved to be a
turning point; by the time 1963 was over, there was no longer
a Diemist regime, as things turned out.

PART III

CRISIS IN SAIGON

Chapter 13

VERY SPECIAL WAR

Policy Towards Enemy Soldiers

I was musing over the image of a nearly full moon, framed in the delicate profile of bamboo leaves, glinting in the dark where the moonlight touched them, everything polished and gleaming like a Vietnamese lacquer painting. Suddenly there was a warning signal from our guide; the outboard motor in our little sampan was cut and we veered sharply towards a bamboo thicket on the river bank.

There was the sound of many more outboard motors coming from the opposite direction and this was disquieting. We were supposed to be in "safe" territory. Cigarettes were doused, complete silence ordered. Within a few minutes, the first couple of a long, double line of sampans appeared around a bend about 500 yards distant. They kept rounding the bend until the first couple were only 20 or 30 yards away from our hiding spot. But long before that, we heard the sound of women's voices and as they grew nearer we caught glimpses through the leaves of sampans filled with women and girls. Each was holding a stick with a papered-over frame on which slogans had been printed in red and black; in some the slogans were printed on cloth banners stretched between two sticks across the front of the boats.

Our sampan slid out again into midstream and jocular greetings were exchanged as the outboard motor started up again and we moved on past the convoy. By the way the exchanges were shouted back and forth and the bursts of laughter that followed some of them, it was clear we really were in "safe" territory. "They're off to the district center for a demonstration," explained the interpreter. "About half a dozen villages are represented here, but there are other convoys moving in by road and river from different directions."

"At this time of night?"

"They have to travel at night to avoid planes and they like to be in the town well before dawn, before the authorities are around to give orders."

I asked what the demonstration was about and after a few more exchanges with the boats, he explained that a few days previously a village in the district had been bombed and a new school and library had been wiped out. No one had been killed but they were going to protest about destruction of public property, as the school and library had been built by the villagers themselves. The others were coming "out of solidarity" and to protest against bombings in general. At my request, he translated some of the slogans: Apart from those demanding an end to destruction of "public," "government" and "people's property," there were others such as: "Higher Pay for Our Sons in the Army"; "Regular Leave for Armymen"; "Pensions for Wounded Armymen"; "Compensation for Mothers and Wives of Armymen Killed and Wounded in Action"; "An End to Beatings in the Army."

"But these are people from Liberation Front areas?" I asked.

"Yes," agreed Huynh, my well informed journalist-interpreter.

"And they are demanding higher pay for the soliders that come and shoot them down and burn their villages?"

"That's right," he replied. "First of all the population never admit to being 'Viet Cong.' They all claim to be loyal subjects of Saigon with the right to protection by the 'legal government.' If there are 'Viet Cong' around, this is only because the 'legal' government has run away. Also it is a Front policy to gain the sympathy of the puppet troops. Such slogans also give them the idea that they ought to struggle for better conditions. But as a means of struggle it is also very effective. Troops find it difficult to repress a demonstration when half the slogans demand better conditions for them.

"This is more than just a tactic. The Front has a whole policy for such things. In cases where there are families in our areas whose sons or husbands have been killed while serving with the enemy forces, we help them materially. There is a special organization that visits bereaved families, and recommends what form the material help should take."

We had left the last of the sampans behind by that time and had the river and the moon to ourselves again. I probed Huynh about further illustrations of political strategies and tactics and of combined military-political struggle.

"In many areas," he continued, "there are posts which we could easily wipe out. If the soldiers don't start shooting and plundering but listen to the explanations given by the people, we don't shoot. If they shoot, we shoot, and we win. Almost the whole population, except for the armed forces take part in the explanations. It goes on day and night. In theory, the Saigon troops are forbidden to have any contact with the local population, even their own relatives. In practice there is contact all the time. For the past couple of years, the top brass is so worried by the disaffection rate that garrisons are rotated every three months. But that doesn't help because if they leave one area for another, the people there will continue the good work started at the post they have just left.

"Our people live among the enemy; they have carried out land reform and work for themselves. The enemy troops are peasant conscripts. When they see this free life going on all round them, you think this doesn't have an effect? Especially when it is drummed into them day and night by fellow-peasants, working in the fields right up to the gates of their posts. Our liberated areas sometimes reach within a hundred yards of a post and the garrison has to depend on air-dropped supplies, which fall into our area. We could prevent them collecting those supplies, cut them off completely if we wanted, but we allow two or three to come out and pick them up, although we often take the parachutes ourselves. The troops appreciate this attitude. We always make it clear that we are against Vietnamese killing Vietnamese and so they adopt our live-and-let-live attitude. We understand that they are conscripts who practically have no choice but to serve Diem but who also don't want to die by being forced into combat with us."

When there are holidays the villagers visit the troops, Huynh told me. They are not too cordial towards them, but courteous and explain things to them. "They might even bring some small gifts, fruit or cakes. They will tell them that if they come to the village to stick to the main 'traffic lanes' and if they come without shooting or pillaging everything will be alright, they will be well received and given tea. But if they leave the main tracks and start uninvited towards the houses, the pigsties, poultry yards, orchards, etc., then they will be in for trouble with the traps. And if they start shooting, they will be in for even worse trouble, if not on that particular occasion then certainly the next time they move out of the post. The troops know by bitter experience that this is true.

"The chief of garrison often knows who are the 'activists' in any village. Posts are always built on an elevation; he has good binoculars and can see who sticks up posters or writes slogans on the wall or addresses meetings. But if he is in a position to send in a patrol to interrogate the people they will reply: 'Sure, there are some "Viet Cong" here. Come and arrest them if you like. But in fact they do no harm and if bullets start flying innocent people may get hurt. You might get hurt, too, because it seems they have good military training.' If troops do come and kill someone, the body will be carried to the post and the whole village will turn out in a big protest demonstration. They will let the troops know they are in for real trouble the next time they move out. But the population is well educated by the Front not to stick their necks out, never to provoke trouble, always to be tactful. The villagers make contributions to the Front, usually in rice. But for anything they provide we give them a receipt. They will take these to the post and show them to the troops. 'You see, the "Viet Cong" made a levy last night. They made us pay up. They said this is necessary for the liberation of the country; to get the Americans out. We had to pay, we couldn't help ourselves.' Another little arrow goes home.

"These are important tactics," Huynh continued, "but are only possible because although the people oppose the administrative, political and ideological positions of the Saigon regime, they are still technically in enemy-controlled territory; they have to maintain a correct legal position to keep alive. So we encourage them to tell the officers in the posts all sorts of things. 'Yes,' they will say, 'we have guerillas in our village. My husband is a guerilla. My son is a guerilla. Yes, they have guns.' But when they are asked what is the strength of the unit, where the guns are hidden, this they 'don't know.' Before, people would have been slaughtered for admitting such things. But once the worst of the tyrants were dealt with, this is possible. So we encourage the villagers to pass on certain facts—it is good propaganda—but never to reveal the strength of units or locations of weapons.

"When the armed resistance first started the villagers encouraged their sons to escape from the villages and join the guerillas. The enemy then started shooting the fathers of sons who had disappeared. We countered this by protests, claiming that the Diemists themselves had killed or kidnapped the sons. A mother would sit up half the night, preparing her lad's clothes and food for a few day's journey to the mountains; pack him off in the small hours of the morning and a few hours later lead a delegation of wailing women to the district chief demanding the return of her son who must have been 'arrested.' Or complain about the lack of security in the village when the 'Viet Cong' could come in and 'kidnap' young lads and demand that the post commander send a patrol to 'rescue' him. The people's initiative and ingenuity in such matters has no limits," Huynh said and went on to explain that in virtually every village, including the Saigon-controlled ones, there were special propaganda teams and they exchanged experiences between them as to the most effective way to get the "line" across with the minimum of danger, in the most disarming way possible.

"The enemy knew for instance," he continued, as we lay stretched out under the brilliant stars, the water rippling by and the outboard motor softly puttering away, "that virtually everybody in the village takes part in making traps. When they are charged with this, they will speak up: 'Yes, the "Viet Vong" make us do that. We have to do it.' If they are asked where they are, they will show one or two, but not the main ones. They will show some spikes, for instance. 'These are rejects,' they will say. 'The "Viet Cong" refused to pay for these. All the best ones they have taken away.' They can reply like this because of our strength now. But even before, when there were all sorts of acts of savagery, from indiscriminate killings to plunder and

acts of hooliganism, the people took advantage of their legal
position and based themselves on what was declared official
policy. They would go to district chiefs and accuse their underlings of acting 'contrary to Saigon policy' and demand that complaints be forwarded to the National Assembly and even
government ministers. Quite a few officials had to be withdrawn
because of this and it had a chastening effect on the others. But
the real breakthrough came when the people themselves started
punishing the worst of the bullies.

"This sort of work never lets up," Huynh said, "and it helps
to compensate a lot for the enemy's overwhelming superiority
in arms." He recalled that before the armed resistance had become general, he had worked for a time in the coastal plains
area of Central Vietnam. "At that time we had no arms at all,"
he said, "but we knew the tribespeople in the hills had started
to defend themselves. Punitive expeditions used to pass through
our areas on the way to the mountains and people used to work
on the troops, warning them in the most tactful way possible
not to start committing atrocities against the tribespeople: 'We
know them,' some old chap would say. 'They are proud, cour-
ageous people; if you do anything wrong they will certainly kill
you. They have terrible traps full of spikes and poison arrows
that make you suffer terribly for a few minutes and then you
are dead. A pity for fine young chaps like you. We only give
you a friendly warning because we are Vietnamese.' And when
they came back again, carrying their wounded and with plenty
of them not coming back at all, our people would be full of
sympathy, tend their wounds, give them tea and make plenty
of remarks: 'What did we tell you? Better never go into those
places. Keep away from their villages or you'll all be killed.'
It was the best sort of propaganda," Huynh concluded, as our
sampan headed into a little cove, "because it was true."

MONKEYS AND BEES

The question of original and ingenius forms of propaganda
was one which cropped up all the time. On one occasion, I had

been talking with some tribespeople about their hunting methods
and Kpy Plui, a famous Jarai hunter from Kontum province,
after an exciting account of how his people hunted tigers and
elephants, came to the less dangerous business of the monkey
hunt. Once a monkey colony is discovered, usually in a dense
grove of bamboo on a slope, big converging swathes of bamboo
are cut out at each side, leading up from the bottom so the
monkeys are concentrated in a triangular-shaped patch. Another
swathe is cut out at the tip of the triangle: While the "hunters"
start hacking their way into the triangle itself, working their
way down from the top, the rest of the village turns out with
gongs and drums and start working their way up from the base
of the triangle; the terrified monkeys, with an ever diminishing
number of bamboo stems and branches to swing from, are concentrated into an ever smaller place. "They will break off bits
of branches to fight back and chatter and jump about," said,
Kpy Plui, a compact, muscular figure with high cheekbones and
a wisp of black beard, "but the noise continues from the bottom
and bamboo and undergrowth is hacked down from the top.
Eventually the old man of the tribe comes down to earth,
and that means the whole tribe has surrendered. All the rest
then come down and we can just pick them up as we like, 500
to a thousand and more." I wondered what they did with such
a quantity of monkeys.

"We keep them in cages," said Kpy Plui, who spoke some
French from having served for a brief period in the French
army, "and eat them as needed. The bones are boiled down for
medicine. But the bigger ones, we hand over to the cadres for
their propaganda teams." A Vietnamese cadre who was present
explained that medicines against anaemia and impotence were
developed from the monkey bones.

"And what about the propaganda aspect?" I asked.

"We choose the biggest ones, about 30 to 45 pounds. We
dress them up in black pants and shirts, color their faces up
a bit to make them look like caricatures of Diem in his time,
or it might be Harkins, draw more caricatures on the back of
their shirts, tie slogans to their legs and smuggle them into

Saigon and provincial capitals. We turn them loose around the market place early in the morning, or in main centers as people are going to work. The monkeys are a bit puzzled at first, but then they start leaping around with their slogans. People are delighted as they always are with monkeys and the police don't know what to do. It is awkward shooting at them, because it is like shooting at the President or Harkins. Anyway it would be ridiculous to shoot them. They start chasing around trying to catch the monkeys and rip off the slogans and the more they chase them the more the people enjoy the spectacle.

"It is a very good form of propaganda but useful for other things, too. In the market places no more than three people can get together normally. The police will arrest them, even if they have only gathered around because of an argument or some bargaining. But when the monkeys are jumping and the police after them, people can get together and our propaganda teams can move into action. Sometimes we do the same thing with dogs, but they are much easier to catch. We also prepare little rafts made from banana palm trunks lashed together, with caricatures and slogans stuck up on little masts and release hundreds of them to float down rivers that pass through provincial and district centers. The police have to make extraordinary efforts to round them up so the people have double entertainment again."

Even lowlier creatures than dogs and monkeys figure in the fantastic arsenal of weapons the people of South Vietnam are using—and not only for propaganda—in this nuclear-age war. There are Front-controlled villages—in Mo Gay district of Ben Tre province, for instance—the defense of which are primarily entrusted to bees. Chi Nguyet (Sister Moonlight), another of those flawlessly beautiful girls from Ben Tre, explained how from 1960 on, the Diemists had tried to convert her village into a strategic hamlet. "A lot of us women and girls went in protest to the provincial capital, but we were all arrested," she said. "Then all the women of the village came to Ben Tre with their children, demanding our release. They kicked up such a row that the governor was glad to get rid of us all. The Diemist troops kept coming to our village, stealing pigs and chickens and always trying to force us to build fences and dig moats. We refused.

"In our area, as in many others, there is a specially big fierce type of bee. They are more than twice as big as ordinary bees; they don't store honey, but their sting is terribly painful and the sting of half a dozen can be fatal. We studied the habits of these bees very carefully. They always have four sentries on permanent duty and if these are disturbed or offended, they call out the whole hive to attack whatever disturbs them. So we set up some of these hives in the trees alongside the road leading from the Diemist post to our village. We covered them over with sticky paper, from which strings led to a bamboo trap we set on the road. The next time an enemy patrol came, they disturbed the trap and the paper was torn from the hive. The bees attacked immediately; the troops ran like mad buffalo and started falling into our spiked traps. They went back carrying and dragging their wounded.

"From the post, they must have radioed for help, because the district chief sent a company by road from another post and some more by helicopter. By that time we had set up quite a few more hives. When the enemy came, they saw piles of dirt that looked like freshly dug traps so the officer ordered the troops to clear away the earth and uncover the traps. But the hives were hidden under the earth and there was a terrible commotion when they were disturbed in such a rough way. They attacked, many hundreds of them, and in no time at all, 30 enemy troops were out of action. They had to withdraw again.

"We were very encouraged by this and started to rear the bees specially for our defenses. When I left," she concluded, "we had over 200 hives and the enemy had not dared come near us for a long time."

When I met Sister Moonlight she was far from her native village, taking part in a regional conference where experiences of such ususual types of warfare were being exchanged to see to what extent they could be applied in other areas. The use of monkey propagandists and bee garrisons are further illustration of just what a "people's war" entails. I doubt that any general staff in the world, including that of the Liberation Front, could plan from on top the employment of such weapons. It is the grass roots nature of the struggle in South Vietnam that produces them. But once they are developed and used successfully, the word quickly passes round and they are used extensively.

The political and military aspects of the struggle go hand in hand at every level. Writers, journalists and art workers, for instance, take part in military and political activities almost simultaneously. After putting on a show realistically portraying the technique of dismantling a strategic hamlet, the actors will take off with the audience—come illegally from an enemy-controlled village—and re-enact in real life what they have just portrayed on the stage by helping the villagers tear down the hedges and barbed wire. If there is armed opposition they will drop their stage trappings for their guns; if there is none they will probably put on a new show during a pause in the work to depict how a strategic hamlet is transformed into a fortified one.

I met these groups many times in my travels; their instruments and stage trappings on their backs, cheerful young men and women, everyone of them with a gun, sometimes carrying sick members of the troupe with them. Their first job on arriving anywhere for a performance is to dig protective trenches for themselves. They take part in military operations, often giving a show just before it starts to pep up morale; then into the fray with their guns. Tran Huu Trang, president of the Writers and Theater Workers Association, himself a well-known writer and dramatist and a member of the Liberation Front's Central Committee, told me that members of the Association, arms in hand, took part in all major attacks and that: "Their first job, once a post has been penetrated, is to make for the paper supplies and carry off as much as possible. Shortage of paper is a major and constant problem for us."

Journalists also collect their stories of military operations while actually taking part themselves and almost literally work "with a pen in one hand and a rifle in the other." A pig-tailed girl who was introduced to me as Sister Thien—not her real name because her family is still in Saigon and she goes in herself from time to time—told me something of the difficulties of a student paper which she helps edit. "For a long time we printed secretly in the center of Saigon itself," she said, "right in Diemist printing shops. But things got too hot, so we bought a printing plant and smuggled it out of Saigon into the jungle."

"You smuggled it out of Saigon?" I asked, knowing that Saigon is probably the most tightly controlled city in the world today, with military and police patrols on round-the-clock duty and secret police at almost every street corner.

"Yes," she said with a cheery smile, "we took the whole thing to pieces. The type was taken out on the backs of scores of 'market women'—actually they were us girl students—in baskets topped off with unsold fruit and vegetables. The rollers were a bit of a problem, but we greased them well and attached them to the bottoms of sampans. They had a long ride in the water, but later they cleaned up alright. We shipped the whole thing out right under the noses of the flics. Our problem before was to print in Saigon and smuggle copies out into the countryside. Now it is the opposite; we print outside and smuggle the copies into the city. We publish 5,000 copies and once they get down to our 'letter boxes,' our liaison workers, they are distributed and pass from hand to hand until virtually every student reads them. It is a very popular paper and our main correspondents are the students themselves who smuggle articles out by the same network we use to smuggle the paper in. Of course we keep changing the communication channels in case of a slip up. But so far there have been none."

WAR ON FOOD CROPS

One of the means devised by the U.S. command for its "special war" is the use of air-sprayed chemical against food crops—to destroy where they cannot control. I saw plenty of evidence of this—entire orchards where the trees were bare of leaves or fruit when those in neighboring villages were flourishing and heavy with fruit; of papaya trees, for instance, which were mere withered stalks with fruit shrivelled to the size of walnuts clinging drooped around leafless trunks; of pineapples shrunk to the size of small oranges whereas those of neighboring gardens were full grown and ready to be harvested. I did not, however, personally witness any attacks nor was I in those areas of the Mekong Delta where attacks are most frequent. But I was able to interview a South Vietnamese woman scientist, Dr. Thuy Ba, a member of the Executive Committee of the South Vietnam Liberation Women's Association, head of a big hospital and Secretary General of the Association for Defense of Mothers and Children. She had made a special study of the chemical warfare problem, mainly in order to plan protective measures.

"Although these poisons are aimed primarily at food crops and livestock," said Dr. Thuy Ba, a sensitive-faced young woman, who like many of her colleagues had left a comfortable home and practice in Saigon for the rude conditions in the jungle, "they also seriously affect human beings, especially children and old people. Three thousand children were affected in the Ca Mau area in the first two months of 1964 alone. The main symptoms are skin burns, diarrhea and pulmonary complaints. Since the beginning of the year the enemy has greatly stepped up its campaign virtually all over the Mekong Delta.

"Our Public Health Committee has worked out some counter-measures," she continued. "We don't have any gas masks but we use handkerchiefs soaked in water and held over mouth and nose to reduce and filter the amount inhaled. We use lemon juice on skin burns. Smaller children are wrapped up in nylon sheeting when a spraying attack starts and others are taught to run up wind from the spraying areas. The enemy pretends they are spraying insecticides or only 'defoliage' agents, but in fact they are out to destroy food crops in the areas they cannot control. In Ca Mau, for instance, after they withdrew from a large number of posts following the anti-Diem coup, they started systematic destruction of rice crops and orchards in the whole area from which they withdrew, and this activity gathers momentum every day. It was intensified still more after Nguyen Khanh took over. Probably," concluded Dr. Thay Ba, "because they find it more and more difficult to carry on the war by normal means now that the puppet troops have lost all will to fight."

Occasionally the curtain of secrecy with which the Americans cloak the more ruthless of their activities, is ripped aside and the outside world gets a brief glimpse of the truth. Thus on March 19, 1964, Saigon troops, with U.S. "advisers" directing the operation, attacked the Cambodian village of Chantrea. After a preliminary napalm bombing, in which several children were burned to death, a dozen tanks trundled in, crushing under their treads any who could not flee in time. Thirteen villagers were crushed, shot or burned to death. "Sorry, we thought you were Vietnamese," was the laconic excuse of the Americans on the spot, while the U.S. State Department tried to deny that any Americans were involved. Later the State Department had to concede the "presence" but not the "participation" of Americans.

Even more horrifying and significant was the confirmation of Dr. Thuy Ba's charges of chemical warfare. M. Huot Sambath, the Cambodian Minister of Foreign Affairs, revealed that between June 13 and July 23, 1964, U.S. planes had dumped "toxic powder" on six villages in the Cambodian province of Rattankiri, killing 76 people, many of them children. The State Department countered that only "herbiage defoliant" was being used and the Cambodian villages had been sprayed by mistake.

The latest information I was able to obtain before leaving the Liberated areas was that new methods of crop destruction were being tried out, including the dropping of eggs of certain types of insects that attacked rice in the water and the use of white phosphorous in napalm containers, the napalm often having little effect in rice fields that remain water-logged even during the harvesting period.

Asian opinion will be shocked at the spectacle of the USA solemnly taking part in world conferences on how to raise food production in underdeveloped countries while their military chiefs in Saigon are doing their best to poison and burn the rice crops in one of the greatest food-producing areas in the world.

So it goes on. A ceaseless, relentless battle waged for the minds of everyone from soldiers to students; from peasants to government officials and career army officers, with never a trick left unplayed. And this battle, the Front is winning hands down. The Saigon regime has little to offer in return and no real means of counter-attack.

Chapter 14

COUPS IN SAIGON

END OF DIEM REGIME

It was the unbroken series of military defeats since Ap Bac that spelled the doom of the Diemist regime, not the repression of Buddhists and students. For over 12 months, the American press had been more and more openly critical of Diem's ineptitude in handling the war, of his resistance to U.S. strategy and tactics. The mixture of medieval and fascist police methods he used to repress all whom he considered his opponents, for the most part, went unnoticed in the U.S. press, or was reported approvingly. But he was losing the war, and this was a real crime. "Can We Win With Diem?" was the title over one anguished editorial in the *New York Times*, hinting at the shape of things to come. The papers were full of wrangles between Harkins and Diem's top military officers and of Diem's resistance to a complete take-over of military affairs by the Americans. These were the real issues.

The suppression of the Buddhists would have gone unnoticed —it had been going on for years—had it not been for official U.S. dissatisfaction with Diem, plus the fact that the Liberation Front's organization in Saigon went into action. The latter broadened the demand for more religious freedom into one for democratic liberties as a whole, and called out its supporters in vast mass demonstrations which ended in fierce street battles with the police. The size of the demonstrations, the energy and militancy of the crowds, was a great shock to the U.S. command in Saigon. The "Viet Cong" was right amongst them, in Saigon itself, in many tens of thousands, slugging it out with Diem's shock troops.

Diem was not only losing the battle in the countryside; he was losing it in Saigon itself. He had to go. But official U.S. opinion was not unanimous about this. The Pentagon wanted

Diem disciplined, but not out and dead. Harkins in fact was against the coup. His own argument with Diem was on two main points.

Harkins wanted to cut losses; to pull out of hundreds of those encircled posts. He correctly regarded them as "arms supply points" for the Liberation forces; they tied up dozens of his helicopters in daily supply operations. But Diem opposed this; it meant abandoning even nominal control in much of the richest part of the country, because it was precisely from Mekong Delta areas that Harkins proposed withdrawing. Even Harkin's promises to win it back later with the mobile reserves accumulated from the "unemployed" garrisons did not impress Diem. Diem also resisted Harkin's other demand, that U.S. officers should have complete operational control, down to company level, and administrative control at district level—about the extreme limit to which "special war" could be pushed. Harkins was confident that with enough pressures applied, Diem would give way. He was against the coup and in this he was supported by a very mediocre brigadier-general, Nguyen Khanh, who had been rapidly promoted by Diem after he played a vital role in saving the latter in the abortive officers' coup in November 1960. Nguyen Khanh was Harkin's closest friend among the Diemist officers.

The State Department demanded the coup, however, and it was Ambassador Cabot Lodge's role to be at his new post in time to arrange it. The State Department had become convinced that "we cannot win with Diem" and the suppression of the Buddhists and jailings of thousands of students from "respectable" Saigon families was hurting U.S. relations with other Buddhist states. More embarrassing still and decisive for the State Department was that the matter of persecution of the Buddhists was before the United Nations; by the skin of their teeth, American UN officials avoided a vote and had the matter temporarily shelved. But a UN mission of inquiry was already in Saigon. The State Department wanted, needed desperately in fact, to have Diem overthrown and thus liquidate half a dozen embarrassing problems with one coup. So the Buddhist crisis, though not the cause of Diem's downfall, probably fixed the date. Cabot Lodge's "two men in Saigon" were Generals Duong Van Minh and Tran Van Don, both of them southerners as opposed to Centralists like Diem and others with whom leading posts in the army and bureaucracy were staffed.

The CIA, usually so enthusiastic where coups are concerned, was divided about this one. The chief of the CIA in Saigon was against the coup and was subsequently packed off home by Cabot Lodge. Many top CIA men thought Diem was "too good to lose" and from their point of view they were right. Those in the CIA Saigon team who favored the coup had as their man Major General Ton That Dinh, a Centralist feudalist like Diem, a ferocious anti-Communist and, as Diem's Acting Chief of Staff, in a position to move the divisions about.

How the coup was carried out, Ngo Dinh Diem and his notorious brother Nhu murdered, is past history and better known than its background, though it quickly faded out of the world headlines after another more important president fell to an assassin's bullet just ten days later.

In the first month that followed the murder of the Ngo brothers, the guerillas cut great chunks out of all roads leading from Saigon towards the Mekong Delta, turning some sections back into water-logged rice fields. They blew up railway bridges and built dams across canals, planting banana palms and bushes on top of them; cut or blocked all road, rail and river communications, and launched a great campaign to wipe out posts and dismantle strategic hamlets. Virtually all posts in the Delta became dependent on helicopter-borne or parachuted supplies.

By the time some of the communications had been restored, a great number of former strategic villages had been converted into "fortified villages"; posts that used to control them were now controlled themselves, with guns pointing at them from all directions. All the bright predictions after the fall of Diem that "military action will be immediately stepped up" were correct but in a contrary sense to that intended. The initiative was with the Front. Lots of operations were launched by Saigon, true, but they all ended in failure. From the month starting November 25, 1963, the U.S.-Saigon forces launched 180 operations, many of them involving three to seven battalions in Tan

An and Cholon provinces, one of the main gateways to Saigon. In counter-attacks, the guerillas destroyed a dozen posts—20 more had to be abandoned; 82 strategic hamlets were either dismantled and peasants went back to their original villages or were converted into "resistance" villages.

"In that month of November," said President Nguyen Huu Tho, "the Liberation armed forces and the population destroyed 1,662 strategic hamlets; wiped out hundreds of posts; in Cochin-China alone we wiped out or the enemy was forced to abandon 401 posts, including very important ones in My Tho, Long An, Ben Tre and Ca Mau provinces. During that same month our compatriots and troops killed 5,495 soldiers and officers, including 31 Americans; wounded 2,849, including 15 Americans; captured 990, of them 4 Americans; seized 2,172 arms of all types, including 16 mortars, 47 machine guns and automatic rifles; knocked down 32 planes and helicopters and damaged 30 others. Apart from this, 6,358 enemy soldiers and officers, deserted." And he went on to list some important battles in which the Front had come off on top.

Those happy U.S. voices after Diem's downfall started now to sing another tune. "During the next six months," commented the *New York Times* on December 9, only five weeks after the coup, "the new government faces an uphill struggle to regain the initiative." The military junta never regained the initiative nor did it last six months. General Harkins and Nguyen Khanh were working quietly in the background. They could both say, "I told you so" to Cabot Lodge, as the military reverses piled up. Within the junta, formed mainly by Minh, Dinh and Don, a fight for power was going on; as they were all of the same rank and none had any more prestige than the other, there was a complete deadlock.

Cabot Lodge was trying to persuade the old-time politicians —some returned from exile in France, others like Dr. Pham Quan Dan and Hu Huu Thong from Diemist prisons—to play a hand. In the first weeks after the coup, Cabot Lodge desperately tried to sell them on the idea of a two-party system "just like our Republican and Democratic parties, with bipartisanship on key issues." They all refused. Each wanted to have his own

party with himself as head, "in the French tradition." The
only few politicians known in the country whom Lodge was
able to round up, rejected both the American two-party system
and the Diemist one-party system and refused to collaborate
anyway as long as power remained in the hands of a junta.
Lodge also had been against the latter. His idea was to put in
a substitute for Diem, as prime minister, so that military and
civil power would be divided. The American choice was Nguyen
Ton Hoang, quietly groomed for the job by an American
Catholic archbishop as Diem in his time was groomed under
the personal tutorship of Cardinal Spellman. Hoang headed
the main faction of the Dai Viet (Greater Vietnam) party,
an extreme right-wing collection of former mandarins, big landowners and political opportunists. Duong Van Minh, who headed
the junta generals, had promised to appoint Hoang as premier,
but went back on his word once he had power in his own hands.

THE KHANH COUP

Nguyen Khanh and Harkins were now plotting to overthrow
the junta generals and Khanh promised that he would give
Hoang the job as premier. So preparations for a new coup went
ahead; its code name should have been "Harkin's Revenge."
Khanh was prepared to accept what the junta was still resisting,
a pilot plan under which U.S. officers would take over complete
operational and administrative control in 28 districts, Saigon
officers and troops to be placed unreservedly at their disposal,
and to have Nguyen Ton Hoang as prime minister.

U.S. Defense Secretary McNamara came to Saigon at the end
of the year and *Newsweek* of January 5, 1964, quoted him as
telling the junta generals: "The dry season has started and
pursuit of the enemy is easier than ever. Forget your concern
for casualties and fight the war as if it were your last chance—
for well it might be." And well it was!

On January 17, the "greatest heliborne assault in military
history," as UPI described it, was launched at Thanh Phu, in
Ben Tre province. Fifty helicopters, 3,000 troops, 26 M-113
tanks, 26 naval craft and dozens of planes were employed against

what was described as a "guerilla base." This was to be the
supreme justification for Harkin's "withdraw, concentrate and
reoccupy" tactic. The mobile "strike force" had been knocked
together from the withdrawn garrisons. The Liberation forces
allowed the first four waves of helicopters to come in, then
opened up on the fifth wave, knocking down two and damaging
fifteen. Had they wanted to avoid combat, of course, they could
have opened up on the first wave and with such helicopter losses
the battle would have ended then and there. "One of the worst
days of the war in U.S. helicopter operations," reported AP.

As the assault waves moved up, the defenders waited until
the officers, urging the troops on from behind with weapons
ready to shoot any who wavered, were also within range. The
defenders then opened up and the assault wave crumbled. This
started the classic pattern: more bombing and shelling; attacks
from the center, from the right flank, the left flank; extreme
right and left flanks together, and bomb and shell barrages in
between. The action lasted two days before it was broken off
by the Saigon forces. U.S. reports called the results—apart from
the "blackest days ever in helicopter losses"—"meagre and dis-
appointing." In fact it was a shattering defeat. The junta had
obeyed McNamara's instructions to forget their "concern for
casualties." The Saigon forces lost around 600 killed and
wounded, according to Liberation Front figures. The junta's
chief of staff, Le Van Kim, who personally commanded the
action, went back to Saigon to brood over matters with his
fellow junta members. Did this mean they had lost their last
chance?

About ten days after the Thanh Phu debacle, there was a
stormy session of the military junta. President de Gaulle, in the
meantime, had launched his bombshell about neutrality for
Southeast Asia, including South Vietnam. Half a dozen Saigon
papers had just been closed down for mentioning the possibility
of a neutralist solution. But the junta chiefs, all of them French-
trained, discussed the impossible military situation and in-
evitability of a negotiated settlement based on some form of
neutrality. Not that they all agreed on this; some, like Nguyen
Khanh, fiercely opposed the idea. But Minh, Don, Dinh and

Kim supported it in various degrees. This was sufficient for
Harkins to break down any last resistance from Ambassador
Lodge to a sort of "back to Diemism" coup—back to individual
strong-man dictatorship rather than muddled junta dictatorship
and flirtations with neutralism. Khanh was to be the new military
chief, ready to accept without reserve U.S. direction of the war
at all levels; Nguyen Ton Hoang would be made premier and
some sort of a political machine would be brought back into
the picture.

So, while Harkins was conveniently "out of town," the coup
was made, no one firing a shot in defense of the junta. The
leading junta generals were all arrested. They had "had their
chance" and muffed it. Nguyen Khanh, however, once in power,
proved to be a reluctant puppet in one matter. Lodge's con-
sent had been obtained in return for the promise of some pretense of a civilian regime. Harkins probably did not care a fig
about this, so Nguyen Khanh refused. He would not divide
power. He would be military and civilian chief; it is the latter
job that yields rich financial rewards from handling U.S. dollar
aid. He did bow to pressure, however, to release Duong Van
Minh, the former junta chief, from house arrest, and make him
a figure-head "chief of state," with no powers at all.

LIBERATION FRONT'S ASSESSMENT

After Khanh had been in power for a month or so, I asked
President Nguyen Huu Tho if he could sum up, from the
Liberation Front viewpoint, the result of the two coups.

"They were gifts from heaven for us," he said. "Our enemy
has been seriously weakened from all points of view, military,
political and administrative. Their armed forces have suffered
heavy losses on the battlefield and from desertions. The special
shock troops which were an essential support for the Diem
regime have been eliminated. The military command has been
turned upside down and weakened by purges.

"For the same reasons, the coercive apparatus, set up over
the years with great care by Diem, is utterly shattered, especially at the base. The principal chiefs of security and the secret

police, on which mainly depended the protection of the regime and the repression of the revolutionary movement, have been eliminated, purged.

"Troops, officers and officials of the army and administration are completely lost; they have no more confidence in their chiefs and have no idea to whom they should be loyal. Their morale, already shattered even before these events because of the repeated victories of the patriotic forces, has fallen to a new low.

"From the political viewpoint the weakening of our adversary is still clearer. Reactionary political organizations like the Labor and Personalism party, the National Revolutionary movement, the Young Republicans, the movement for Women's Solidarity and others which constituted an appreciable support for the regime have been dissolved and eliminated. . . . In any case, placed in power because of U.S. intervention in the internal affairs of South Vietnam, the regime of Nguyen Khanh is disqualified at birth; it is faced with total isolation inside the country and abroad."

When I asked Tran Nam Trung, of the People's Revolutionary Party, what he thought of the results of the coups he was even more forthright. "The Americans were accusing Diem and Nhu of responsibility for the defeats; Diem and Nhu were accusing the Americans. The Americans were demanding they adopt more up-to-date policies in order to pull the wool over the eyes of the people; they wanted to check the falling morale and also to hand over to more docile puppets. So they chose the dangerous course of 'changing horses in midstream.'

"But in fact," said this veteran revolutionary, "they will search in vain for a more efficient horse than Diem. With all his faults and criminal stupidities, in nine years Diem did succeed in setting up and maintaining an army, an administration and some sort of a political machine, with all the reins of power in his hands. One U.S. idea—probably Lodge's too—was that it would be enough to get rid of brother Nhu and this would make Diem more docile. Nhu, although a champion anti-Communist, was regarded as a 'hard head,' a 'tough nut' who obstinately refused to be docile enough in executing Washington's orders, especially towards the end. But the first coup went a bit contrary to Washington's expectations. It was the military who did it and they wiped out Diem as well as Nhu.

"There were motives of personal vengeance in this; also of fear as to how Diem would react if he remained alive and how to face the fury of the people if they made an anti-Diem coup but did not finish him off. For these same reasons, the new junta decided to liquidate the whole system by which Diem maintained power and which they feared might be turned against them by pro-Diemists seeking to regain power. Over 100 officers up to the rank of colonel were kicked out of the army. At provincial and district level, many officials faithful to Diem were eliminated. The whole apparatus of the secret police was dissolved—not that in doing this the junta was acting out of any sympathy for the people against whom this machine had been used so ferociously in the past, but because they feared it might be used against them.

"Each of the three groups among the junta generals had his own satellites fighting for him within the army and administration and that is why there was complete confusion there and a total lack of confidence in the power at the Center. It explains also how we were able to exploit the situation for large-scale activities in the countryside and in Saigon itself. Many hundreds of 'strategic hamlets' were liberated in groups of ten and 20 at a time and we scored important military victories on all fronts. In Saigon factories, universities and schools, there was a big upsurge of activity by workers, especially the textile workers, by teachers and students, struggling for improved economic conditions, democratic freedoms, a purging of police spies in their organizations.

"A new and important development is the very strong movement for 'peace and neutrality' among different sections of the urban population. This movement, in fact, started several years ago, but in the crisis which followed the two coups it was possible to transform this into a very strong mass movement. There is great scope now for radical activity in the cities, based on the struggle for democratic liberties and improved living conditions. The press is already raising its voice in this sense, demanding an end to censorship, among other things. The enemy was unable to stabilize the situation after the first coup; in all fields, but especially the military one, things had taken a rapid turn for the worse. That was the reason for the second coup, plus the fact that the Americans wanted a more docile servant, a more efficient puppet free of suspected pro-French leanings."

Another point made by the Front leaders was that U.S. prestige among some sections of the population rose slightly after the anti-Diem coup, because Diem was so hated that "nothing could be worse." Similarly, Duong Van Minh gained a certain amount of prestige because he had got rid of Diem. So popular feeling was against Nguyen Khanh from the start, especially when he arrested Minh and killed the latter's bodyguard because it was he who had executed Diem and Nhu. Anger against the USA then rose to new heights because it was so clear to everyone that this was an authentic "made in USA" coup.

"We had little difficulty in persuading people of this," said Nguyen Huu Tho, "but the greatest gift for us was when McNamara came and toured the countryside, holding up Nguyen Khanh's arm and shouting, 'This is our man.' This saved our propaganda cadres a great deal of effort." McNamara felt it was necessary to come and "sell" Nguyen Khanh to the population; to assure them in a dozen different variants that Khanh had the complete backing of the USA, precisely because Washington knew that he had no popular support at home. But he was the one general prepared to continue "killing Communists" on U.S. terms. "He doesn't need your support, he's got ours," was what McNamara was saying in effect to the South Vietnamese people. However, when Khanh's troops refused to go into action and, despite some extra blood money, the rate of desertions was sharply stepped up, Washington probably realized that something more than only their support was needed.

The political vacuum created by the dismantling of all Diemist organizations has not been filled, nor can it be within a short time. Washington is aware of the desperate weakness that results from this and Americans on the spot have been thrashing round to try and fill the vacuum. Immediately after Khanh took over, U.S. correspondents wrote that he was the man to rally the sects and within days there were announcements that this or that Cao Daist or Hoa Hao leader had rallied to Khanh. As the sects had previously been crushed by Diem with U.S. arms and official U.S. approval the new hopes smelt of cynicism. But within seven days of taking over, Khanh's American-piloted air force had dropped 60 tons of bombs on Ben Can, the second largest Cao Dai center after Tay Ninh—in Saigon-controlled territory—burning out 1,000 homes, killing 84 and wounding 200 people. There was such a tremendous outburst of rage, that Khanh, Cabot Lodge and Harkins rushed to Tay Ninh and promised to pay 2,000 piastres for every adult and 1,000 for every child killed, while photographers took pictures of Khanh handing out candy to Tay Ninh children. As the uproar continued, even at a public meeting addressed by Khanh, the price of South Vietnamese corpses was raised to 5,000 piastres for an adult and 2,000 for a child. And as an extra gift, Khanh appointed a discredited Cao Dai general, Le Van Tat, as governor of Tay Ninh province. The area of his control, as of April 1964, ended a couple of miles outside Tay Ninh city.

Khanh did succeed in buying over a few Cao Dai and Hoa Hao leaders, but they were the same who have been bought and sold over the years by Japanese, French—and now Americans. Whether these leaders could carry the rank and file with them and thus create some sort of political support for Khanh—or whoever Washington chooses to succeed Khanh—is another matter. It was a question I put to Tran Nam Trung:

"The Cao Dai and Hoa Hao people," he replied, "have had years of experience of their chiefs changing sides according to who paid most. And each time they changed sides, it meant more deaths and distress, more exploitation for the mass of the Cao Dai and Hoa Hao population. They suffered great disasters in the past while the cash dividends went to the leaders. In the days of their greatest sufferings, Le Van Tat was never there to share their griefs or help the people overcome them. The Cao Dai and Hoa Hao people are peasants who have now got their own land because of the Front. They will defend this land as other peasants do. The fact that they are peasants comes first, the question of their sect allegiance is secondary. Most of those Cao Dai leaders who really helped their people have rallied to our Front, the others support it. And this is the same with the Hoa Hao. As for the Binh Xuyen, it is affiliated to the Front. The Americans and Khanh would love to win the sects over, but it is impossible."

The other political force on which U.S. hopes are based is the Dai Viet party mentioned earlier. A tiny party without any grassroots support at all—"dollar hunters par excellence," Trung expressed it—the Dai Viet is already split into several factions, each of whom has its nominee for future premier. One of them, Nguyen Chanh Thi who helped organize the abortive officers' coup in November 1960, tried his luck again on February 10, 1964, against Khanh, eleven days after the latter took over. He was doubtless encouraged by the ease with which Khanh had done the job, but he failed again. But even if a Dai Viet coup succeeded, it can not fill the gap caused by the dismantling of the Diemist organizations nor can it pretend to represent even a class in Vietnamese society. As a counter to the Front, it would be like "trying to push back the ocean with a fire hose," as one of the Saigon Liberation Front leaders said.

A major difficulty for the handful of generals and politicians that are willing to play any role for dollar dividends, is to know to "which" USA they should be "loyal." Because of the many warring factions and the uncertainty of the future, Washington has a stake in every faction and will back any coup-minded group which has a chance of success, providing they make a show of being efficient and docile. But Embassy, Military Command and CIA all have different evaluations in judging potential efficiency and docility. Even the most zealous puppet is faced with an agonizing choice as to which of the three he should play with. Pick the wrong one and however loyally one works, and no matter how lavish the praise for faithful service, one may end up in a pool of blood like Diem and Nhu, or be handed over by an American consul to be guillotined like the third brother, Can; or laid out in lines by the execution squads as were many from the "Special Force" of the late, also executed, Colonel Le Quang Tung, even though it was the private creation of the CIA. That was the reward for loyalty to the wrong service.

And the junta generals? All jailed within three months for having hitched their stars to the State Department and some of them were very lucky to have had only their immediate underlings executed and not themselves. And Nguyen Khanh himself? Could he have felt very safe when his chief backer, comrade-in-arms and co-plotter was relieved of his Saigon command in May 1964? Khanh knew the reason why! Because he, General Nguyen Khanh, who had made the most fire-eating speeches about "crushing Communists," suffered more defeats faster than any of his predecessors. If Khanh did not realize that by mid-1964 the CIA experts were thumbing through the dossiers of generals and colonels for the next choice, he must have been naive in the extreme. The CIA, incidentally, had not yet had its coup.

If Washington was then having difficulty in persuading a new figure to have a try, the dilemma of even those avid for power at any price must be recognized.

A major effort to coordinate State Department and Pentagon policies was the appointment in June 1964 of General Maxwell Taylor, Chairman of the U.S. Joint Chiefs of Staff and chief ideologist of "special war," as a sort of super-ambassador in Saigon to replace Cabot Lodge. Maxwell Taylor thus had military and civil affairs in his hand: a striking parallel to what the French government had done just ten years previously when they sent their Chief of Staff, General Paul Ely, to Saigon to take over civilian and military authority.

In sending General Taylor as ambassador, President Johnson was saying to him in effect: "You got us into this mess, now get us out of it." Just as "special war" was Taylor's brainchild, the main strategy for winning it—the Staley-Taylor plan of 1961—was also co-fathered by him. Both had failed. General Taylor is doubtless a good general; so was France's de Lattre de Tassigny, but he was sent on a hopeless mission. The most brilliant strategies and tactics could not be effective when Washington had already lost the battle for the minds of the people of South Vietnam.

Chapter 15

HOW WILL IT END?

How long will this war go on and how will it end? These
were questions which I obviously discussed at length with the
most responsible of the Liberation Front's military and political
leaders. Replies varied. "It will go on as long as necessary until
the Americans have pulled out or are driven out and a really
independent government based on peace and neutrality is
formed" was Nguyen Huu Tho's first reply. "We are capable of
fighting for a very long time," Ybih Aleo, the leader of the ethnic
minorities, emphasized the same point. "If our generation cannot
finish the job, then our sons or our grandsons certainly will."

It is clear that the plans of the Front's Military Affairs Committee are based on several more years of fighting. But they are
completely confident they will win. And the changing colors on
the military maps, even during the period in which I had access
to them, the gradual expansion of red and corresponding shrink-
ing of the green patches, certainly justifies their confidence. So
did everything else I could see and hear during my visit.

The Front claims to control two thirds of the territory and
over a half the population, as of the beginning of 1964. It is
a government in everything but name, with Committees of
Military Affairs, External Affairs, Public Health, Culture, Information and Education, Post and Tele-Communications, Economic Affairs and others functioning as ministries, with their
various departments and sub-departments. The Committee of
External Affairs already has its "ambassadors" abroad—in Cairo,
Havana, Algiers, Djakarta, Berlin, Prague—and the setting up
of more bureaus of the NFL abroad is limited only by shortage
of cadres. Most of the bureaus also have representatives of Liberation Press, the official news agency, who act as press attachés.

The question of transforming the Front's Central Committee

into a provisional government is obviously only a question of time. It was under study when I was at Nguyen Huu Tho's headquarters. "It exists already in embryo form," he said. "We have our own administrative organs. We are starting to work on certain economic problems, improving the technical level of agriculture, opening up virgin lands. Everything is on an absolutely democratic basis. Where conditons permit, and it is almost a general rule today, the villagers elect their own self-management committees. The methods of ensuring public security and putting the economic and cultural life on a sounder basis are improving daily. A big question for us now is to organize life in the liberated zones as it should be—we are starting to have a plan for this. The self-management committees are in line with old resistance traditions and represent a transition to a more rational form of administration. The essential problems of public order and security have already been solved; economic and social life is being organized on a systematic basis.

"Well over one third of the arable land in the whole country has been affected by our land reform measures—distribution of the common lands and those of absentee landlords who have turned traitor, rent reduction and other measures. We have started to build schools, especially in the Mekong Delta area, also clinics and hospitals. We lack material means but this reconstruction work is also starting to take on a clear profile. The formation of a provisional government is now on the agenda, but is a matter which has to be carefully studied."

Over the greater part of the country, in fact, there is a stable administration in the hands of the South Vietnamese people, with social and economic reconstruction already under way. Matters in the Liberation Front-controlled areas will continue to develop this way, even as the war goes on. The really big question mark, however, is what the USA intends to do.

"Special warfare" has been pushed to its fullest development and has failed. The original plan called for the use of 11,000 U.S. "advisers," but by 1964 these had reached over 25,000 and were operating at company, in some cases, at platoon level. The equivalent of two air divisions was being employed; U.S. personnel were running transport and communications. To go any further, to employ combat troops, would be to move beyond "special war" and engage in "limited war" with U.S. ground troops. But how many troops would they need? And how could they guarantee the war would be "limited"?

In Algeria, the French committed 800,000 troops against a population of 10,000,000—and had to negotiate a withdrawal. The population of South Vietnam is 14,000,000, vastly more experienced in warfare than the Algerians and with infinitely more favorable geographical conditions, mountains and jungle covering two thirds of the country. The experience of Korea is still fresh in every American's heart; 54,246 Americans died in Korea and another 103,284 were wounded, according to U.S. Defense Department figures; the dead included 5,884 airmen. The result was a negotiated settlement along the 38th parallel where the war started. The terrain in Korea was infinitely more favorable for the UN troops than the jungles of South Vietnam.

There are another 16,000,000 Vietnamese in the North, including the cream of the fighting forces from the South. And there was nothing in the Geneva Agreements that prevented them continuing their training in modern military techniques after they were regrouped in the North! It is worth noting that in the program adopted by the NFL congress early in 1962 there is the following paragraph:

"Congress affirms that . . . if the U.S. imperialists and their agents plunge deeper into their bloodthirsty aggression . . . the people of South Vietnam and the NFL will use all forms of struggle, will take all measures to fight resolutely to the end to save themselves and their country—to liberate South Vietnam, to defend independence and democracy and completely overthrow treacherous dictators. In case of necessity, the people of South Vietnam and the NFL will use their legitimate and effective right to appeal to the people and the government of North Vietnam, to peace-loving and democratic peoples and governments the world over . . . requesting that active support, including material and manpower support, be afforded to the just struggle of the South Vietnamese people. The U.S. imperialists and their agents would have to bear the full responsibility for any disastrous consequences."

One could hardly doubt that in the event of moving "special war" up to "limited war" this paragraph would be invoked and, at the very least, the USA would find itself involved in a war with 30 million Vietnamese. At the very least!

INTERVENTION FROM THE NORTH?

From the moment the big military defeats started, the Americans charged officially that these were due to aggression or intervention from the North and at the time this book goes to press the threats are mounting to "push the war to the North." So far there has not been an iota of evidence to support the charge of intervention from the North. There is any amount of evidence to show it is absurd.

If the main military activity were in the upper parts of South Vietnam near the 17th parallel or even close to the frontier regions of Laos where the other side of the border is controlled by the Pathet Lao, then suspicions might be justified. Militarily, this would be shown by the red patches on the maps appearing first there and spreading southwards. But it has never been so; on the contrary, the movement has been in the opposite direction. And there are only two roads leading south from the 17th parallel area, with Saigon forces in solid control of both, except for occasional ambushes. The main military activity from the very beginning has been in the deep South; this has been the major scene of the big defeats for Saigon. The first liberated area, in fact, was the Ca Mau peninsula, the southernmost tip of South Vietnam. This was the area of the big military sweeps made by Diemist forces long before armed resistance was started; the main part of the fighting has gone on there ever since, despite the fact that it lies closest to the greatest concentration of U.S. military power at Saigon. There are no roads, except those in U.S.-Saigon hands, that link the Mekong Delta with North Vietnam. And a major part of the guerillas' activity is to cut and destroy such roads as do exist. A strange tactic if they depended on them for supplies! The guerillas wage a ceaseless struggle to sever all communications with their areas because their operations are essentially defensive—in defense of their own homes and villages. The tendency from the beginning has been for the red splotches to spread from south to north and not vice versa.

Perhaps arms come from the North? All western press reports agree that at first the guerillas' arms were of a most primitive type. So much so that the Diemist government ordered a special exhibition of "Viet Cong" arms in Saigon to show its own superbly equipped troops that they had nothing to fear. (Certainly Diem omitted to state that these were arms abandoned by the guerillas as new U.S. weapons fell into their hands, but that is beside the point.) All Western press reports also stressed that those "superbly equipped" troops have been, voluntarily or involuntarily, parting with their arms to the Front forces at an increasingly rapid tempo.

In a commentary on the Loc Ninh battle, referred to earlier, David Halberstam of the *New York Times,* in a dispatch dated October 27, 1963, referred to the "bloody nose" which U.S.-Saigon forces received and, attacking the official U.S. optimism, he commented: "There is too much dependence on artificial statistics. . . . For two months now, the weapons capture ratio has been running against the Government at an alarming rate, around two to one. Just today it was announced that in the last week, the Vietcong had taken 225 weapons from the Government while the Government had captured 100 from the Vietcong." Halberstam concludes: "Anyone who knows what the guerillas can do with 125 weapons or who has tried to take 125 weapons away from the Communists, will know why there is a disquieting feeling. If there is a light at the end of the tunnel [President Kennedy's expression] it is hard to tell from this end whether it has been turned on yet."

When I asked Nguyen Huu Tho about charges made by Secretary of State Dean Rusk a few days previously concerning "intervention" from the North, including supply of arms, he replied: "According to recent statistics published by the Pentagon, during the last three months of 1963 our armed forces seized an average of 234 weapons every week. This rate, taken together with our own arms production, is more than enough to equip Liberation forces. Besides, the Americans have never furnished the slightest real evidence of their charges."

It is obvious that on the question of arms supply, even if it were possible to transport weapons in sufficient quantities, no military commander could ever base operations on supplies carried on human backs over a supply line of well over 600 miles of jungle and steep mountain trails, leading across the formidable Annamite Chain. In any case the Front forces need weapons for which there is a constant supply of ammunition on the spot. "Our main arsenals are in the United States itself; our logistics depend on their trucks, helicopters and parachutes," one of the Front's military leaders said to me. "They deliver the most excellent weapons and the munitions which fit them, right at our front door, just where we need them." The main reason given by General Harkins in evacuating so many posts in the Mekong Delta was because they were a major source of arms supply for the Front. Wiping the whole of North Vietnam off the face of the globe could not change the situation as far as arms supply is concerned.

The inspiration, leadership and technical know-how—surely this at least comes from the North? It is the one question that perhaps could be argued. Manpower is clearly not needed; the Mekong Delta is one of the most densely populated areas in the world and in general there is no lack of manpower in the Front-controlled zones. Rank and file troops that I saw—and there were plenty—were in their late teens and very early twenties; officers up to battalion commanders in their late twenties and early thirties. The troops had graduated into the regular forces from their local self-defense units; commanders had graduated during the present fighting and as guerilla leaders in the war against the French. But there is another side to the question of inspiration and leadership.

The Mekong Delta, especially the provinces of My Tho and Ben Tre, are the most revolutionary areas in all of Vietnam, North or South. It was here that in November 1940 the first major revolt against the French was launched. The peasants took advantage of the withdrawal of some French troops from the Delta to Cambodia (to counter a Japanese-Thai threat to the French in Indo-China) to launch an uprising against conscription and unbearable taxes. The yellow-starred, red flag of today's

Democratic Republic of Vietnam was born during this armed revolt. (The villages that were the center of that revolt were among the first to start armed resistance against the Diem regime.) Then as now the red splotches on the military maps first appeared in the south, not the north.

The first resistance war against the French also started in the Mekong Delta, in September 1945, a full year before it started in the North. And the first armed action against the Diem regime also spread to the Delta after Diem's crushing of the armed religious sects in 1955. Revolt has not been exported from the North in the past, but started spontaneously where conditions were ripe. It was Diem who launched a full-scale war against the sects which, as noted earlier, withdrew to the Delta and continued to wage sporadic guerrilla warfare until they merged their armed forces with those of the Front in 1960.

As for technical know-how, the Delta peasants have been waging almost continuous warfare for nearly a quarter of a century. They are the most experienced and probably the best guerilla fighters the world has ever known. A whole series of French generals and marshals, including the greatest of them all, de Lattre de Tassigny, were in no doubt about that even in their day. But today, their know-how of military technique is on a much higher level. By my own observations I am convinced that every armed unit is capable of handling whatever type of weapon is likely to fall into its hands. A "Viet Cong" guerilla unit is infinitely more sophisticated than his Viet Minh elder brother ever was. And the latter were not bad! The difference is due to technical instructors from the North? I do not believe so and found no evidence of it.

The superior technical know-how is another product of "special war." If you are going to fight with a local army, you have to develop local officers, local NCO's and technicians in all branches, many of which specialties in the old days would remain the exclusive preserve of the Expeditionary Corps. The French, in other words, had no interest in teaching Vietnamese how to handle heavy machine guns, bazookas, mortars, artillery and so on. They might be turned against them. But "special war" requirements forced the Americans to train local military technicians by the thousands. As time went on an increasingly high proportion of the trainees passed over to the Front forces; even if they cannot bring their complicated weapons with them, they bring their know-how. They are used as instructors in Front training courses, and in a surprisingly short time U.S. advisers were complaining about the astonishing accuracy with which mortar shells were lobbing on their positions, the efficient use of bazookas and the technically excellent disposition of firing positions. In fact, the technical know-how comes from the same source as the arms munitions.

General Harkins, who has the distinction of being the first general in the world to have been beaten in "special war," was sacked in May 1964. If he is philosophic, he can draw support from the following: He was beaten by the world's best guerillas, armed with superb U.S. weapons, trained—indirectly at least —by U.S. instructors in their use. And after all, a whole list of illustrious French generals had the same experience—none of them, however, was left so long with so many defeats to their debit as General Harkins. Finally, he can be certain that he will not be the last U.S. general to lose his reputation in the jungles of South Vietnam. His replacement, General Westmoreland, was fortunate to escape with his life on the very day before his appointment was announced. Three officers sitting alongside him were wounded when his plane came under ground-fire, with an even chance that it came from the troops the general was about to command.

Until some concrete evidence is produced of "aid from the North" one can discount the accusations as a cover up for very embarrassing and otherwise inexplicable defeats. After all, the U.S. command in Saigon has a complete monopoly of planes, helicopters, tanks, artillery (except for such pieces as can be carried on a man's back), naval power and motor transport. The Liberation forces have none of these, not even a single motor truck, as far as I could see. The U.S. command has an overwhelming superiority in effectives. And yet they have been pushed back to the gates of Saigon. It is very embarrassing, but the answer will not be found by either blaming or bombing Hanoi or by U.S. air attacks in the Gulf of Tonkin. There are no railway networks, bridges, factories or anything else to bomb in the Front-controlled areas. If the Americans really want to bomb the Front's source of supplies they would have to bomb their own arms factories; but it would be much more effective to pull out of South Vietnam and take their arms with them.

Although there has been no case of a soldier from the North having been found in the South, there have been innumerable cases of the contrary. In the seven months between June 1963 and the end of January 1964, thirteen U.S. trained commando and sabotage groups, parachuted from planes or landed from craft, were rounded up in North Vietnam and tried by military tribunals. On one occasion a U.S. plane was brought down north of the 17th parallel, complete with its commando group and parachutes. General Vo Nguyen Giap, North Vietnam's Minister of Defense and commander-in-chief of the armed forces, told me that such activities had been stepped up since Nguyen Khanh took over in Saigon. In general they are sent in squad-sized groups he said, adding:

"I can assure you that all such sabotage groups have been wiped out, in the vast majority of cases being dealt with by our civilian population or local self-defense forces. They aim at acts of sabotage, collecting military information but also at organizing 'discontented elements' which exist only in the imagination of those that sent them." General Giap said that Saigon was planning the use of Kuomintang agents and some from Laos also, but he was confident they would also have short shrift. In most cases the groups had been rounded up within a matter of hours.

The U.S. threat of taking the war to the North, however, was being taken seriously in Hanoi. The incidents in the Gulf of Tonkin and the U.S. air attacks against North Vietnamese oil storage depots and coastal installations in the first week of August 1964, showed how well justified Hanoi was in taking those threats seriously. It also showed how far Washington was prepared to go in testing a policy of extending the war. As a means of affecting the struggle in the South, however, the effect was the opposite to that intended. The first direct reaction was a great upsurge of popular wrath culminating in the wave of stu-

dent demonstrations in Saigon, Hue and other cities which forced
Nguyen Khanh to step down, even if only temporarily. The size
and vigor of these demonstrations in the major cities, coordinat-
ed as they were with military operations by the Liberation Front,
signaled that the struggle had moved up to a new level. Henceforth urban workers and intellectuals could be expected to play
a much more direct role than previously.

If the USA takes the initiative of "unifying" the war, of creating a single military front by pushing the war to the North, it
seems the first logical consequence would be the military unifica-
iton of the country. And certainly not on Washington or Saigon
terms! And in so far as U.S. planes based in Laos take part in
attacks on North Vietnam, the Americans would have taken
the initiative of creating a single war front in Indo-China.

PROSPECTS FOR NEGOTIATED PEACE

In short, having failed with "special war," Washington has to
make up its mind what to do next. The series of top-level conferences that took place in the first half of 1964 were evidence
that Washington was having difficulty in making up its mind.
And they do not have all that many choices. High level voices
were being raised in the United States warning that no U.S. security or any other interests would justify a "second Korea" in
South Vietnam which is what moving up from "special war"
to the stage of "limited war" would mean. And how to guarantee
that "limited war" would not automatically lead to the stage
of "global nuclear" war? In talks with Liberation Front leaders,
I was interested to what extent they were prepared to make it
"easy" for the Americans to leave without too much loss of face.
I also wanted to know to what extent they felt the war might be
shortened by some sort of coup in Saigon which, although not en-
gineered by the Front, might bring to power a regime with which
they could negotiate. What would be the basis for negotiations?
What role could an international conference play in bringing
about a solution?

Nguyen Huu Tho said that with the way things were developing in Saigon—the demoralization in the army, the contradictions

between the generals, the general dissatisfaction of the population and the ease with which Khanh made his own coup—the possibility of another one, or even a series of coups, could not be rejected, even including one not to the taste of Washington.

"As far as the Front is concerned," he said, "we are prepared to negotiate with all parties, groups, sects, patriots, without considering their political tendencies or their past activities, if we can bring about a peaceful solution based on national independence, democracy and neutrality. But we consider that the internal affairs of South Vietnam should be settled by the South Vietnamese themselves without any foreign interference. The basis of any eventual agreement must be the withdrawal of all American troops, with all their arms and equipment. The Front is not opposed to an international conference to help find a solution, but the role of the foreign powers taking part should be limited to submitting proposals and recording any agreement reached between the South Vietnamese parties concerned and guaranteeing the execution of such agreements."

He explained that under the Alliance for Unity of Action which was being developed the Front was prepared to work with all groups, including those who were hostile to various parts of its program. "We do not claim the exclusive right either to win the war or form the government afterwards," he said. "We are prepared to forget the past and even the present. We say: 'It is enough that you want to end the war and foreign intervention. We will march shoulder to shoulder with you.' And what we say we do. When we define a policy, we apply it. This is not just a propaganda stunt. To officers serving now in the U.S.-Saigon armed forces, we say: 'Even if you have killed our compatriots, even if you have committed crimes, if you regret and return to the patriotic path, we accept you.'" Nguyen Huu Tho went on to explain that the Front recognized that those within the ranks of the adversary were there for a variety of reasons. The rank and file soldiers were mainly press-ganged conscripts. Many officers were forced because of financial reasons into the army when all other avenues of making a living were deliberately closed to them, leaving the army the only way out.

"The front pays great attention to trying to win such elements back to the side of the people," he continued, "individually or in groups. When enemy units are prepared to break away from the Saigon command, we are ready to support them. If they need material aid, we will supply it. They can keep their own formations, operate independently; they need not join the Front. They can retain their political, ideological tendencies, we will not interfere. Our only condition is they oppose the U.S. interventionists and their puppets in Saigon. As for the higher administrative officials, we oppose only those whose hands are really drenched in the blood of our compatriots, but there are only a few of these. With the others we are prepared to cooperate. This policy has received wide support from elements within the Saigon army and administration, from rank and file elements up to senior officers and officials."

He revealed that as military victories piled up and the prestige of the Front grew, many in the Saigon administration felt the way the wind was blowing and began to make adjustments accordingly. Feelers "at quite a high level," he said, were constantly being put out for contact with the Front. He gave me as an instance the fact that the Front ran courses to educate civil servants, ostensibly to staff public administration in their own zones. "But officials now serving the Saigon administration find ways and means of attending these courses secretly. They have their eye on the future."

I asked if any army units had in fact broken away and accepted Front support to operate independently. He referred to a Cao Dai force as an example. "It is quite a big unit," he said, "not affiliated to the Front. It has its own command, fights under its own flag, but it gets material support from us, coordinates its military activities with those of the Front. Another unit, a platoon in Can Long village, Tra Vinh province, recently killed its officers and deserted and appealed to us for help. We support it and it carries on independent activities; as it builds up into a bigger unit, we continue to give support. There are numerous other cases and this will develop into a big movement once our 'Alliance for Action' policy becomes better known. It is quite a new development."

The commander-in-chief of the Binh Xuyen forces, Lt. Col.

Vo Van Mon, several times reported killed by Saigon, happened
to be with Nguyen Huu Tho during this conversation. I asked
him about the relations between his forces and those of the Front.
"After the Diemist forces gave us a bad beating due to all-round
treachery," he said, "what was left of us regrouped and continued
to fight independently until the Front was formed. Then we
affiliated with it. The enemy propaganda machine warned us that
it would be impossible to remain independent, we would be
swallowed up by the Communists. In fact we still have our own
organization, our own cadres at all levels, but we fight under
the unified command of the Front. After several years of coop-
erating with these people (and he indicated Nguyen Huu Tho
and some other members of the Presidium who happened to be
there), I was convinced they were on the right track. We had a
meeting and decided to affiliate with the Front. But we still retain our independent character and it was just a big lie that we
would be swallowed up by the Communists. What is true is
that the Front grows in strength and popular support every day."

I brought the conversation back to the question of how to end
the war and make it not too hard for the Americans to execute a
face-saving withdrawal. It was clear the Front attracted support
from a very broad cross section of the population and its anten-
nae were probing out way beyond the main body of its influence.
Was it not possible that a quite unknown personality might
emerge from the coups and counter-coups, possibly any day in
Saigon, with a program the Front could support? Would they
throw their Saigon machine into action in such an event?

The reply was that certainly they would; that the Front leadership worked day and night to create favorable conditions for
such an eventuality, and was in a position to give effective and
immediate support to any "favorable coup." But it was explained
also that long-range political and military planning could not be
based on this possibility, only on the "relation of forces." They
had to think in terms of a long-range politico-military struggle,
then possibly a military uprising at a higher political level than
anything so far. But if the Americans wanted a face-saving
way out, they had already staged two coups. Why not a third,
with someone prepared to negotiate on the basis of peace, democ-

racy, independence and neutrality? The latter was thrown out as a joke, but Washington could have done worse than to think it over. In general, Nguyen Huu Tho thought Washington would probably try out a few more personalities and have to suffer some more defeats before they would be willing to permit negotiations on any realistic basis.

I asked about the ideas of President de Gaulle for neutralizing Southeast Asia, including South Vietnam. Nguyen Huu Tho pointed out that the Front had already approved the suggestion of the Cambodian Chief of State, Prince Norodom Sihanouk, "for the formation of a neutral zone to include Cambodia, Laos and South Vietnam. The recent views expressed by President de Gaulle," he continued, "seem realistic to us. The NFL welcomes them." And in referring to the future developments of relations between an independent South Vietnam and France, he said: "Good relations between South Vietnam and France, especially in the economic and cultural fields, have existed for a long time. The Front looks forward in the future to developing such relations on the basis of equality and mutual advantage. We hope that France will always occupy a privileged position among countries friendly to South Vietnam. All that depends, of course, on the attitude of France towards the present struggle of the Vietnamese people against American aggression, for our liberation and national independence.

"In this connection we follow with great interest the recent steps and efforts of the French government in helping to find a peaceful solution to the problem of South Vietnam."

President Ho Chi Minh, whom I subsequently saw in Hanoi, also remarked that President de Gaulle's views "were worthy of serious attention," and that the best solution was that proposed by the Liberation Front, namely, "that the South Vietnam question must be settled by the people of South Vietnam on the basis of independence, democracy, peace and neutrality. And as a first condition, the U.S. imperialists must withdraw all their troops and arms from South Vietnam and respect the 1954 Geneva Agreements."

If U.S. policy-makers were motivated by a grain of realism, it seems, they could find a solution along these lines. It is the optimum solution they can have in South Vietnam and Southeast Asia as a whole. Absurd talk of continuing the war "until all the Communists are driven out of South Vietnam," as repeated with wearisome monotony from Washington, is a bankrupt, hopeless business. Nguyen Huu Tho pointed out that in the American context of what represented "communism" in South Vietnam, "this threat means they intend to continue this war until all South Vietnamese are expelled from their own territory. Vietnamese patriots will give a fitting reply to this sort of braggadocio," he said.

Short of using the H-bomb and wiping out all Vietnamese and many of their neighbors, the Americans will never succeed in South Vietnam by trying to impose a military solution.

EPILOGUE

An Advanced Base of the Liberation Army,
January 15, 1965

During the latter part of November 1964 and the first half of January 1965, I revisited the liberated zones and the battle-fronts of South Vietnam. Great changes had taken place in every sphere. Liberation Army companies I had visited before had blossomed into battalions, battalions into regiments. The enemy-controlled strategic hamlet which I visited last time, some seven miles from Saigon, had been liberated and the two posts guarding it had been wiped out.

Roads which had been cut to pieces as defensive measures last time had been repaired because they were now safely far in the rear of the liberated areas; but other roads like the major strategic highway No. 13, which leads from Saigon north to the strategic center of Ban Mé Thuot in the High Plateaux, had been put out of action. The guerillas over a length of several miles had built mud and stone barricades across the road at regular intervals and posted sharpshooters to deal with any attempts to remove them. American pilots, while I was in the area, were trying to blast away the barricades by firing rockets at them from low-flying fighters. But whatever they could blast away was put back again within minutes at night.

Northbound civilian traffic from Saigon was halted at the start of the barricades; bus passengers could get out, walk a few kilometers to the end of the barricades and catch another northbound bus from there. The aged and mothers with babies were helped by the guerillas. But military traffic was ambushed long before it arrived at the barricades and had to make an enormous detour.

The famous McNamara plan, with the modest aim of "pacifying" for a start the single province of Long An, had failed; the

238

liberated areas in Long An were in fact extended during the attempted "pacification." And, taking advantage of the withdrawal of regular troops from Central Vietnam for the Mc-Namara plan, the Liberation Army launched a series of sharp attacks and in the four months preceding the tragic typhoon and flood disaster in October-November 1964, they liberated territory with 1,200,000 inhabitants.

Incidentally, I met refugees from the flood areas and they were unanimous that the high death toll, over 7,000 according to Saigon figures, occurred almost exclusively where the population was herded into "strategic hamlets," which in many cases were kept locked from the outside when the water was six or seven feet deep. I heard of several incidents in which the people tore down the walls and made a break but were machined-gunned as they fled. One of the worst cases was in a "strategic hamlet," 30 miles west of Quang Ngai provincial capital where there were only three survivors out of over 300 Hre minority people. The rest were shot down as they tried to escape. And in a prison at Tam Ky village in Quang Ting province, 407 political prisoners were drowned in the prison because the guards refused to open the doors as the water steadily rose. In the old and newly liberated areas where the "strategic hamlets" had been torn down, there was virtually no loss of life.

The only answer the U.S.-Saigon command had found to the "wipe-out-enemy-posts-and-annihilate-reinforcements" tactics of the Liberation Army was to continue abandoning, or being forced out of, smaller posts; instead it concentrated on battalion or regimental size cantonments. These in turn were encircled by the guerillas, but from several such posts the Saigon forces could concentrate artillery fire on individual villages, firing up to 500 shells within an hour or so. More and more the war was being waged, from the U.S.-Saigon side, by air and artillery strikes. During 1964 ground operations, except defensive actions in reply to Liberation Army attacks, were on a very small scale, with only four major operations attempted and one of these a defensive one, compared with a dozen major operations in 1963. Throughout 1964, the U.S.-Saigon command did not score a single victory but suffered the most crushing defeats of the war, defeats which were on an ever bigger scale as the year came to its close. The year 1965 was ushered in with major Liberation Army victories at Binh Gia and Soc Trang.

As the war is waged more and more by the U.S.-Saigon Air Force and artillery units so it begins to take on the character of an open war of aggression waged by the United States, since every pilot and at least half of all air crew members are American and every artillery unit is in fact officered by Americans. Although the "officer" may only be a sergeant, he has absolute authority over Saigon junior officers.

When I interviewed President Nguyen Huu Tho—on December 20, 1964, the fourth anniversary of the founding of the Liberation Front—I asked him if super-ambassador General Maxwell Taylor, the father of "special war," had brought any new ideas to Saigon with him. He replied:

"He brought nothing new at all. The French changed their commanders several times and each time a new general arrived he brought a new plan with him. But we are still waiting to see something new from General Maxwell Taylor. Even after his last much publicized visit to Washington, he has brought nothing new. A few hundred more U.S. 'advisers,' a few more planes, tanks, artillery. But it is not bombs and artillery that win wars; it is infantry that can occupy territory. And here they are in a real impasse. The fact is that the defeats since Maxwell Taylor came here have been greater, more important than the disasters before he arrived. I would like to add that this is not the fault of Taylor. It is the fault of a war of aggression, an unjust war. It is not a question of sending top-rank strategists; not a question of highly-trained troops and ultramodern arms in a war of this type. Of course the relation of forces is decisive, but these are not only material forces. Above all it is morale that counts; it is the human factor that is decisive. If one could take into account only material forces we would have been crushed long ago, given the enormous disproportion. In fact it is they who are being crushed. No Maxwell Taylors can change that."

The interview was interrupted twice, once by a bomber that

came circling low overhead and once by a courier who came with the news of the "Young Generals" coup in Saigon and the arrest of members of the High National Council. The courier arrived like a punctuation mark just as Nguyen Huu Tho was explaining the absolute impossibility of the Americans bringing about political stability in Saigon and that it was impossible for them to wage the war without that stability. (As for the bomber, we were well protected from its sights by the branches of a huge banyan tree and from its bombs, if necessary, by splendid air raid shelters a few yards away.)

As an example of morale, I would cite the attack on Bien Hoa airfield a few minutes before midnight on October 31, in which 21 B-57's—the pride of America's nuclear bomber fleet—were destroyed and another 15 planes irreparably damaged. I later interviewed Huynh Minh, who commanded the Liberation Army unit, a slight, merry man, his face covered with smiles as he recounted the attack. It is noteworthy that Huynh Minh a few years ago was a peasant, tilling his rice fields on the very spot where he was later to blow up $26,000,000's worth of nuclear bombers. His home, as with virtually every other member of the unit, was bulldozed out of existence, the rice fields destroyed to make way for extensions of the then small Bien Hoa airport. The families of the unit members are today concentrated in "strategic hamlets" in the area—and if Huynh Minh is not the commander's real name, the reason will be understood.

To build this super air base, the Americans cleared 35,000 peasants off 320 hectares of land and later the base was used to bomb and spray toxic chemicals on liberated villages in Bien Hoa province. Almost every member of Minh's unit had relatives killed or tortured and still rotting in fascist jails. His unit started as a very small guerilla band, but gradually built up, with captured arms, to a compact, well armed unit. "At first, when we captured mortars," Minh said, "we had no idea how to use them. We handed them over to the regular army. Later we decided to master them. We can now use mortars, if necessary even without tripods or base plates, with complete accuracy."

The Bien Hoa air base was one of the most heavily guarded in all South Vietnam. The U.S. press later revealed that the presence of B-57 bombers there was a top military secret. But Minh and his men knew they were there, they had shot one down a few days earlier and captured documents which revealed the unit's presence at Bien Hoa. There were three main defense lines to be penetrated, rows of blockhouses and watchtowers, integrated with "strategic hamlets." The second defense line with 18 towers and 12 blockhouses was manned by two battalions of Saigon regulars. The third line consisted of five rows of barbed wire entanglements with minefields in between the rows. Behind that lay the runways, the installations and garrison headquarters for 2,500 Americans—pilots, administrative and service personnel. A third battalion of regular troops was stationed about 800 yards outside the base and two more battalions were stationed in Bien Hoa town, a few miles away. Also for the defense of the base, there was a battery of 155mm artillery pieces at Tan Uyen, the provincial capital of Phuoc Thanh, seven miles to the north. (Their range is nine miles.)

"Once we decided to attack the base," continued Minh at our little press conference in a jungle clearing not too far from the scene of the action, "the first thing was to outline the task to our unit. All troops took part and we had the fullest possible discussion. We decided the attack should be to avenge Nguyen Van Troi [the Saigon worker, executed by a firing squad a few weeks earlier]; to avenge the U.S. piratical attacks in the Gulf of Tonkin; to avenge the massacre of our compatriots at Nhon Truch village, Bien Hoa province [where 400 fishermen and their families had been massacred in an air attack on their sampans, a few weeks previously]. Everyone, even the sick, demanded to take part. We had to have a special meeting to explain to the sick that they might only hamper the action. We would have to move fast; everything must be done with complete precision." Obviously Minh could not go into details of exactly how they filtered through the network of posts and defense positions, but a major factor was the help they had from those in the "strategic hamlets."

"We had to carry out very complicated infiltration movements," Minh continued, "but when the order was given to open fire, every team was in position. Our mortars and artillery were all concentrated at the same moment. The planes had first priority. Within split seconds there were thunderous explosions and flames shooting high into the air; crewmen could not contain themselves with excitement. As they scored direct hits, they jumped up: 'Take that for my wife, you swine,' 'That for Nguyen Van Troi,' 'You'll never drop bombs again,' and so on, as the giant planes burst into flames. Planes started exploding, some of them with bombs; there was a roaring tornado of flames. Within minutes we had switched our fire to the enemy barracks, knocking out the observation post with the first salvo. The Americans panicked, the puppet troops ran for the trenches. The Americans thought the puppets had revolted and started shooting them down; the puppets fired back and killed or wounded 21 Americans. The Americans ordered planes to take off, but we shot down the first Skyraider as it was taking off and it blew up, blocking the runway.

"At the same minute that our mortars opened up at Bien Hoa, another unit attacked the artillery at Tan Uyen and within the first minutes the two 155mm cannon were destroyed. Under cover of the attack, which continued at Tan Uyen, we were able to withdraw our forces and later joined up with the Tan Uyen unit. Neither force had suffered a single casualty, and the flames at Bien Hoa airfield lit up our hearts as well as the tracks we had to follow to reach our base.

"Puppet heads fell like rice before the sickle afterwards," he concluded. "The Lieut.-Col. in charge of Bien Hoa base was sacked; so was the chief of province, the commander of the battalion stationed 800 yards away, the commander of the two battalions stationed at the airport and a captain in charge of security forces. Not a single unit lifted a finger in defense of the base"—a graphic illustration of the point made by Nguyen Huu Tho.

Another example was the wiping out of an amphibious tank group—14 in all on Dec. 9, 1964—by a unit armed only with light infantry weapons, but attacking at such close quarters that the heavy tank weapons could not be angled sharply to fire back. All 14 tanks were destroyed and nine Americans were killed.

More and more the U.S.-Saigon forces are pulling back to try and form "iron rings" around Saigon, Hue and other major cities. The Front forces and the population counter the bombing threat by going underground and the artillery threat by ever more frequent attacks against the district and garrison centers, with destruction of the artillery pieces a major target. The fact that a base like Bien Hoa could not be defended, and even the super-security measures at "The Brink" officers Hotel and Club in the center of Saigon could not prevent it being blown up on Christmas Eve, show that the Front forces can penetrate where they like and at will. Obviously this is only possible due to the solidarity between the population and the armed forces.

The Saigon forces can no longer make good their losses on the battlefield, since the countryside on which they counted most for recruits is almost completely in the hands of the Front. And every manpower raid in the cities drives more recruits into the Liberation Army. The U.S.-Saigon command would show a deficit of some 80,000 regular army troops in 1964; that is, battlefield losses exceeded their recruitment figures by at least that figure. Many units exist on paper only, regiments are really battalions, battalions are companies. All units, according to officers with whom I spoke, who had crossed over to the NFL, are on the average down by from 30 to 50 per cent. Of the 11 "elite" or "shock" battalions which comprise Saigon's strategic reserves, two—the 33rd Rangers and the 4th Marine Rifles—were entirely wiped out during the Binh Gia battles of December 29 to January 1, and two companies of a third—the 35th Rangers—were wiped out in an ambush on January 3, 1965. The Liberation Army, on the other hand, is expanding rapidly in effectives and above all in fire power. In many regions parity in effectives has already been achieved with the U.S.-Saigon command. The fire-power of companies in regiments that I visited is now superior to that of their adversary; at battalion level, it is at least equal and only at regimental level, where the adversary has the advantage of tanks, heavy artillery and air support, is he superior.

The value of air support, however, is extremely limited. After the Bien Hoa disaster, the puppet chief of the Saigon Air Force, General Nguyen Cao Ky, personally commanded one of the greatest bombing raids of the war. In a night bombardment, supposedly of the unit which attacked the airport, 125 tons of bombs were dropped. Ky claimed "hundreds of Viet Cong killed." In fact, there was not a single casualty.

I have had plenty of personal experience of bombing raids. From that viewpoint, my second trip was somewhat more exciting even than the first. At one stage of the trip, the Americans became aware of the presence of our little party, which included the French writer and resistance heroine Madeleine Riffaud, who was reporting for *l'Humanité*, and some South Vietnamese photographers and cameramen. On one occasion, after having been shadowed all day by reconnaissance planes, the little clump of trees where we sheltered for the night was bombed in the pre-dawn hours of the following morning—specifically for us; there was no preliminary circling. The planes made precisely for our little corner of the woods and unloaded their bombs. While the first burst—about 300 yards away—was still thundering through the forest, we had fallen out of our hammocks into deep shelters. That was a raid I was able to record from start to finish on my tape-recorder, as I was trying to record the voice of an intriguing night bird when I heard the sound of the planes.

On another occasion, whether by precise bombing or by luck, they blew to pieces the table our little group had been dining at an hour or so earlier. A group of two Ranger (commando) platoons headed by four Americans once arranged a neat little ambush for us, but they had no idea that while they were stalking us with the most elaborate precautions, a highly amused Front patrol was stalking them. On still another occasion a raid, complete with planes, M-113's and river boats was laid on for our benefit, but this time we were saved by secret tunnels. One learned to feel very safe with a few feet of earth overhead during the bombing raids. The indiscriminate use of airpower can make no difference at all to the final outcome.

Nothing the Americans or their puppets can do can halt the political degeneration within the puppet government. The endless series of coups and counter-coups, of political crises, of increasing friction even between puppets and masters, reveal more clearly than ever the bankruptcy of the American position in South Vietnam. The best they can do is to go home.

INDEX